W9-ANQ-036

Trail Guide
Cuyahoga Valley
National Park

3rd Edition

Trail Guide
Cuyahoga Valley National Park

3rd Edition

Cuyahoga Valley Trails Council

Gray & Company, Publishers · Cleveland

Copyright © 2007 by Cuyahoga Valley Trails Council, Inc.

All rights reserved. No part of this book may be reproduced or trans-mitted in any form or manner without written permission from the publisher, except in the case of brief quotations embodied in critical articles and reviews.

Gray & Company, Publishers
www.grayco.com

The first edition of this publication was made possible through a gener-ous grant from The George Gund Foundation, Cleveland, Ohio.

Library of Congress Cataloging-in-Publication Data
Trail guide to Cuyahoga Valley National Park.—3rd ed.
    p. cm.
Title of first ed.: Trail guide handbook : Cuyahoga Valley National
Recreation Area, 1991.
Includes index.
ISBN 978-1-59851-040-9 (softcover)
1. Outdoor recreation—Ohio—Cuyahoga Valley National Park (Ohio)—
Guidebooks. 2. Trails—Ohio—Cuyahoga Valley National Park (Ohio)—
Guidebooks. 3. Cuyahoga Valley National Park (Ohio)—Guidebooks.
I. Cuyahoga Valley Trails Council.
GV191.42.O3T73 2008
796.5109771'31—dc22   2007030797

Printed in the U.S.A.

There are some who find a trailhead,
or a path through the woods which
curves invitingly out of sight,
simply irresistible.

Charles Little,
Greenways for America

The Cuyahoga Valley Trails Council (CVTC) is a non-profit all-volunteer organization dedicated to building and maintaining trails in the Cuyahoga Valley. CVTC was formed in 1985 from the Ad Hoc Trails Committee of the Cuyahoga Valley National Recreation Area (now named Cuyahoga Valley National Park) Advisory Commission just after the completion of the park's trail plan. Since its founding, CVTC has assisted Cuyahoga Valley National Park in implementing the trail plan by helping to build sections of new trail and maintain existing trails. The group holds monthly volunteer trail work sessions, helps coordinate the Adopt-A-Trail program, trains new volunteers, and encourages stewardship of the trail system.

Cuyahoga Valley Trails Council
1403 West Hines Hill Road
Peninsula, OH 44264
www.cvtrailscouncil.org

Contents

Foreword

A Brief History of Trails in the Cuyahoga Valley

Joseph D. Jesensky, artist, park ranger, and local historian, has been exploring the Cuyahoga Valley for many decades. In 1923, Joe and a small band of fellow artists made their treks into the valley. Together these young men ventured by train from Cleveland, disembarking in Bedford. From there, with sketchbooks and sandwiches in their knapsacks, they explored on foot every nook and cranny of the Tinkers Creek valley, from the Great Falls of Tinkers Creek to the stream's confluence with the Cuyahoga River. Joe has been exploring ever since. In 2007 he celebrated his 101st birthday. This foreword is from the first edition of the Trail Guide, published in 1991.

The earliest trail builders in our valley were the buffalo (bison) who had a natural knack for the best trail locations, including fording places in the streams. The Indians adapted these trails, followed by the early settlers. Many of these trails played an important part in the early history of our nation—as shown on the ancient maps of early North America.

By 1923, when our small band of adventurers sought to "re-explore" the hidden places in the valley, these trails were long ago taken over by the area roadways, or grown over by the natural vegetation. Our small group of art students, garbed in the toughest clothing and shoes available in those popular "Army & Navy" stores of WWI vintage, ventured forth into this tanglewood of dense brush and trees—with barbed-wire-like vines and poison ivy—formidable enough to make even Brer Rabbit look twice before entering! Our slogan was from the line in Kipling's poem, "The Explorer," which went something like this: "Something hidden—go and find it—Lost and waiting for you—Go!" and go we did, paying a dear price for the sweat-stained pages in our sketch books!

By the mid-1930s, some trail work was done in the valley, but only within the various parks existing then. This didn't help us much, and we had only the vegetation-choked towpath which ran through the full length of the valley. This trail work was done by the various work relief agencies—the Works Progress Administration (WPA) and Civilian Conservation Corps (CCC). The latter did much trail work in the Kendall Ledges area.

It wasn't until Cuyahoga Valley National Recreation Area was established that trail work was begun within the valley proper. (How we could have used such trails years ago!) By the year 1991, there were many types of trails within the valley. Ski trails, short trails, long trails, trails to fit all shoe sizes, and even boardwalk trails where needed. Trail building had progressed much from our own early days. They no longer just "grew like Topsy" and ran helter-skelter over the hills and valleys. They are carefully planned now, by park architect and engineer, and carefully built by park crews, aided by groups of volunteer trail builders. (Their combined efforts and results deserve our heartiest thanks!)

The trails described in these pages, remember, are merely "paper trails." To get the feel of the real trails, you should walk them, savoring each new view along them, views changing from day to day and season to season. Go and find for yourself that "something hidden" which Kipling spoke of!

—Joe Jesensky

Preface

Visitors to Cuyahoga Valley National Park (CVNP) are astonished at the variety of scenery to be found. The Cuyahoga Valley Trails Council (CVTC) produced this guide with the hope that it will encourage people to explore CVNP.

The CVTC published the first two editions of this guide in the 1990s, when the park was known as Cuyahoga Valley National Recreation Area and the Ohio and Erie Canal Towpath had just been completed. Since then, new trails have been added and many of the existing trails have been re-routed in places.

The park's name changed in 2000, and CVNP is now one of the ten most visited national parks. The publication of this new edition fulfills part of the CVTC's mission, which is to promote, coordinate, and participate in the building, inspection, maintenance, improvement, and enjoyment of trails in and around the Cuyahoga Valley.

The CVTC's main function is to do the physical work of building and improving trails. The CVTC is an all-volunteer organization, and we schedule monthly trail work sessions from March to December in CVNP, in cooperation with the National Park Service (NPS). We take great pride in augmenting the tremendous work of the NPS trail crew.

We clear new trail corridors, dig drainage ditches, install culverts, spread gravel, grade the trail surface, build bridges and boardwalks, and construct steps with logs or rock, all to make the trails solid and dry underfoot.

Our quarterly trail work schedules are distributed to all of the visitor centers in the CVNP. They are also found on our Web site at: www.cvtrailscouncil.org

Whether or not you volunteer with us, we hope you will use this guide to enjoy the trails in Cuyahoga Valley National Park.

—Dave Daams, President
Cuyahoga Valley Trails Council

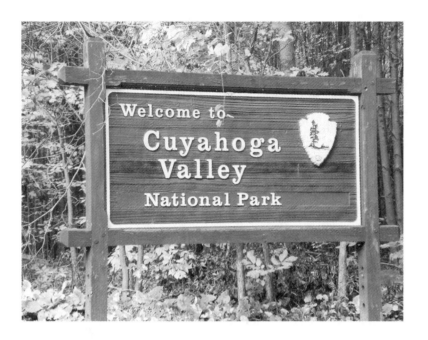

Introduction

Newcomers to northeast Ohio are often surprised to find a large green spot on the map between Akron and Cleveland. If curious enough, they will discover that the green place between the two cities is the Cuyahoga River valley. Exploring the river valley, they are soon forced to give up the "steel mills and cornfields" impression of Ohio. What may also come as a surprise are the sheer cliffs and hemlock groves that look like they belong in Canada, the clear, rippling streams coming from forested hills that look like smaller versions of the Appalachian and Allegheny Mountains, and the farmsteads and canal villages suspended in time.

Much of this green valley between Akron and Cleveland is now protected within Cuyahoga Valley National Park (CVNP), a unit of the national park system. Of the Cuyahoga River's entire length, one-fourth, or about twenty-two miles, is within the boundary of Cuyahoga Valley National Park. The surrounding 33,000 acres of CVNP are a microcosm of northeast Ohio, both in human and natural history. The national park was created in 1974 through the combined energies of citizens and legislators, all with a strong desire to preserve and protect the green, open space, along with the recreation opportunities and the rich history of the valley. It was originally named Cuyahoga Valley National Recreation Area, and was created at a time when the National Park Service (NPS) was seeking to bring parks closer to people. It became one of several such urban national recreation areas, and soon became all of northeast Ohio's backyard, here for everyone to enjoy. In 2000, the park's name was changed to Cuyahoga Valley National Park, acknowledging its prominent place in the national park system. It now receives over two and a half million visits a year and is typically ranked in the top ten most visited national parks in the country.

CVNP is a unique park: within its bounds are federally owned land, privately owned land, and park units owned and operated by Cleveland Metroparks and Metro Parks, Serving Summit County, partners in managing the public areas. In this guide, we describe all the trails within the boundary of the national park, including those managed by the metropolitan park districts. In doing so, we have put in one place information on over 200 miles of trails in the Cuyahoga Valley, hoping to clarify the many choices available to you for hiking, skiing, bicycling, and horseback riding. With guidebook in hand, you can plan your outings, from a short lunch-time walk to an all-day trek.

The trail system in CVNP has been developed over the years through a partnership between volunteers and the National Park Service. In the early 1980s, the founders of the Cuyahoga Valley Trails Council (CVTC) assisted the National Park Service at CVNP in exploring the valley's existing and potential trails. The result of this joint effort was the National Park Service's *Trail Plan and Environmental Assessment (1985)* for Cuyahoga Valley National Park. The trails have been developed and improved over the last twenty years, often with the help of the trail volunteers. Every month, CVTC volunteers do a work project to help maintain and improve the existing trails and construct new trails in accordance with the *Trail Plan*. When the *Trail Plan* was written, there were 105 miles of trails in CVNP, with another 115 miles proposed. Of the 115 miles of proposed trails, 82 miles have been completed, some by NPS staff and contractors, and some by volunteers. In addition to building new trails, CVTC volunteers maintain existing trails through the Adopt-a-Trail program. We encourage you to help build and improve the trail system by volunteering your time and talents to the volunteer work crews.

In this guide, we describe the long distance trails first: the Ohio & Erie Canal Towpath Trail, the Buckeye Trail, and the Bike & Hike Trail. These are followed by the rest of the trails, grouped geographically, north to south. For each trail, you will find a map and description, and directions for reaching the trailheads shown on the trailhead map at the back of this book. The first few lines of the trail description offer an overview of the trail's general character and special attributes. The difficulty ratings on the maps are, of course, subjective. However, we have taken into account the distance covered and the steepness and frequency of climbs—the shorter and flatter the trail, the easier. In the case of skiing and horseback riding, our ratings assume some beginning competence in controlling your skis or horse. We also note on the maps facilities located at the trailheads, using universal park symbols. See the legend on page 14 for a full listing of symbols. Where there are a number of trails in one area, we suggest you read the general information on the area first, then refer to the particular trail you are interested in. Our guide will be most helpful when used along with CVNP's free "Official Map and Guide," available at visitor centers.

Our route descriptions are meant to keep you from getting lost by highlighting the general route of the trail and making note of intersections or confusing spots. If the trail is circular, we note in which direction it is described. Once you are familiar enough with the trail, try it in the opposite direction. You'll be surprised how different it looks! This is not advised on one-way ski trails, however. In those cases, the trails are laid out in one direction to make the best use of the terrain and to ensure safety and a sense of solitude on the trail.

Keep in mind that the soils in this valley, some of which are loose deposits of glacial material, are unstable and "flow" when saturated. Flooded streams can erode banks and deposit trees where they were absent a day ago. The valley is always changing, and this means the trails can be changing too. What we describe today may be a little different when you go out to hike.

We hope that presenting all these options will help disperse hiking traffic throughout the valley. Some familiar areas can become crowded on beautiful summer weekends, placing

stress on natural resources and visitors alike. This can be avoided with a little advance planning and by seeking the lesser-known areas on busy days. The effects of heavy use in an area are obvious and can detract from your experience of the trails. You can help minimize your effect on an area by a few simple considerations: Please carry all trash out with you (as food refuse left in receptacles at the trailheads tends to get redistributed by scavenging animals), control your pets on a leash, and stay on the trail.

In our trail descriptions, we also point out historic features, plants, and animals that you might find along the trail, especially those unique or well-represented in that area. We cannot be all-inclusive, but instead we try to bring your attention to a portion of the rich natural life and cultural history in the valley and hope to whet your appetite for learning more. You will find in your ventures that your enjoyment of the trails increases as you become more aware of the other lives that share this piece of the planet.

The Footsteps Before You

Before you begin exploring the trails, we would like to tell you some things about this river valley. As you follow the trails of the Cuyahoga Valley, you will be following paths that have seen many other feet before yours. Evidence of human habitation here goes back to about 10,000 BC, following the last glacial retreat. The glaciers, which intermittently covered the area with ice two to three million years ago, ground down and rearranged the hills and drainage patterns. The last glacial retreat exposed a drainage divide, separating the waters that flow to the Gulf of St. Lawrence from those that flow to the Gulf of Mexico. This is the same divide that causes the Cuyahoga River to make a U-turn halfway along its circuitous course from Geauga County to Lake Erie.

Following that last glacial retreat, prehistoric Native Americans hunted mastodons and mammoths. After these early peoples, other native populations emerged, surviving off the rich resources of the river and Lake Erie, and eventually farming and coming together in small villages. Throughout these many years, plant life evolved to the point that the area was covered by a dense, unbroken forest of massive trees. Some of the sycamores along the river were so huge that their hollowed trunks were used for shelter.

The first white explorers, followed by settlers, arrived in this valley in the late 1700s. Following the Revolutionary War, surveying parties made their way to the mouth of the Cuyahoga River to begin to measure and map an area known as the Connecticut Western Reserve. The Western Reserve, stretching 120 miles west of the Pennsylvania border and between the 41st parallel and Lake Erie, was land retained by the state of Connecticut when it surrendered the rest of its land claims to the young federal government. Connecticut then sold the wilderness reserve to the Connecticut Land Company to divide up and sell to eager easterners, both settlers and speculators.

The Cuyahoga River valley was truly "the West," and witnessed a typical phase of pioneering. In 1800, there were twenty-four million acres of seemingly unlimited forest in Ohio. Seeing these forests as an impediment to raising crops and livestock, the early settlers embarked on an intense slash-and-burn campaign. By 1883, the forest cover was reduced to four million acres. If you look at canal-era pictures of the valley, you see mostly bare hillsides.

The early settlers could subsist, but could not progress economically without a means of transporting agricultural products to eastern and southern markets. The canals were a short-lived but successful solution: the first section of the Ohio & Erie Canal was opened in July of 1827, connecting Akron to Cleveland, and by 1840, Ohio led the nation in agricultural production.

The white settlers left other effects upon this land besides transforming forests to farm fields. They quarried stone, then later made use of sand and gravel for concrete building materials. They eradicated predators (at one time there were bears and mountain lions in the valley) and hunted fur-bearing animals, extirpating the beaver. Industries developed and grew, and the towns of Akron and Cleveland began to spread out towards each other.

Beginning around the 1920s, some Ohioans began to value the Cuya-

hoga Valley in a different way. Seeing an oasis of green space between the two industrial cities, they began a conservation movement centered mostly on creating metropolitan park districts. A number of these early conservationists were private citizens who owned large retreats in the valley and wished to see them preserved for public use and enjoyment. Their pioneering preservation efforts led to the establishment of our exemplary metropolitan parks, and eventually to the creation of Cuyahoga Valley National Park.

The Natural Valley Today

The deforestation trend that occurred in the Cuyahoga Valley during pioneering times has been reversed, and the valley now supports a diverse wildlife population owing to the variety of habitat types and the many "edges" between forest, field, stream, and wetland. The forests today are second- and third-growth, different from the virgin oak, beech-maple, and pine woods. Today we have more than one hundred species of trees, including red maple, tulip tree, ash, wild black cherry, mixed oaks, hickories, and beeches. Dry uplands are dominated by oaks, while along the river bottoms you find sycamores, willows, cottonwoods, and Ohio buckeyes. The ravines hold relics of the cooler post-glacial period, such as Eastern hemlock and yellow birch.

Birds and Beasts

The diversity of habitats in CVNP makes the area one of the best in the state for birdwatching. The National Audubon Society has named CVNP an Important Bird Area, their designation of areas that are crucial to the survival of many bird species. Of the 230 or so bird species that have been found in the valley, several especially prefer this area of the state. One species is the elusive veery. You may not see it, but if you're lucky you'll hear its ethereal, flute-like song. The woodcock is another—famous for its spiraling mating display performed in early spring. Turkeys had disappeared from the valley, but they have been reintroduced in the area, and now are seen more frequently, though they too are quite secretive.

New wetlands, some created by beavers and some created by park biologists, are providing a valuable habitat for a number of species, such as green heron, Virginia rail, and sora. Likewise, a large restored grassland area, where the Richfield Coliseum was removed, is now hosting several species of rare sparrows. In winter a northern species, the short-eared owl, visits the grassland. The large, unbroken tracts of forest in the valley are important to woodland nesting birds, such as the wood thrush. Most significant perhaps, and emblematic of the environmental improvements in the Cuyahoga Valley, is the return of the bald eagle. Eagles are sighted more frequently now in the valley, and in 2007 a pair of bald eagles nested in CVNP for the first time in over seventy years.

Your chances of observing other wildlife in CVNP are quite good, especially if you take some care in your efforts. The best times are early mornings or evenings around dusk. For the best advantage, be quiet, go slowly, and even better, sit still. You won't see wolf or elk, but you could see a beaver working on its dam or a fox or coyote stalking prey. White-tailed deer are plentiful. Raccoons, opossums, skunks, and bats are most active at night.

Along with the forests and meadows, your hikes will take you through or past wetlands, including streams, floodplains, beaver marshes, and many man-made ponds. These wet habitats are where you can find one of our largest birds, the great blue heron, plus kingfishers, Canada geese, wood ducks, tree swallows, and many warblers. Several species of native frogs, salamanders, reptiles, and amphibians moving and mating among the cattails and willows are just part of the highly productive wetland world.

At any time of the year, something is happening in the valley, but spring sets the fastest pace. In just the brief period from late March to early June, the valley is transformed from its open, sparse, gray, winter look to a dense, lush, emerald garden. In the midst of this transformation is a window of time in which dainty spring wildflowers bloom. It is also about this time that migrating birds pass through the valley, resting and feeding for a while once insects begin to hatch. The co-occurrence of warblers and wildflowers in early May strains the necks of naturalists gazing up, then down; up, then down. In summer, animal activity appears to slow down, especially midday. Early morning, before the mist has burned off, and late evening, when the insects and tree frogs begin their serenades, are good times for experiencing summer in the valley. Autumn brings the bittersweet excitement of change and cooler weather, along with the animals' preparations for winter. The height of fall color occurs about mid-October, a popular time for taking to the woods again for the sheer beauty of the scenery. Again, you might sight unusual birds in the valley as they migrate south to wintering grounds. More and more visitors are discovering that winter offers its own special rewards to those who venture out. The starkness and silence are a welcome contrast to the fullness of the leafed-out seasons. You can observe animals by following their signs left in the snow, and given enough snow, you can enjoy the exhilaration of gliding over familiar terrain on skis. There are even special field guides to help you identify plants, trees, fungi, birds, and animal tracks during the winter months.

Rock-hard Facts

For those of you who love rocks, the geology in this area tells the valley's history in deep layers of time. Some of that history is buried far beneath the surface in shales formed from muds deposited in shallow seas 375 million years ago. These Devonian Period deposits are exposed in places where the Cuyahoga River has cut through the layers. Above these are Mississippian shales and sandstones, 330 million years old. The sandstones resist erosion, and when softer rock underneath is eroded, the sandstones sheer off to form cliffs such as those along Tinkers Creek. On top of these layers are the shale, sandstone, and conglomerate laid down in the streams and swamps of the Pennsylvanian Period. These form the surface bedrock wherever they are not overlaid by the younger glacial till. Sharon Sandstone and Conglomerate compose the familiar rock ledges of the valley.

After these Pennsylvanian Period deposits there is a long gap in the geologic record in Ohio—a gap of about 225 million years! In the Rocky Mountains, there are layers of rocks created during that time period, but not in Ohio. It is believed that during this time Ohio was undergoing extensive erosion, up until about two million years ago when climate changes spawned enormous polar ice caps which spread southward as glaciers.

These frozen masses, 1,000 to 8,000 feet thick, moved across northern

Bicycling the Towpath

Ohio like giant bulldozers, advancing and retreating in several different ice ages, with the most recent entering Ohio about 25,000 years ago. By the end of their final retreat, they had altered the landscape tremendously, in a scale difficult to imagine. Glaciers changed the course of streams and created new hills, called kames, by depositing tons of till (soils and ground rock). The Cuyahoga River today follows a course that is partly ancient, and partly altered by the glaciers. Underneath part of the Cuyahoga Valley, buried by 500 feet of till, sand, and silt, is a much older valley.

Bedrock in Canada is often exposed over large areas, but here it is only seen in knobs or ledges, and is usually buried by glacial deposits brought down from Canada in the ice sheets. Every time you find a boulder in the valley, you are finding a piece of Canada, usually composed of granite or granite gneiss, brought here during the ice age.

Animals were plentiful along the edge of retreating glaciers, but these animals were quite different from what we see today. Known as megafauna, these included giant mammoths, beavers, mastodons, and saber-toothed tigers. They are now all extinct. The vegetation changed within a few centuries from predominantly needle-bearing trees to the present day broad-leaved trees. A few of the cooler climate plants still remain, usually found in the cooler ravines.

We have mentioned only a few of the many species of plants and animals you may find here and have simply highlighted the natural and cultural history. This is meant to get you started on a long and enjoyable period of exploration. To learn more, stop at any of the visitor centers in CVNP. There you will find rangers leading guided walks, exhibits on the natural and cultural history of the park, a schedule of programs, general information, and bookstores with field guides and local history. (See appendix for addresses and phone numbers.)

The Cuyahoga River valley holds many surprises. There are those who have repeatedly tramped these "fuzzy green hills," to borrow a phrase from Edward Abbey, and on each return find something new and exciting. We invite you to discover your own special places in the Cuyahoga Valley.

Before You Head Out

What to Wear, What to Take

Before you go hiking in Cuyahoga Valley National Park, guidebook in hand, remember "If you don't like Ohio weather, wait a few hours. It will change!" This is particularly true in northeast Ohio, where because of our topography and proximity to Lake Erie the weather changes by the hour, not the day. So it's good to prepare for these changes before you set out. John Muir was known to set off into the Sierra Nevada Mountains with just some tea and bread, but most of us are far less tolerant of discomforts than he. A few select items in a daypack or fannypack can help ensure a pleasurable day.

First determine the time you will be out—all day or only a few hours. The longer you are out the more protection from changing weather you will need, but even short hikes require a few basics to keep you comfortable and safe. There are fourteen basic items that provide you with comfort and protection from almost anything on hikes from five to fifty miles. These essentials include a lightweight shell top and pants (or a poncho in a pinch), gloves, a hat, spare socks, a thermal vest (or midweight wool shirt), sunglasses, sunscreen, bug repellent, a flashlight, a lighter or matches, a map and compass, a one-quart water bottle, snacks, and a small personal first aid kit.

A lightweight shell top and pants of a waterproof-breathable fabric (such as Gore-Tex) provide the ideal protection for you, doubling for wind and rain protection in one garment. Though the temperature may seem warm, a quick rain shower with no protection leaves you wet and chilled. At this point you are a prime candidate for hypothermia. Remember that most cases of hypothermia occur in temperatures of 30 to 50°F.

If additional warmth is required, slip on a down, wool, or fleece vest, or wear a wool shirt under your shell jacket. A little wind goes a long way to chilling you. With a temperature of 40°F and a wind of 15 MPH, the wind-chill factor is 25°F. Gloves and a hat will help keep your extremities warm. A balaclava—a stocking-type cap that can be worn as a hat, or pulled down over the face and neck for added protection and warmth—will do the duty of a hat and scarf in cold weather and offers more versatility.

Abundant precipitation in this temperate climate creates ground conditions which you will come to know well, and perhaps even tolerate. Mud is prevalent almost any time of the year, especially where the soils do not drain well, like in the stream valleys and even on some of the higher ground. Take care to wear adequate footwear and carry spare socks. A change of socks halfway through a long hike will help prevent blisters on tender feet (and is a good excuse for a rest stop!). If your feet do get wet, the change of socks will feel especially welcome. Also, some people find that wearing a thin pair of liner socks under heavier socks helps prevent blisters.

Eyestrain can drain your energy reserves quickly. However, wearing sunglasses can help lessen eyestrain, as well as reduce the cutting effect of winds on your face. Protection for your skin is also important: sunscreen and insect repellent should be included in your bag.

One quart of water and some high energy snacks (dried fruits, nuts, or a sandwich) will help keep you going. Choose foods that give quick energy boosts such as items high in carbohydrates and sugars. Many of the trailheads in the Cuyahoga Valley do not have drinking water, and even where there is water, the supplies are shut down in winter, so carrying water is especially important. When hiking, remember that even if you don't feel thirsty, it's a good idea to take frequent drinks to prevent dehydration. Unless you are familiar with the trail, take along a map and compass. A small flashlight may come in handy if you become lost, for reading a map in the dark, or locating trail markers. Your first aid kit should include items for blister care, for minor cuts and scrapes, and some aspirin. These items take little space but can make a big difference if needed.

There is not a lot of space in a daypack, so choose clothing with minimal bulk. When hiking in warm weather, make sure there is room for clothing you may want to remove after you start. When you are moving you generate more heat, but when you stop to rest or enjoy the view, you may need an extra layer for chill protection. Remember it is better to be prepared than to get caught short.

Trail Etiquette and Safety

Proper trail etiquette promotes good trail safety; the two go hand in hand. Due respect among all trail users is a wise investment, and the returns include a pleasant, enjoyable, and safe trail outing.

The most common type of trail where different types of users will meet is a multi-use trail, although most trails do have more than one use. Therefore a review of some of the common-sense points of etiquette is essential.

Multi-use Trails

- Travel in a normal traffic pattern as on a regular roadway.

- Bicyclists should always voice their presence and what they are going to do when approaching a slower moving user, especially when passing from behind (for instance, "passing on your left").

- In winter, cross-country skiers should do the same.

- If possible, get off the trail or as far to the right of the trail as possible when stopping.

Bridle Trails

- Horses are like people. They all react differently in any given situation. Always bear this in mind when using a bridle trail for any purpose other than horseback riding.

- When encountering a horseback rider, stop, step off the trail, and let him pass. Ceasing activity will prevent any sudden noise or movements that may cause the horse to shy. Stay away from the horse unless the rider invites you to approach him. When the horse has passed, continue on your way.

- Horseback riders should voice their presence if they are not seen when approaching another trail user.

Cross-country Ski Trails

- When hiking, the main point of courtesy that should be practiced on trails designated for cross-country skiing is to avoid walking in the ski tracks. Footprints in the tracks make a more difficult time for the skier. Walk to the side of the trail, out of the tracks.

- Skiers should voice their presence if not seen when approaching another user.

In General

- Be aware of others who will be encountered on the type of trail you are using.

- Any transport equipment or animals with you should be under control. Keep dogs on a leash, and equipment in safe working condition. Avoid excessive or uncontrollable speed on bicycles, horses, and skis.

- Stay only on trails that are permitted for your use.

- When trails approach private property, please respect the landowner's privacy.

- Pack out trash: garbage placed in trailside containers tends to get strewn through the woods by scavenging animals.

With trail use on the rise, recreational enthusiasts will experience increased interaction with other trail users. Good attitudes and actions on the trail are indeed an investment—in safety, in camaraderie, in future enjoyment of the trails.

Off-Trail Hiking

In the valley you'll find old roads and animal trails that cross or come near the official trails. There are also picturesque ravines that offer their own little rewards, some with delightful waterfalls. The temptation to go off-trail sometimes becomes overwhelming—that enticing animal trail that follows down the ridge, that old roadway that goes up the edge of the gully. But, if you decide to follow this whim, there are several things to consider first.

The land within the boundaries of Cuyahoga Valley National Park is owned by many different entities, so be aware of just where you are and who owns the property. Most areas are clearly posted and signed. Metro Parks, Serving Summit County, has a strict policy of staying on official trails. Their annual ranger-led Stream Stomp is an exception to this policy. Elsewhere throughout the valley, keep in mind that if you leave the trail you may be straying onto private property, so take care not to trespass. If in doubt, ask permission to pass through a particular area. At all times, please remember that you are sharing this wonderful valley with many other creatures who call it home. Move carefully to minimize disturbance to vegetation or to nesting or resting animals. In harsh weather conditions, disturbing an animal could jeopardize its survival.

Also, be careful! There are obstacles in the woods— fallen trees, multiflora rose briars, poison ivy, stinging nettles, stumps, and holes, to name just a few. Waterfall and stream bed exploring has its own set of hazards including slippery footing. Go prepared: dress to protect yourself against insects and unfriendly plants.

And please, don't get lost. If you leave the trail, go prepared with a map and compass and know how to use them. There are excellent books on learning the use of map and compass, and the North Eastern Ohio Orienteering Club (see appendix) specializes in cross-country map and compass exploring. You can purchase U.S. Geological Survey maps online from the USGS store at www.store.usgs.gov or from local retailers listed on the USGS Website. Most of the valley is shown on two maps, the Northfield and Peninsula Quadrangles. Be aware, however, that these do not show the public and private boundaries, so do some research before leaving the trails.

There are several areas in CVNP that lend themselves well to cross-country exploring, and these make good practice areas for learning to use a map and compass. In the northern part of CVNP is an area known as Terra Vista Study Area. It sits on a plateau above the corner of Tinkers Creek Road and Canal Road, and includes a couple of small fishing ponds and acres of shrubby, open area that was once a gravel pit operation. Farther south, in central CVNP, is the Kendall Hills area—acres of mowed hills, all interconnected, with splendid views across the valley. And in the southern part of the park, on Riverview Road just south of Bolanz Road, is the Indigo Lake area. Indigo is another good fishing pond surrounded by some open fields connecting to the Howe Meadow special events site.

Map Legend

Main trail	![main trail]
Intersecting, continuing trail	
Trailhead	**P**
Canal (watered/unwatered)	
Picnicking	
Restrooms	
Park Boundary	
Structure, pavilion, shelter	
Scenic View	
Camping	

The Trails

Ohio & Erie Canal Towpath Trail

On a clear, crisp afternoon in October of 1993, for the first time in over 80 years, a mule crossed over the Cuyahoga River in Peninsula just south of Lock 29 of the Ohio & Erie Canal. The mule and his driver were followed by a procession of people, some in period costumes, some in park ranger uniforms; some walking, some riding bicycles. The event marked the official opening of almost twenty miles of the Ohio & Erie Canal Towpath Trail. Today this popular multi-use trail is the heart of Cuyahoga Valley National Park (CVNP), and it now continues outside the national park as part of the Ohio & Erie National Heritage Canalway. Eventually the trail will be 101 miles long, connecting Cleveland, on Lake Erie, to New Philadelphia, on the Tuscarawas River.

Within Cuyahoga Valley National Park you can access the Ohio & Erie Canal Towpath Trail at any of eleven trailheads. The trail is designed for hiking, bicycling, and cross-country skiing and is graded and surfaced to comply with the Americans with Disabilities Act of 1990. Some sections are also shared with equestrians. When planning your trip, you might also consider using the shuttle service offered by the Cuyahoga Valley Scenic Railroad (800-468-4070; www.cvsr.com).

A Quick Look

Within the boundaries of Cuyahoga Valley National Park the Ohio & Erie Canal Towpath Trail passes near the remnants of a full range of canal-related structures including lift locks, aqueducts, feeder canals, and various weirs, sluices, overflows, gates, and other devices used to control water levels. (North of Station Road, where the canal is still watered, these water-control devices are still in use today). Your trip will take you past much of the valley's human history, such as the site of South Park Village, a Native American settlement dating to AD 1000; or Pilgerruh, site of the first known Moravian missionary settlement in the valley; plus a canal-era mill, farmsteads and fields in production since the 1800s, and historic homes in canal villages.

National Park Service facilities along the way help interpret the valley's natural and human history: Canal Exploration Center has in-depth, interactive exhibits for children and adults, focusing on exploring canal history. The Boston Store tells the story of the canal through its boat builders and watermen. The Stephen and Mehitable Frazee House has exhibits on settlement, building construction, and the vernacular architecture in the region. Hunt House presents the life of the farming community. All along the Towpath Trail are numerous informational panels, or waysides, that will help you understand what you see and, in some cases, what you can no longer see.

As you travel along the canal, the evolution of transportation in the valley is all around you. You parallel the first transportation route through the valley—the Cuyahoga River—and the one that put the canal out of business—the Valley Railway. The development of bridge engineering in transportation is evident from an 1882 wrought iron structure, to the graceful form of a 1931 concrete arch, to major interstate highway bridges whisking today's travelers from rim to rim across the valley.

The Ohio & Erie Canal Towpath Trail connects a large number of trails, facilities, and other points of interest. Among the many sites and attractions you will be able to reach, via back roads or connector trails are Hale Farm & Village, Brandywine and Boston Mills Ski Resorts, Brandywine Falls, and the Stanford House. Along the way you might see deer, coyote, beavers, great blue herons, or even a wild turkey. In spring, look for woodland wildflowers, such as spring beauties and trout lilies; in summer look for the purple and white dame's rocket. Fall is the time for the yellow of wingstem and the purples of joe-pye weed, ironweed, and asters; and winter brings the muted colors of dried goldenrods and grasses.

Things to Keep in Mind

Sandstone mileposts along the trail mark the approximate location of the original mileposts as recorded on earlier survey maps. These mileposts measured miles from the beginning of the canal near the mouth of the Cuyahoga River in Cleveland's industrial flats. The original mileposts were determined using the chain and link method. Washouts and other changes over the years necessitated rerouting some parts of the historic towpath when the trail was constructed. As a result, the distance between mileposts is not always 5,280 feet.

Canal locks were always numbered starting from the high point, increasing in the direction of the flow of the water. Hence, lock numbers within the park *increase* as the canal heads north, or downstream.

The Ohio & Erie Canal Towpath Trail is a very popular trail, with 1.5 million visits per year. Less busy times include weekdays, before noon on weekends, and days with less than ideal weather. Remember, it is a shared trail used by hikers and bicyclists and by visitors of varying ages and abilities. Some short sections are also open to horse and rider.

A few tips will help make your trip on the Ohio & Erie Canal Towpath

Trail safe and enjoyable. All are based on the golden rule of a shared trail: be courteous.

- Travel at a safe speed. Adjust your speed to match traffic flow.
- Keep to the right except to pass others.
- Give a clear warning before passing on the left.
- Everyone yields to horses. If you need to pass, make sure the rider knows in advance that you are passing. Be especially cautious, as horses can be startled by sudden movements or sounds.
- Travel single file when passing or being passed.
- Park regulations require that pets be kept on a short (six-foot or less) leash.
- Move completely off the trail when stopped.

Back to the Future

The 1996 legislation designating the Ohio & Erie National Heritage Canalway has enabled the park's neighboring cities, counties, and park districts to extend the Towpath Trail north into Cleveland and south through Akron and Massillon into New Philadelphia. Seventy-five percent of the trail is completed, and progress continues on the remaining twenty-five percent. When the trail is finished, you can start in Cleveland and along the route be able to sample food in the ethnic neighborhoods, visit restored historic sites, and rest in small towns and villages. You will pass through a variety of preserved natural areas—forests, wetlands, open fields, and stream corridors. Using connector trails or side roads, you can catch a baseball game, visit an indoor rain forest, or explore a world-class art museum.

Yesterday we wrote about the Towpath Trail yet to be. Today we write of a national heritage canalway that will extend the Towpath Trail from New Philadelphia to Cleveland and connect the region and its people through their shared natural, cultural, industrial, and recreational heritage. For more information on this project, visit the Web site of the Ohio & Erie Canalway Association at: www.ohioanderiecanalway.com.

Lock 39 Trailhead to Frazee House Trailhead

This section of the Ohio & Erie Canal Towpath Trail follows part of the only watered section of the canal in the national park. Our description begins at the Lock 39 Trailhead on Rockside Road and follows the trail north to south. At the southern end of this section, there is limited parking at the Frazee House Trailhead on Canal Road. Additional parking can be found at Canal Exploration Center.

Just north of Rockside Road is the boarding site for the Cuyahoga Valley Scenic Railroad, an excursion train running on the historic Valley Railway. The railroad operates a seasonal shuttle service for hikers and bicyclists using the towpath. See appendix for information.

The section of canal you are about to explore is a National Historic Landmark. This designation recognizes the property as being nationally significant, and although there are many structures and areas listed in the National Register of Historic Places within the park boundaries, this is the only one listed as a National Historic Landmark.

Directions: I-77 to Exit 155, Rockside Road. East on Rockside Road about one mile to Lock 39 Trailhead on the south side of Rockside Road, just west of Canal Road.

Trail Description: Your journey begins at Rockside Road in Valley View, near canal mile marker eleven. Nearby, the Cuyahoga River is flowing north to Cleveland and Lake Erie. From this trailhead, the Towpath Trail to the north is under the jurisdiction of Cleveland Metroparks. Traveling south, you enter Cuyahoga Valley National Park. Soon the noise of traffic from Rockside Road recedes as you travel south back into a quieter, simpler time. Lock 39, also known as 11-Mile Lock, is just a quarter of a mile down the trail. Here you find the remains of a small metal bridge at the north end of the lock. This bridge was used by canallers to cross from one side of the lock to the other when the lower gates were open. Less than a mile farther on, a road bridge crosses the canal on your left. Stone Road was so named because it was the road used to haul stone to the canal from the quarries west of here. Across Canal Road is the Abraham Ulyatt House built in 1849. This house is built of stone in the Greek Revival style and is a reflection of the quarrying industry that thrived in Independence in the 1800s.

Just south of Stone Road, a wayside exhibit marks the general location of Pilgerruh, or Pilgrims Rest. In 1786, somewhere in this vicinity, Moravian missionaries and their Christianized Indian followers built a temporary

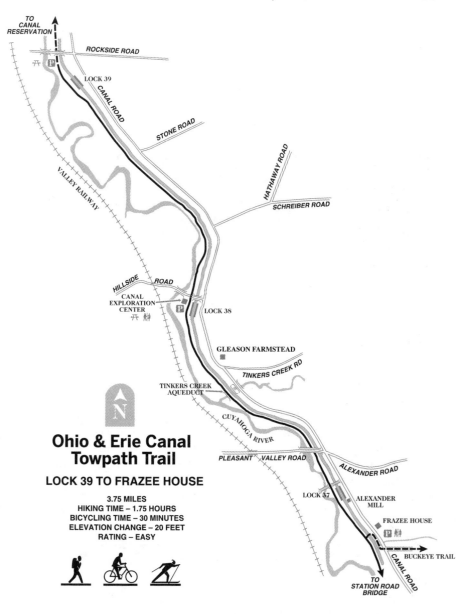

**Ohio & Erie Canal
Towpath Trail**

LOCK 39 TO FRAZEE HOUSE

3.75 MILES
HIKING TIME – 1.75 HOURS
BICYCLING TIME – 30 MINUTES
ELEVATION CHANGE – 20 FEET
RATING – EASY

settlement in the Cuyahoga Valley. John Heckewelder, one of the missionaries, drew a map of the settlement, but its exact location is unknown.

Just past Mile 12 the restored 1853 canal-era building located at Lock 38 comes into view. This is Canal Exploration Center, operated by the National Park Service. You may want to stop in and enjoy the canal exhibits

Lock 38 and the Canal Exploration Center

on the first floor (including a working lock model), visit the bookstore, or learn more about human history of the valley from the exhibits on the second floor. It's a good place to stop, with picnic tables and year-round restrooms.

Take a moment to look over Lock 38 before resuming your journey. In front of you is something that may seem quite simple, but was the evolution of many centuries of trial and error. Coming from Europe, this lock type, known as the two-gate lock, is a remarkable piece of engineering. Restored in 1992 to its 1905 condition, Lock 38 is the only operating lock in CVNP. On summer and fall weekends, costumed park rangers and volunteers demonstrate how the power of gravity was used to gently raise or lower a fully loaded canal boat eight feet in the lock.

Less than a half mile south of the visitor center is Tinkers Creek Road. The bridge across the canal opposite Tinkers Creek Road once carried vehicular traffic, but when the bridge across the river was removed the canal bridge was also closed to vehicles. It is still used by pedestrians and fishermen. Just beyond, the canal and towpath cross over Tinkers Creek on the Tinkers Creek Aqueduct. Aqueducts, or bridges of water, were designed into the original canal as a way to carry the canal over larger creeks or rivers. This aqueduct is one of twenty-three that were originally used on the 309-mile canal between Cleveland and Portsmouth, four of which were located on the 38-mile Cleveland-to-Akron portion. Only this one and the smaller Mill Creek Aqueduct (north of the national park, near Lock 40) are in use today. The Tinkers Creek Aqueduct has been repaired and rebuilt many times during the past 175 years, with the most recent reconstruction completed in 2011.

To your left, on the hill above the intersection of Canal and Tinkers Creek Roads, stands the historic Edmund Gleason farm, marked by the huge red dairy barn with its distinctive gambrel roof. The Greek Revival farmhouse was built between 1851 and 1855 and features dressed sandstone. The barn was built in 1905 by Edmund's daughter and very likely replaced an earlier one.

After a gentle swing to the east, the Towpath Trail again swings west and passes under Pleasant Valley/Alexander Road, bringing you to the only remaining mill structure along the watered portion of the canal. Alexander Mill (now Wilson Feed Mill) was constructed in 1855 and used the excess, or waste, water which bypassed Lock 37 (14-Mile Lock) to power its overshot wheel. The mill used water power up until 1972 to grind grain but switched to electricity since floating debris kept clogging the water power mechanism. Now grinding has ceased altogether at the mill, but it remains a popular place to purchase feed and seed.

Immediately south of 14-Mile Lock is a bridge on the towpath over a water control structure know as a floodgate. The matter of keeping just the right amount of water in the canal was a never-ending battle. Side creeks, leakage, animal holes, floods, and droughts all had to be accounted for, and a floodgate was one mechanism to drain excess water from the canal, or drain the canal for repairs. This remains true today, as this one is still used to regulate the level of water in the canal.

South of Lock 37, stop a moment to take in the view. The open pasture to the northeast, above Canal Road, represents what most of the area looked like 150 years ago. With a little imagination, you can erase the power lines in front of you and turn Canal Road into a narrow dirt path. On a knoll east of Canal Road sits the stately red brick Frazee House, built around 1825, just as the construction of the Ohio & Erie Canal was under way. The route of the canal split Frazee's property, and Stephen Frazee sued the state of Ohio. He might have used his settlement to pay for construction of this house, very fine for its time. The Frazee House is open to visitors on summer weekends. Just north of the Frazee House was a "wide-water" in the canal, a basin used for layovers and transfer of cargo. The utility poles mark the original location of Canal Road. The basin has been filled in and the road relocated.

There is a small parking lot and restroom next to the Frazee House.

Frazee House Trailhead to Station Road Bridge Trailhead

In contrast to the section of trail north of here, this part of the Towpath Trail is out of sight and sound of any roads. Just south of the Frazee House the canal and path swing sharply away from Canal Road and enter a much narrower portion of the Cuyahoga Valley known as the Pinery Narrows. The Towpath Trail continues through the narrows for about two and a half miles before reaching the next road.

Directions: I-77 to Exit 153, Pleasant Valley/Alexander Road. East on Pleasant Valley to Canal Road. South on Canal Road about half a mile to Frazee House. Park at the north end at the Frazee House Trailhead on Canal Road, and at the south end at the Station Road Bridge Trailhead, located on Riverview Road just south of State Route 82.

Trail Description: From the Frazee House, reach the Towpath Trail by crossing Canal Road. A short bridge takes you across the canal to the trail. Turn left (south) to begin. Here the Buckeye Trail (BT) joins the Towpath Trail from the east on the BT's 1,400-mile journey around Ohio. Be aware that portions of this section of the Towpath Trail are also used by equestrians. Remember: hikers and cyclists yield to horses.

Cross a concrete-lined sluice and a wooden bridge over floodgates, then follow the canal in a gentle curve to the west. Here you enter a section of the Towpath Trail that will carry you away from the sounds of internal combustion engines. The Pinery Narrows, or simply the Narrows, is a secluded part of the national park where the canal, the river, and the Valley Railway closely parallel each other, confined by the cliffs and hills on either side. The name, Pinery Narrows, dates at least as far back as canal days, and it is believed that the name derives from the many white pines that once covered the hillsides. Pines were one of the valley's most treasured trees, tall and straight and useful for everything from sailing ship masts to furniture. A few white pines can be seen on the steep slopes near the trail, but equally beautiful are the Eastern hemlock trees that do especially well on the cool, moist, shaded slopes. An 1880 railroad guide referred to this area as Little Packsaddle Narrows and suggested it was "the Eden of the Cuyahoga valley." In 2007 an event occurred that helps confirm this—for the first time in over seventy years, a pair of bald eagles nested in the Pinery Narrows. A young pair had checked out the area in 2006 and began a nest in the great blue heron nesting colony, but did not

Ohio & Erie Canal Towpath Trail

FRAZEE HOUSE TO STATION ROAD BRIDGE

2.5 MILES
HIKING TIME – 1.25 HOURS
BICYCLING TIME – 20 MINUTES
ELEVATION CHANGE – 8 FEET
RATING – EASY

follow through. In 2007, a pair chose a slightly different location, still in the herony, and established their nest and raised one eaglet. This was the first bald eagle nest to be built in the national park.

Just before Mile 15 the trail swings sharply to the east. This is Horseshoe Bend, also known as the Devil's Elbow. The next two miles in the Narrows are good for spotting wildlife. In mid-summer look for turtles sunning on logs. During a spring evening you might spot a great blue heron silently

State Route 82 bridge

returning to its nest colony. Winter's snow captures tracks for later observation. Try traveling quietly to see what you can find.

Soon the graceful arches of the State Route 82 bridge, carrying traffic 145 feet above the Cuyahoga River, come into view. This is one of the few remaining bridges that use parabolic arches of reinforced concrete. Stop for a moment and look around. To your immediate right is the Cuyahoga River. Three hundred years ago you may have seen Native Americans passing by in canoes. To your left is the canal. One hundred and fifty years ago, standing where you are, you may have had to move to let a team of mules pass by. West of the river is the Valley Railway. One hundred and twenty years back it would have been carrying goods and people up and down the valley faster than the canal. Ahead, the Station Road Bridge crosses the Cuyahoga. One hundred years ago you might have seen it carry one of the first Model T Fords across the river. Today, you hear and see traffic of all kinds on State Route 82 above. Where else can you stand in one location and see more than three hundred years of the history of transportation?

Just north of the high-level bridge is Lock 36, or 17-Mile Lock (buried during the construction of the bridge). Seventeen-Mile Lock is also the location of the Brecksville feeder canal and dam, one of three original feeder systems in the Akron-to-Cleveland stretch of canal. The footbridge here is actually spanning the feeder canal. The main trunk canal is not

Towpath Trail

watered from this point south. Follow the feeder canal to the river to see how the canal gets its water.

To reach the trailhead from the Towpath Trail, turn west on the old Station Road and cross the Station Road Bridge, restored by the National Park Service for pedestrian and equestrian traffic in 1992. The parking lot is just beyond, south of the bridge. Here the Buckeye Trail leaves the Towpath Trail and enters the splendid Brecksville Reservation. Those looking for longer, more challenging loop hikes should consider combining the Buckeye and Towpath Trails in the areas south of Station Road Bridge.

Station Road Bridge Trailhead to Red Lock Trailhead

South of Pinery Narrows, the scenery along the Ohio & Erie Canal Towpath Trail changes compared to that in the Narrows. The canal is not watered here as it is to the north, although small sections of canal intermittently retain shallow water from the many side creeks draining off the hills to the east. The towpath, formerly used as a road in this section, is now lined with trees on both sides, which in some places create an arched canopy to shade the trail. This portion of Towpath Trail serves as access to the Old Carriage Trail, a 3.25-mile cross-country skiing and hiking trail.

Directions: I-77 to Exit 149, SR 82. East on SR 82 to Riverview Road. South on Riverview Road a quarter of a mile. Left into Station Road Bridge Trailhead. Or take I-277 to SR 82; west on SR 82 to Riverview Road, and south to the trailhead as above.

Trail Description: Starting from the Station Road Bridge Trailhead, head towards the bridge. The old road takes its name from a railroad depot once located here west of the tracks. A newer station serves the Cuyahoga Valley Scenic Railroad and has restrooms and a drinking fountain. The iron bridge, originally erected in 1881 (the date of 1882 on the plaque probably marks the dedication), was restored by the National Park Service and reopened for trail use in 1992. Note the wooden pavers used as flooring for the bridge, to reflect a practice common at the time the bridge was originally built. Cross over the Cuyahoga River and continue on the old Station Road until you reach the intersection of the Towpath Trail. Beavers are busy here on both sides of the trail. Turn right to go south.

It was somewhere in this general vicinity that there were nineteenth- and early twentieth-century powder works. The Civil War-era powder works was on the west side of the river, and a later works was here on the east side. Local historian Joe Jesensky relates a story that the ravine near here became known as "Crazy Man's Hollow" because of a story about a soldier left here alone to guard the magazine who scribbled graffiti and diagrams all over the walls of the building.

Travel is easy on this path, and from the trail you can soon see the confluence of Chippewa Creek and the Cuyahoga River. Soon the river and canal part company as you head towards Lock 35. Also called Kettlewell Lock, after a local resident, this lock also gained another nickname, Whiskey Lock, from a still that was located nearby.

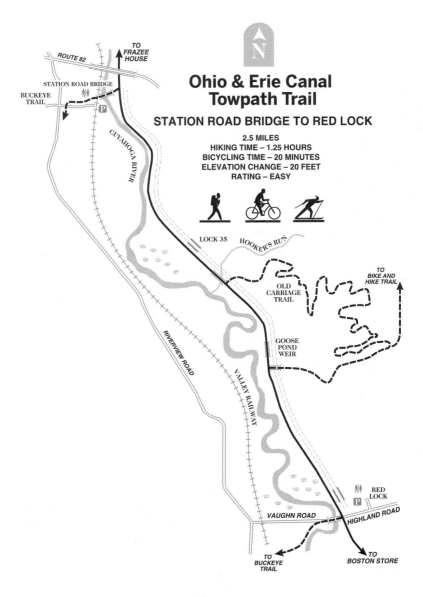

Ohio & Erie Canal
Towpath Trail

STATION ROAD BRIDGE TO RED LOCK

2.5 MILES
HIKING TIME – 1.25 HOURS
BICYCLING TIME – 20 MINUTES
ELEVATION CHANGE – 20 FEET
RATING – EASY

Northwest of the lock is a wide meadow-like area lying slightly below the level of the trail. A mining operation removed topsoil from here before the area was integrated into the national park. The river flooded the lowered land creating a large marshy area and a pond. In some places the low land is thick with shrubs, and in other places beavers are working the area, damming around the pond and creating beaver canals throughout the area. This mixture of open water, marsh, and shrub meadow attracts

Bike Aboard at Brecksville Station

waterfowl, songbirds, and raptors. Near Lock 35 is a bench where you can rest and enjoy this particularly scenic spot.

Past Mile 18, the Towpath Trail crosses Hooker's Run on a bridge built on the concrete remains of a floodgate dating from sometime between 1905 and 1909. Here, the northern connection of Old Carriage Trail takes off to the east (for foot traffic and skiers only). Ahead, the Towpath Trail is well away from cars and commotion, providing hikers, bicyclists, and skiers a chance to experience a piece of solitude and watch natural habitats quietly reassert themselves after being displaced by the canal.

Just north of Mile 19, you cross a wooden bridge built on the concrete remains of a water-control structure called Goose Pond Weir, probably named after a nearby pond. Immediately after the weir is the intersection with the southern connector of the Old Carriage Trail. This trail is paved and open to bicycles. It connects the Ohio & Erie Canal Towpath Trail to the Bike & Hike Trail. A small contemporary wooden bridge takes the connector across the canal.

Soon your trip on this section ends as traffic on Highland Road brings you back to the present century. Just ahead are the remains of Lock 34, also known as Red Lock. The reason for this name is not entirely clear. Although the lock gates were at one time painted red, many gates were so painted, so the name remains a mystery. The condition of the remaining masonry on the lock is a testament to the early use of concrete as a repair material. From 1905 to 1909, extensive repairs were made on the Cleveland-to-Akron locks—deteriorated stone was removed and replaced with a concrete facing. One hundred years of weathering have shown their effect. To reach the parking lot, follow a short trail to the left. The small concrete bridge that you cross carries you over the remains of the spillway that formerly carried water around Red Lock.

Red Lock Trailhead to Boston Store Trailhead

After the canal ceased operation, this stretch of Towpath Trail was used as a road by farmers and mill workers up until the 1970s. Now hikers and cyclists use the towpath passing through a scenic mix of swampy fields, wetlands, and horse pastures. It is also here that, just south of Red Lock, on April 18, 1990, the first spade of earth was turned marking the start of the restoration of the Ohio & Erie Canal towpath as a multi-use trail.

Directions: I-77 to SR 21 (Brecksville Road). North three-quarters of a mile to Snowville Road. East on Snowville Road to Riverview Road, then north on Riverview Road one quarter mile to Vaughn Road. East on Vaughn Road, across the Cuyahoga River, and left into the Red Lock Trailhead. Or on the east side of the park, take I-271 to the SR 8 exit. South on SR 8 one quarter mile to Highland Road. West on Highland, jogging right and left to go under I-271, about two and a half miles to Red Lock Trailhead. There is trailhead parking at the north and south ends of this section of the Towpath Trail.

Trail Description: The trail leaving the end of the Red Lock Trailhead parking lot takes you immediately past Lock 34 (Red Lock) and onto the Towpath Trail. This description begins with a left turn, south, toward Highland Road. Immediately after crossing the road, look through the trees to your left. The small concrete structures just on the other side of the remains of the canal prism mark the beginning of the spillway for Lock 34. The spillway was a side channel used to carry excess water around the locks. Just beyond, the Towpath Trail swings to the right slightly and joins a road that workers used to drive to reach the Jaite Mill. At this location, Brandywine Creek slips almost unnoticed under the trail. A historic, graceful, arched stonework culvert carries Brandywine Creek under the trail and road, towards the Cuyahoga River.

The Jaite Paper Mill was built in 1905 and used well water, which was plentiful here, in the paper-making process. The mill was one of the earliest and largest industries in this valley. The company town just west of here, built to house the workers and company officers, now houses Cuyahoga Valley National Park headquarters. The paper mill closed in 1984. After a fire destroyed much of the mill itself, the National Park Service demolished the buildings and has begun to restore the site. The Fourdrinier paper machine remains as part of an outdoor exhibit.

The next mile or so of trail carries you past old farm fields and pastures (some now wetlands) to Lock 33 (Wallace Lock), where there is a bench

and a fine view towards the Cuyahoga River. One half mile farther is the short connector trail to the Stanford House and the Stanford Trail (trail open to hikers only). The house is a historic Greek Revival-style farmhouse, once home to an early settler, George Stanford. It is open to the public on a limited basis. (For more information call the Cuyahoga Valley National Park Association, 330-657-2909). A one-and-a-half-mile hike on the Stanford Trail takes you to 65-foot-high Brandywine Falls, a scenic reward in any season.

Continue south on the towpath. A small wooden bridge over Lock 32 (Boston Lock) provides a good vantage point from which to watch for wildlife or view the inside of the lock, known as the lock chamber. On the east side of the canal prism, you find the remnants of the concrete structure marking the spillway. Ahead and across Boston Mills Road is the Boston Store. Originally built in 1836, it served the canal in a variety of ways and has been restored as a museum of canal boat building, an activity for which the village of Boston was well known. The parking lot and public restrooms are behind the Boston Store.

The Stanford House

Boston Store Trailhead to Lock 29 Trailhead

Between the two canal towns of Boston and Peninsula, the Ohio & Erie Canal Towpath Trail snakes its way alongside the Cuyahoga River. There is parking at either end for trail visitors.

If the Boston Store is open, a visit is certainly in order, particularly if your interests include either canal history or boats. The exhibits will give you the true flavor of the art of canal boat building. You can even measure your skill as a craftsman using the many hands-on exhibits. The porch is also a perfect place to meet friends or just reconnoiter before heading out.

Directions: I-77 to Exit 145, Brecksville Road. North one quarter mile to Boston Mills Road. East on Boston Mills Road, jogging left and right to go over I-80, about three miles to Riverview Road. Cross Riverview Road and the Cuyahoga River. Right into the Boston Store Trailhead. From the east side of the park, take I-271 to SR 8. South on SR 8 three and a half miles to Boston Mills Road. West on Boston Mills Road three and a quarter miles to the trailhead.

Trail Description: As you leave the parking lot, turn south (right) onto a well-used section of the Towpath Trail. After passing over a foot bridge, a trail to the left leads to an overflow parking lot. You will soon notice that, unlike the canal north of this point, there is no longer a canal prism to your left. Construction of the two sets of highway bridges (I-271 and the Ohio Turnpike) and erosion caused by the meandering Cuyahoga River have obliterated about one half mile of canal bed here. Between the two highways, the Buckeye Trail, which rejoined the towpath in Boston, heads off to the east (left). Just after you pass under the turnpike bridges, the canal prism reappears as a ribbon of wetland on your left, only to be lost again as the trail drops down onto a long, winding boardwalk through Stumpy Basin.

Canallers probably called the area Stumpy Basin for the many stumps of trees removed when the basin was originally built. Such basins were used for boat layovers during the active seasons and boat storage during the winter. The towpath, which in many places was the only barrier between the river and the canal, was breached here in the great flood of 1913. The basin is now an active wetland as seasonal floodwaters enter the area. The interpretive wayside on the boardwalk tells how ice was cut from the canal in winter.

Leaving Stumpy Basin, you pass Lock 31, or Lonesome Lock, and just before Mile 23, pass through a tunnel under the Valley Railway. At Lock 30

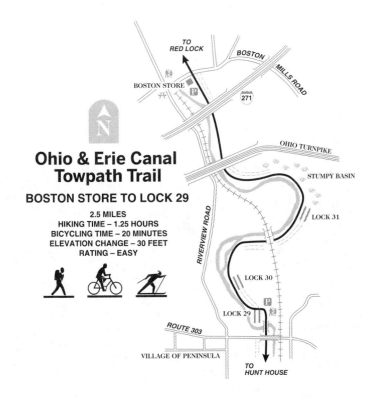

Ohio & Erie Canal Towpath Trail

BOSTON STORE TO LOCK 29

2.5 MILES
HIKING TIME – 1.25 HOURS
BICYCLING TIME – 20 MINUTES
ELEVATION CHANGE – 30 FEET
RATING – EASY

are the remains of another feeder complex like the one still in use north of Station Road Bridge Trailhead. Although none of the river dam remains, with a little imagination (and help from the wayside exhibit) you can piece together the remaining ruins to see how water was diverted from the river into the canal.

This segment of trail ends in the village of Peninsula at Lock 29 Trailhead. Don't miss the opportunity to explore the chamber of Lock 29 before ending or continuing your journey. Lock 29 is unique, because in 1882 it was completely rebuilt with new masonry. This meant the masonry was in good condition during the 1905-1907 repairs when all the other locks had their deteriorated sandstone replaced with concrete. Therefore Lock 29 is the only lock in the Cleveland-to-Akron section of canal that is still made entirely of sandstone. Inside the lock chamber, the wayside tells how masons' marks were used to measure productivity and determine how much the masonry crews were paid.

Restrooms and water are available at the trailhead. In the village you can find food, shops, a museum, visitor center, and bike rentals. Peninsula is proud of its arts heritage, making it a delightful place to explore, as it is filled with many historic buildings, shops, and galleries. A walking tour takes you past historic homes and public buildings. Allow time for shopping for exquisite art and locally-grown farm products.

Peninsula Depot

Lock 29 Trailhead to Hunt House Trailhead

The section of the Ohio & Erie Canal Towpath Trail from Peninsula to Everett travels through the Deep Lock Quarry area and is also used by the Buckeye Trail as it continues its 1,400-mile loop of Ohio. Parking for the trail in Peninsula is at Lock 29 and at the south end, at the Hunt House Trailhead. The Hunt House, just across the road from the trailhead, is open seasonally for park visitors. There is additional parking at Deep Lock Quarry Metro Park, half a mile south of Peninsula.

One hundred and fifty years ago, canal travelers between Cleveland and Akron—moving at a steady three miles per hour—found Peninsula a perfect place to break the journey. It is no wonder that hotels, mills, boat yards, and other businesses soon flourished. It is not hard to imagine that this little village, an island of history spared from mega-developments and su- perhighways, was once the major hub of canal activity for miles around. It still is—when trail visitors flood the village on warm summer days. A walk around town may pique your interest in its history. The Peninsula Library and Historical Society operates a museum at the corner of SR 303 and Riv- erview Road in the restored Boston Township Hall, and the National Park Service staffs a visitor center (seasonally) in a restored train depot.

Directions: I-77 southbound, take Exit 145 to Cleveland Massillon Road. South on Cleveland Massillon Road one and a quarter miles to SR 303. East on SR 303 four and a half miles to Peninsula. If northbound on I-77, take Exit 143, Wheatley Road. East on Wheatley Road three miles to Riverview Road. North on Riverview Road two and a half miles to Peninsula. In Peninsula, go east on SR 303 to Locust Street. Left on Locust and another immediate left, winding west a couple blocks to the trailhead just beyond the railroad station/visitor center. From SR 8, exit at SR 303 and go east three miles into Peninsula. Right on Locust Street, following the above directions to the trailhead.

Trail Description: Heading south from the parking lot you will immedi- ately pass Lock 29 and then cross the Cuyahoga River on a trail bridge. This is the location of the Peninsula Aqueduct, one of four aqueducts that were located in the Cleveland-to-Akron section of canal. (The bridge's shape, by the way, was chosen to resemble the curved profile used on one of the other aqueducts, the one over Furnace Run.) Standing in the mid- dle of the bridge looking downstream, you can still make out the trough of the aqueduct by the shape of the massive stone abutments on either side of the river. Looking upstream you will see that the river makes a rather unnatural turn after passing over the remains of a mill dam. This is the result of a rerouting of the river that occurred in the 1880s when the railroad was built. The Cuyahoga River used to make a winding bend to the east and back west, creating a peninsula for which the village was named. When the railroad was built, workers cut through the neck of the peninsula, rerouting the river's flow and cutting off the peninsula. A dam was also built across the river, the remains of which can still be seen from this bridge. Wetlands near the Lock 29 Trailhead parking lot lie in part of the old river bed.

Pass under the State Route 303 bridge. To your right (west) and above you stands the historic Fox House (c. 1880). Restored by the National Park Service in 1985, this slate-roofed house stands near the site of one of the Peninsula boat yards.

Along this section you will see that the canal bed, or prism, is to the west of the towpath, whereas north of Peninsula, it is to the east. This is because in Peninsula the canal itself crossed the river, and the towpath was always located between the canal and the river. The towpath switched from west to east of the canal at the north end of Lock 29, at exactly the same place the present-day trail crosses the lock. The towpath was located between the canal and the river for two reasons. First, it acted as a dike to keep the canal out of the river and the river out of the canal, and second, this location kept it away from the hillsides and the potential of being washed out by side creeks.

Soon the trail takes you into the Deep Lock Quarry area. Quarrying was an active industry in Peninsula in the 1800s, and one of the quarries was located here, just west of the trail.

This is an especially scenic part of the Towpath Trail. A stand of pines borders the trail right before you come very close to the river and some rapids. This section of trail is popular with bird watchers in the spring, since you can often find flocks of migrating songbirds resting and feeding here.

Just over half a mile from Peninsula, you reach the well-preserved remains of Lock 28, or Deep Lock. This lock had the deepest drop of all the locks on the Ohio & Erie Canal—seventeen feet. The usual drop on a lift lock was eight to twelve feet. Apparently, the additional depth was not economical, and the canal builders never repeated the experiment.

You may want to spend a moment at this lock. Note the holes in the top of the lock wall. These are locations of wooden mooring posts used to tie the boats to the sides to prevent them from bumping about in the

TO BOSTON STORE

LOCK 29

ROUTE 303

VILLAGE OF PENINSULA

DEEP LOCK QUARRY

MAJOR ROAD
LOCK 28

RIVERVIEW ROAD

CUYAHOGA RIVER

Ohio & Erie Canal Towpath Trail

LOCK 29 TO HUNT FARM

3 MILES
HIKING TIME – 1.5 HOURS
BICYCLING TIME – 25 MINUTES
ELEVATION CHANGE – 25 FEET
RATING – EASY

VALLEY RAILWAY

LOCK 27

EVERETT ROAD

FURNACE RUN

HUNT HOUSE

BOLANZ ROAD

TO IRA

VALLEY TRAIL

Great Blue Heron

lock chamber during filling and draining. Other features not visible in watered locks can be seen, such as the square openings in the lock walls used as culverts to move water from high to low level when the gates were closed.

A side trail south of the lock leads uphill to the parking lot for Deep Lock Quarry Metro Park. It is open to bicyclists, but the trail into the Metro Park and quarry is for hikers only. You can leave your bike at the bike rack and explore the quarry by foot.

Back on the trail, cross under the Valley Railway and head south. The scenery here is a pleasant mix of farm fields, river, and floodplain. In winter you might notice your proximity to Riverview Road, which parallels on the west, but summer's foliage hides all but the occasional sound of a car passing by. In this stretch of trail the agrarian setting in the valley is preserved. The rich bottom lands of the Cuyahoga River have been farmed for hundreds of years, and the National Park Service has developed a program to keep these fields farmed.

Just north of Mile 27 stands, coincidentally, Lock 27 (Johnnycake Lock). This marks your arrival at the crossroads hamlet of Everett. Here the canal crossed Furnace Run, by way of an aqueduct. A wayside at the lock tells how the lock got its nickname. From the pedestrian bridge over Furnace Run you can see the remains of the stone abutments of the Furnace Run

Aqueduct. In low water, you can see small iron pins built into the stone used to tie the iron work of the aqueduct to its supports.

The little hamlet of Everett developed in the canal days, grew to a population of 150, and in the early 1970s still had a small population and supported a gas station and general store. Everett was included in Cuyahoga Valley National Park when the park was created in 1974, and the National Park Service later purchased many of the houses. Things were quiet in the hamlet until 1993 when the park service began the process of restoring the houses and outbuildings, two or three each year. Most of the buildings have been converted into residences for the teaching staff working at the Cuyahoga Valley Environmental Education Center on Oak Hill Road. The remaining buildings are used as offices, park library, and park archives. Everett's church is thriving and Szalay's Farm sells corn and other farm products seasonally, making this corner of the park one of the busiest in summer and fall months.

Your trip ends at the Hunt House, located in a restored late-nineteenth-century farmhouse. It is open seasonally. Next to the visitor center, you will find restrooms built into a renovated farm outbuilding.

Best Hikes for . . .
Scenic Vistas

- Bridle Trails, Bedford Reservation (p. 101)
- Buckeye Trail—Egbert Rd. to Alexander Rd. (Tinkers Creek Gorge Scenic Overlook) (p. 53)
- Salamander Loop Trail (My Mountain Scenic Overlook), Brecksville Reservation (p. 129)
- Hemlock Trail (Chippewa Creek Gorge Scenic Overlook), Brecksville Reservation (p. 124)
- Ledges Trail (Ledges Overlook), The Ledges (p. 169)
- Hale Farm Trail, Towpath Trail (p. 45)
- Cross Country Trail (Kendall Hills), Kendall Lake (p. 178)

Hunt House Trailhead to Ira Trailhead

Before beginning your trip south, take a moment to visit the Hunt House (open seasonally). Hunt House was typical of the many small family farms that were found throughout the valley at the turn of the twentieth century. This is a good opportunity to pick up a park map or fill your water bottle, as this is the southernmost towpath facility in the national park with public water.

Directions: From I-77, take Exit 143, Wheatley Road. East on Wheatley Road three miles to Riverview Road. South on Riverview one quarter mile to Bolanz Road. East on Bolanz Road to Hunt House Trailhead on the right. Parking is available at both ends of this length of trail, at the Hunt House at the north end, and at the Ira Trailhead at the south end.

Trail Description: From the parking lot, turn south (left) onto the trail and immediately cross the remains of a stone floodgate historically used to drain excess water from the canal. In a short distance you will pass behind a small trailer park. Just south of the trailer park is a bicycle connector trail to Hale Farm & Village, Western Reserve Historical Society's nineteenth-century farmstead and village. This mile-long trail will take you past a boarding stop for the Cuyahoga Valley Scenic Railroad, alongside Indigo Lake, then over a wooded ridge above Hale Farm, with an exceptional view into the pastoral setting below. If your time permits, a visit to Hale Farm & Village is definitely worthwhile.

Continuing south on the Towpath Trail, you will enter an area of canal that is rich in wildlife. For the next three-quarters of a mile or so, you will travel along a portion of canal re-watered by nature's own engineer, the beaver. This large member of the rodent family has been in residence in this vicinity since the late 1970s. If you are observant, you will see not only beaver-chewed stumps and mud-and-stick dams, but also lodges and possibly tracks and drag marks where the beavers have hauled tree limbs across the Towpath Trail. Here also the trail passes a bend in the Cuyahoga River, another good spot from which to observe geese, ducks, and other birds. A wayside tells of the river's role as a pre-canal transportation route for Native Americans and how it failed to meet the needs of early settlers, leading to the building of the canal.

Just past Mile 28 you enter the heart of the beaver marsh. Before beavers flooded this area, there were old fields here that were probably farmed or pastured in the past. A car repair shop sat at the edge of the fields. After

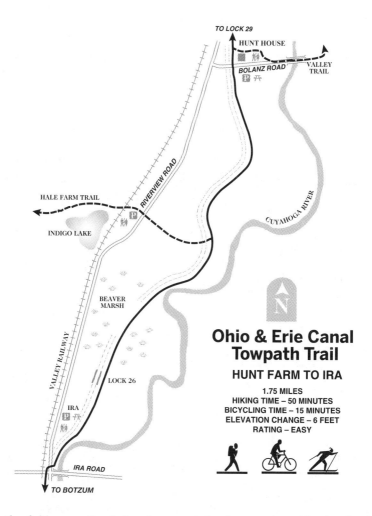

TO LOCK 29

HUNT HOUSE

BOLANZ ROAD

VALLEY TRAIL

RIVERVIEW ROAD

HALE FARM TRAIL

INDIGO LAKE

CUYAHOGA RIVER

BEAVER MARSH

VALLEY RAILWAY

LOCK 26

IRA

IRA ROAD

TO BOTZUM

Ohio & Erie Canal Towpath Trail

HUNT FARM TO IRA

1.75 MILES
HIKING TIME – 50 MINUTES
BICYCLING TIME – 15 MINUTES
ELEVATION CHANGE – 6 FEET
RATING – EASY

the fields were flooded, volunteers helped remove truckloads of refuse that had been dumped or left behind. The beavers, in essence, have completed a wetland restoration project, and humans helped by cleaning up the dumps. Now the wetland is one of the most popular places in the park, an exceptional place to watch the sun rise or to unwind at the end of the day. Visitors come at dusk to see the beavers at work repairing dams, or feeding on water lilies, bark, and twigs.

The National Park Service built the boardwalk here, slightly to the east of the location of the original towpath, to minimize impact on the rich habitat of the extensive wetlands. This is an excellent place to observe wildlife, so much so that the Ohio Department of Natural Resources has selected

Hunt House

the marsh boardwalk as an official Watchable Wildlife site. Beavers share the wetland with muskrats, which are active during the day; turtles and snakes, which like to sun themselves on logs and shorelines; and many species of birds, which feed, rest, and nest here. Benches and an observation platform were built into the boardwalk to provide places for observation or contemplation.

Next, beyond the end of the boardwalk, you reach Lock 26, or Pancake Lock, whose nickname came from a tale not unlike the one attributed to Lock 27's nickname of Johnnycake Lock. The story goes that a flood caused the canal to be temporarily impassable, and the travelers were fed meals made from the freight on board—cornmeal. Another version, however, is that boatmen were fed corn cakes at these ports on the canal, and may also have enjoyed the juice of the corn—whiskey.

The Ira Trailhead parking lot is found a short distance past Lock 26.

Hale Farm

The Hale Farm Trail is one of the newer trails added since the first edition of this guide and is one of the multi-use trails connecting to the Ohio & Erie Canal Towpath Trail. It connects the Towpath Trail to Hale Farm & Village. The section west of the railroad tracks was designed to be used by motorized trams carrying railroad passengers to and from Hale Farm, hence the wide, paved treadway. Much of the trail's alignment follows a cable right-of-way. The Hale Farm Trail is a pleasant little trail which climbs through a scenic stretch of woods with the pastoral view of Hale Farm & Village as a reward.

Directions: From I-77, take Exit 143, Wheatley Road. East on Wheatley Road three miles to Riverview Road. South on Riverview three-quarters of a mile to Indigo Lake. Right into the trailhead parking lot.

Trail Description: From the Indigo Lake parking lot, the trail east leads to the Towpath Trail. The trail to the west goes to Hale Farm & Village. Just across the tracks of the Cuyahoga Valley Scenic Railroad, Indigo Lake comes into view. Indigo Lake was created when a bulldozer struck an underground aquifer during a sand and gravel operation. A local story says the operator of the bulldozer abandoned his machine and scrambled up

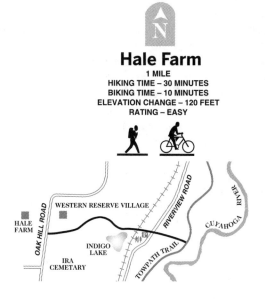

Hale Farm
1 MILE
HIKING TIME – 30 MINUTES
BIKING TIME – 10 MINUTES
ELEVATION CHANGE – 120 FEET
RATING – EASY

Hale Farm & Village

the steep banks to safety. The bulldozer—so the story goes—is still down there! How much of the tale is true is anybody's guess, but there is no doubt that the lake is fed from more than just rainwater. The clarity of the water gives it the color for which it is named.

As you continue west, the trail circles around the north side of the lake and then gently climbs through a mature forest. Along the way are scattered "erratics" uncovered during construction and cast to the side. Erratics are boulders brought here by the glaciers from the north. They consist of a type of bedrock, such as granite, not normally found in northeast Ohio. Soon the trail reaches its pinnacle in a planted stand of black walnut trees. Just as the trail heads down the final grade to Hale Farm, there is a wonderful view of the pastoral setting in which Jonathan Hale chose to locate his home.

An entrance fee is charged to visit Hale Farm & Village. The Gatehouse, which serves as a visitor center, also serves food and includes a gift shop. See the appendix for more information on Hale Farm & Village.

Ira Trailhead to Botzum Trailhead

This section of the Towpath Trail is unique because the canal and towpath south of Ira Road were destroyed by the construction of Riverview Road. The trail here was built west of where the canal used to be, and only comes close to the location of the original towpath at two places, where the trail passes the remains of two locks.

Directions: I-77 to Exit 138, Ghent Road/Cleveland Massillon Road. North on Ghent Road a short ways to Cleveland Massillon Road. Continue north about two miles to Ira Road. East on Ira Road two and three quarter miles to Riverview Road. North on Riverview Road and then an immediate right into Ira Trailhead. Parking at the north end is at the Ira Trailhead, and at the south end at Botzum Trailhead, the largest trailhead in the southern end of the park.

Trail Description: Follow the short trail east out of the parking lot at the Ira Trailhead to the Towpath Trail. Note the wetland in the remains of the canal prism. The trail to the left (north) will take you to a boardwalk over a beaver-created marsh. It is a great place to observe wildlife, particularly at sunrise or sunset, and is popular year-round (see description for previous trail section). To go south, turn right and follow the trail to Riverview Road. The trail crosses Riverview Road and Ira Road, and continues on the west side of Riverview Road. Please use caution crossing at this busy intersection.

Here, near the intersection of Riverview and Ira Roads, was a crossroads known as Ira. It was first called Hawkins, named after a local resident, until it became a mail stop on the Valley Railway. The mail got mixed up because of a town called Haskins in another part of the state, so the railroad changed the stop's name to Mr. Hawkins's first name, Ira.

The trail along here is bordered by a mix of hardwoods and has a few slight changes in elevation not found on the other portions of the Towpath Trail. The trail passes the remains of two canal locks. The east walls of both Locks 25 and 24 were demolished, and the canal prism filled in, when Riverview Road was widened in the 1930s. Halfway between the lock remnants, a drive leads up to the historic Botzum farmstead, now leased to a descendent of Conrad Botzum, who owned the farm in the late 1800s. The Conrad Botzum Farmstead has rental facilities and seasonal activities open to the public. (See appendix for more information.)

Here the trail also parallels the Valley Railway. Built in the 1880s, the

Bath Road herony

railroad carried passengers until 1962 and freight until the mid-1970s, hauling coal to Cleveland from southern Ohio and West Virginia, and iron ore south from Cleveland's harbor. Also in the 1970s, the Cuyahoga Valley Preservation and Scenic Railroad Association began offering excursions through the Cuyahoga Valley, at first using a steam engine. In 1987, CSX (successor to the Baltimore & Ohio Railroad) sold the Akron-to-Independence stretch of railroad to the National Park Service. A scenic excursion train, operated by the Cuyahoga Valley Scenic Railroad, has been operating on it ever since. (See the appendix for information on the Cuyahoga Valley Scenic Railroad.)

Just after passing Mile 30, you will cross Bath Road where, once again, the Buckeye Trail intersects, heading south into Akron on its way to Cincinnati. Your journey ends about one-third mile south of Bath Road at the Botzum Trailhead. A station for the scenic railroad and restrooms are near the parking lot. From here, the Ohio & Erie Canal Towpath Trail continues south, under the jurisdiction of Metro Parks, Serving Summit County.

Ohio & Erie Canal Towpath Trail

IRA TO BOTZUM

1.75 MILES
HIKING TIME – 50 MINUTES
BICYCLING TIME – 15 MINUTES
ELEVATION CHANGE – 25 FEET
RATING – EASY

The Buckeye Trail

When traveling from Cleveland to Cincinnati, most people follow I-71. Few would consider the less known routes that comprise the Buckeye Trail, a 1,400-mile path that encircles the state of Ohio. Buckeye Trail Association, Inc. (BTA), the group that supports the Buckeye Trail, is proud that the trail passes through Cuyahoga Valley National Park, a place as scenic as any in the state.

Within the legal boundaries of Cuyahoga Valley National Park, the Buckeye Trail remains mostly off-road, from its entry into Bedford Reservation near Egbert Road and Gorge Parkway, throughout the length of the park, to its exit just south of Bath Road. Within Brecksville Reservation, the Buckeye Trail forms a three-way intersection from which emanate north, south, and west routes. Whichever direction you follow the Buckeye Trail—north, west, or south—Cincinnati is less than 800 miles away (791 miles via the north route, 489 miles via the west route, and 655 miles via the south route). Along the way to Cincinnati, the trail travels through both glaciated and unglaciated terrain across Ohio's bluegrass country, its plains, and its hills. The trail traverses abandoned homesteads, strip mines, former railroad rights-of-way, towpaths of the historic state canal system, little-used country roads, levees, and even city streets. At present, about 40 percent of the trail is off-road. Through the American Discovery Trail and the North Country National Scenic Trail, the Buckeye Trail links to a nationwide system of long distance trails, making it possible to walk by trail from the Cuyahoga Valley to the far corners of the United States.

The thirty-seven miles of Buckeye Trail within CVNP are described in detail in the following pages. The route runs generally north and south, traversing the length of CVNP from Bedford to Akron. If you want a really long or challenging hike, the Buckeye Trail is ideal. In the Cuyahoga Valley you can link portions of the Buckeye Trail with other trails (particularly the Ohio & Erie Canal Towpath Trail) or roads, to make long loop hikes.

In general, the Buckeye Trail is marked on trees and posts with blue blazes that are similar in color, size, and acceptance to those seen on side trails to the Appalachian National Scenic Trail (a unit of the National Park Service). Where the trail changes direction, the blazes are positioned one offset above the other. The offset of the upper blaze indicates the direction in which the trail turns. Where the Buckeye Trail goes through land either owned by Metro Parks, Serving Summit County or anywhere else along the Ohio & Erie Canal Towpath Trail, the trail is marked by wooden trail signs.

Throughout the state, the Buckeye Trail is maintained, and was often built entirely, by volunteers. Except where the trail follows existing public trails or uses public land, no public assistance has been used to develop or promote the Buckeye Trail. Built primarily for hikers, the trail is open to all without charge. However, users must learn and obey whatever rules are imposed by the landowner. In some places, the blue trail markers may be faded almost beyond recognition. In others, the trail may be overgrown or muddy. However, with some determination, adequate preparation, and trail guides, the hiker will enjoy many wonderful experiences!

Buckeye Trail Association, Inc., which maintains this trail, is a non-profit, tax-exempt, all-volunteer organization that is incorporated in Ohio. The association is organized and operated exclusively for charitable and educational purposes. The goal of the association is to construct, maintain, and encourage use of the Buckeye Trail. For membership information and trail guides (maps) for the Buckeye Trail in other parts of Ohio, write to: Buckeye Trail Association, Inc., P.O. Box 254, Worthington, OH, 43085. Alternately, view the BTA Web site: www.buckeyetrail.org.

Best Hikes for . . .
Waterfalls

- Bridal Veil Falls Trail, Bedford Reservation (p. 96)
- Buckeye Trail—Egbert Rd. to Alexander Rd. (p. 53)
- Viaduct Park Trail, Bedford Reservation (p. 110)
- Hemlock Loop Trail, Brecksville Reservation (p. 124)
- Brandywine Gorge Trail, Jaite/Boston Area (p. 145)
- Blue Hen Falls Trail, Jaite/Boston Area (p. 148)

Egbert Picnic Area (Bedford Reservation) to Frazee House Trailhead (CVNP)

The Buckeye Trail (BT) from Egbert Road to Alexander Road shares the route with Bedford Reservation's Bridle Trail for much of the way. In these sections it is wide, gently-graded, and has a stone surface. From Alexander Road on, through the Sagamore Creek valley, it is a narrow footpath. There the Bridle Trail takes a different route, along the north side of Sagamore Creek. Hemlock ravines, waterfalls, rock ledges, and historic sites all combine to make this a favorite area for beginning the Buckeye Trail. Remember that the trail is linear, requiring you to double back or arrange a return ride to your starting point.

The Buckeye Trail enters the northeast corner of Cuyahoga Valley National Park near the intersection of Egbert Road and Gorge Parkway in Bedford Reservation. (See page 91 for more information on Bedford Reservation.) There are restrooms and picnic tables with grills at the Egbert Picnic Area near the start of the trail.

Directions: From I-77, exit at Pleasant Valley Road and go east to Canal Road. At Canal Road, Pleasant Valley Road becomes Alexander Road. Continue east on Alexander Road to Dunham Road. Turn left (north) on Dunham, then right onto Egbert Road. Take Egbert Road past Shawnee Hills Golf Course and turn left onto Gorge Parkway. The Egbert Picnic Area is on the right. From I-480 and I-271, exit at SR 14 (Broadway Road). Go northwest on Broadway to Union Street. Take Union to Egbert Road. Left on Egbert Road, then right on Gorge Parkway.

Trail Description: The Buckeye Trail extends from north to south through CVNP. Begin this section of Buckeye Trail at the Egbert Picnic Area. The trail runs along the rim of Tinkers Creek Gorge, just behind the picnic shelter. There is an access trail off the northeast corner of the parking lot that connects to the Buckeye Trail, where you will reach a spot with a good view of the gorge. Take this trail down a few steps and across a bridge, towards the gorge, then turn left onto the Buckeye Trail and begin to follow the blue blazes.

For a short distance the narrow trail hugs the edge of the steep gorge and is separated from the cliff edge by a wooden fence. About fifty yards beyond where the fencing ends, make a sharp turn away from the gorge, following the blue blazes. The Buckeye Trail is making a swing around to the south, going back towards Gorge Parkway. The Buckeye Trail joins the

Bridal Veil Falls

Bridle Trail and bears to the left to climb a bit. Near the picnic area, the Buckeye Trail and Bridle Trail now bear right, away from the picnic area, to go out and across the parkway. Just before reaching the parkway, the BT crosses the All Purpose Trail and the Parcourse Fitness Circuit, then crosses the parkway to the south side of the road. For the next couple miles, the BT and the Bridle Trail share the same path. They wind up and down along Shawnee Hills Golf Course, then come back across Gorge Parkway and the All Purpose Trail. About 500 feet beyond this crossing, a footpath leaves the Buckeye Trail, leading down to Lost Meadows Picnic Area. This is an interesting area to explore for its views into the gorge, its sheer cliff, and its waterfalls.

Continue on the Buckeye Trail, combined with the Bridle Trail. Cross the drive leading to Lost Meadows Picnic Area. Now you enter an area of hemlock ravines, with views of Deerlick Creek and its waterfalls to the right. The trail then comes out to the edge of Gorge Parkway, crosses the culverted creek, and follows along the rim of a ravine.

Now about two miles from your starting point, you join the trail coming down from Gorge Parkway leading to the Bridal Veil Falls Overlook. Cross the stream on an arched bridge. The overlook is to your right.

Leaving the overlook, follow the blue blazes on through a mature woods of oaks, hickories, and beeches. In a little more than a half mile, the BT

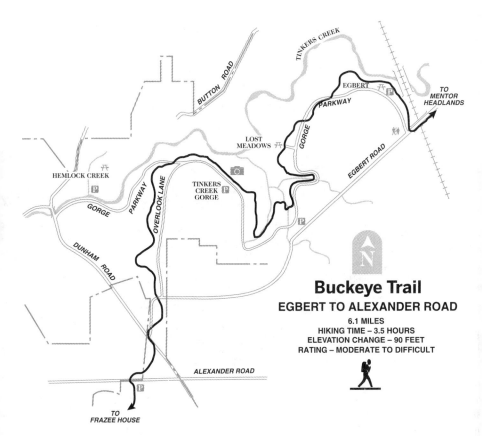

Buckeye Trail
EGBERT TO ALEXANDER ROAD
6.1 MILES
HIKING TIME – 3.5 HOURS
ELEVATION CHANGE – 90 FEET
RATING – MODERATE TO DIFFICULT

and the Bridle Trail part company—the Bridle Trail crosses Gorge Parkway and the Buckeye Trail remains on the north side of the road. Here you reach the Tinkers Creek Gorge Scenic Overlook that provides stunning views across the gorge, a National Natural Landmark.

Past the overlook, the Buckeye Trail, still separated from the Bridle Trail, continues to the intersection of Gorge Parkway and Overlook Lane. Just west of the intersection, the trail crosses the road and rejoins the Bridle Trail. The trail bears away from the road and enters a deeply wooded area. About 1,500 feet after the trail turns south, one branch of the Bridle Trail goes west, while the BT and the south leg of the Bridle Trail continue south. In another 1,000 feet, the BT and Bridle Trail split again, for a short ways. The Buckeye Trail takes a sharp turn away from the Bridle Trail to lead you to an old stone quarry. Watch carefully for the blue blazes, following them around the quarry and back to the Bridle Trail. Shortly after this, you come to a grove of pines, then reach Egbert Road, now over four miles from where you started. Cross Egbert Road, continuing to share

Waterfall along Buckeye Trail

the path with the Bridle Trail as both descend to the end of Egbert Road at Dunham Road. Here the Buckeye Trail again reaches the All Purpose Trail, but in a very short distance leaves it and crosses Dunham Road, heading due south, to rejoin the All Purpose Trail at Alexander Road.

Follow the All Purpose Trail just a short ways west, then cross Alexander Road. The Cleveland Metroparks Bike Trail parking lot is on your right.

At this point the Buckeye Trail joins the Bike & Hike Trail, both using an old railroad grade. (The Bridle Trail is separate here, taking a route on the north side of Sagamore Creek.) In less than a third of a mile, watch for the place where the Buckeye Trail leaves the railroad grade to the west (on the right), descending the embankment. Here the trail changes from a wide, paved trail to a narrow footpath that hugs the very rim of the Sagamore Creek gorge. This part of the trail is very scenic, and especially so in the wintertime when you can get the clearest views into the narrow, wooded creek valley. Two 25-foot waterfalls can be seen from the trail. Winter is also their best season, when ice decorates the cascades and neighboring shale cliffs.

The narrow gorge of Sagamore Creek widens into a broader valley, with the whitish upper branches of sycamores pointing out the floodplain below. Continue on the Buckeye Trail, roughly paralleling Sagamore Road. The BT comes close to the road and descends a hillside as you approach the Sagamore Grove Picnic Area. Watch carefully for the blazes here. The trail is prone to flooding here in the floodplain of Sagamore Creek. If the trail is passable, follow the blue blazes along and across Sagamore Creek, ending at the Frazee House Trailhead. If the trail is obscured or impassible, go out to Sagamore Road and follow it to Canal Road. Turn right (north) and follow Canal Road for a short distance to the Frazee House Trailhead on Canal Road, just north of Sagamore Creek.

Buckeye Trail
ALEXANDER ROAD TO FRAZEE HOUSE
1.5 MILES
HIKING TIME – 45 MINUTES
ELEVATION CHANGE – 200 FEET
RATING – MODERATE

Frazee House Trailhead to Station Road Bridge Trailhead

This section of the Buckeye Trail has two special attributes: it is almost entirely level and it goes through a unique roadless area of the valley known as Pinery Narrows, following the Ohio & Erie Canal Towpath Trail.

To access the north end of this section of Buckeye Trail, park at the Frazee House Trailhead located on Canal Road, just north of Sagamore Road. The historic Frazee House, completed in 1827, is one of the oldest brick residences in the area. The National Park Service restored the house and opened it to the public in 1995. The excellent exhibits tell the story of the settlement of the Connecticut Western Reserve and the architecture and craftsmanship of the time.

Directions: I-77 to Exit 153, Pleasant Valley/Alexander Road. East on Pleasant Valley to Canal Road. South on Canal road about half a mile to Frazee House.

Trail Description: To begin your hike, cross Canal Road and the canal to reach the trail on the opposite side of the canal. Turn south (left) to continue on the Buckeye Trail. The Buckeye Trail follows the Towpath Trail route to the south for the next two and a half miles. Here the canal passes through a very narrow section of the Cuyahoga River valley. You can find a special quiet and remoteness here, with the Cuyahoga River close on one side of the trail, and the watered canal on the other. The hustle and bustle of canal days is far removed from today's trail chatter. Also gone are large stands of white pines that gave this area its name, Pinery Narrows. In the 1800s, the tall, straight pines were cut for ship masts and floated to Lake Erie for the Great Lakes' sailing ships. The area has had other names as well. In the 1880s, the Valley Railway's guidebook referred to this area as Little Packsaddle Narrows.

At the southern end of this section you pass under the graceful arches of the State Route 82 bridge. Constructed from 1930 to 1931, it has achieved recognition for its engineering and design and is listed in the National Register of Historic Places.

Pine Hill Road, which was named Station Road on the other side of the river, intersects with the trail. This is no longer a public road. To follow the Buckeye Trail, turn to the right (west), on the old road, and cross the Station Road Bridge. The National Park Service restored this iron bridge in 1992 for pedestrian, bicycle, and horse traffic. The original bridge, constructed in 1881, served as an important vehicular link from east to west across the Cuyahoga River. A stop on the Valley Railway was located on the west side of the tracks not far from the shelter used by the Cuyahoga Valley Scenic Railroad today.

The trailhead parking is located just south of the bridge. There are restrooms in the railway shelter, and picnic tables along the river.

Station Road Bridge Trailhead to Jaite and Red Lock Trailhead

In this section, the Buckeye Trail leaves the river valley, climbs 200 feet towards the west rim of the valley, wanders through much of the Cleveland Metroparks Brecksville Reservation, then traverses up and down several stream ravines before descending once again to the valley floor. It is as rugged and challenging as any of the trails in CVNP.

To reach this section from the north, park at the Station Road Bridge Trailhead located east of Riverview Road just south of State Route 82. The trailhead is located opposite the entrance to Brecksville Reservation. Since this is a linear trail, you need to arrange to leave a car at the other end or return on the same route. Or, if you are in the mood for a long loop hike, you can return via the Ohio & Erie Canal Towpath Trail, a round trip of ten and a half miles. Parking at the south end of this section is located at Red Lock Trailhead on Highland Road, a half mile from the Cuyahoga Valley National Park Headquarters (located at the intersection of Vaughn and Riverview Roads). From Red Lock Trailhead, a connector trail links to the continuation of the Buckeye Trail heading south.

Here again we describe the Buckeye Trail from north to south.

Directions: I-77 to Exit 149, SR 82. East on SR 82 to Riverview Road. South on Riverview Road one quarter mile. Left into Station Road Bridge Trailhead. Or take I-277 to SR 82; west on SR 82 to Riverview Road, and south to the trailhead as above.

Trail Description: From the parking lot at Station Road Bridge, go back towards Riverview Road by crossing the railroad tracks and following a bridle path that parallels the entrance road. Just before reaching Riverview Road, watch for a post bearing the trail sign of a hiker symbol on a blue background. The trail now cuts diagonally southwest on a mowed path to reach Chippewa Creek and Riverview Road. Cross Chippewa Creek using the road shoulder, then step over the guardrail at the south end of the bridge, where another trail sign directs you into the floodplain woods along Chippewa Creek.

Now the Buckeye Trail is a narrow footpath that starts you on an interesting tour of the lesser-traveled parts of Brecksville Reservation.

Follow the blue blazes as the trail leaves the floodplain, climbs steadily, and swings to the left around a hill. It continues to climb steadily to the

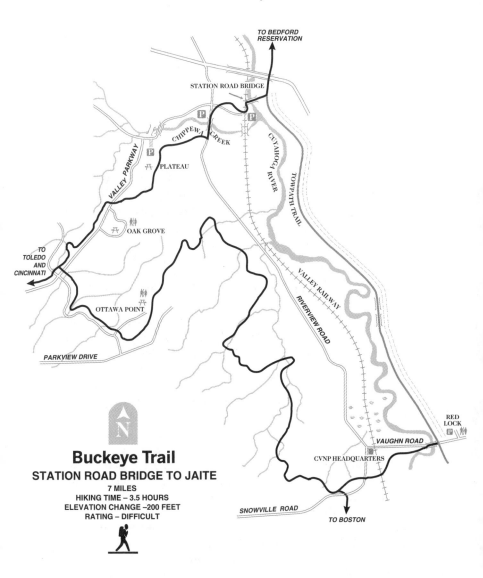

Buckeye Trail
STATION ROAD BRIDGE TO JAITE
7 MILES
HIKING TIME – 3.5 HOURS
ELEVATION CHANGE –200 FEET
RATING – DIFFICULT

top of the ridge. This is quintessential Buckeye Trail here on the backside of this hill—a narrow footpath, away from the roads, with wildflowers and trees as far as you can see. To the south, the forest stretches uninterrupted for many miles.

Towards the top of the climb, the trail crosses over to the north side of the hill and reaches an intersection. A short spur trail named My Mountain Overlook trail, leads to the right. This is a worthwhile side trip. The trail goes out along on a narrow hogback, getting narrower every year as the unstable soils of the hillside slump off to the north. The trail ends at a high viewpoint where there are a couple of benches. The nose of this ridge points towards the SR 82 bridge, visible only when the trees are bare, and to the north are views down into the Chippewa Creek valley. Parts of the ridge are covered with soft mosses and wildflowers, such as rattlesnake weed, with its purple-veined leaves.

Return to the intersection with the Buckeye Trail and continue along the ridge, where you will find another bench from which to enjoy the view. In 360 feet you reach the intersection with the Salamander Trail. The Buckeye Trail turns left with the Salamander Trail, staying on the high ground. In 1996, Cleveland Metroparks began studying and managing this forest area to improve the habitat for wildflowers and the oak-hickory forest. Unfortunately, gypsy moths arrived in the area around the same time and began defoliating trees, especially the oaks. Many of the older oaks suffered so much defoliation that they eventually died.

Continue southwesterly on the Buckeye Trail. In a short distance, you reach another intersection. The Salamander Trail and the Buckeye Trail part company, with the Salamander Trail going to the right, north to Plateau Picnic Area, and to the left, to end at Oak Grove Picnic Area. The Buckeye Trail goes straight out towards Valley Parkway, turns left onto the All Purpose Trail for a short distance, then crosses the parkway just short of reaching the exit road from the Oak Grove Picnic Area. You are about one mile from the start of your hike.

The Buckeye Trail now joins with the Deer Lick Cave Trail, marked with an oak leaf symbol, on the north side of the road. Turn left and follow the trail, running parallel to and just below the level of the road. The Buckeye Trail sticks with the Deer Lick Cave Trail through here except for diverging a short distance along the rim of the slope, then returning to the Deer Lick Cave Trail. Just continue to follow the blue blazes until you come to a three-way intersection of the Buckeye Trail. This intersection marks the spot where the Buckeye Trail was officially completed, linking all four corners of Ohio. The Medina, Akron, and Bedford sections all meet here. If you continue west, you can reach Cincinnati in 489 miles. If you go south, you reach Cincinnati in 655 miles. Turning back and going north, you can reach Headlands Beach State Park in 65 miles.

At this point, if you go straight (west) on the Medina leg of the Buckeye Trail, you reach the Deer Lick Cave area in just a few minutes. To explore Deer Lick Cave (more a rock overhang than a true cave), follow the blue

Buckeye Trail in Brecksville Reservation

blazes west, paralleling Valley Parkway. The trail leads down and through the cave area, a Berea sandstone formation, rich with fern gardens and plush mosses. (This section of Buckeye Trail leaves the reservation in one mile, heading towards Medina.) Return to the three-way Buckeye Trail intersection to continue south on the Buckeye Trail.

From the three-way junction, cross Valley Parkway and the All Purpose Trail, following the blue blazes south. Here the Buckeye Trail joins the Brecksville Reservation Bridle Trail. Turn right on the Bridle Trail and continue with this trail for about half a mile towards the Brecksville Stables. Many of the roads and trails of Brecksville Reservation have been around since the 1930s, when federal work-relief programs employed thousands of men here at Brecksville Reservation and at Bedford Reservation. The work crews constructed roads, trails, culverts, picnic grounds, and shelter houses. At one point along the trail you can see their fine work in an arched stone culvert under the park road.

Before the stables, one branch of the Bridle Trail leaves to the right, looping around the stables. The Buckeye Trail continues along Meadows Drive with the other Bridle Trail, coming very close to the road where it and the Bridle Trail part. This leg of the Bridle Trail crosses Meadows Drive just beyond the drive into the stables parking lot. The Buckeye Trail now narrows to a footpath once again. You can see a small abandoned quarry near the trail, which perhaps supplied stone for the road work and culverts.

White-tailed deer

The trail swings away from the road, then comes back near the road to skirt around the head of a ravine.

At the entrance to Ottawa Point Picnic Area, about a quarter mile from the stables, the Buckeye Trail joins the entrance road into the picnic area and turns to the northeast. This is a reservable picnic area. If it is in use, please respect the privacy of the picnickers. Follow the blue blazes into the picnic area, then again pick up the footpath near the parking lot.

Leaving the picnic area, the trail enters a mixed pine/hardwoods forest, and descends along a creek valley, then crosses at creek level. After leaving the creek, the Buckeye Trail parallels, then goes onto, an abandoned section of Parkview Road. Watch for the next turn, to the right—the Buckeye Trail leaves the old road and heads back southeast. Here in the lowlands, the Buckeye Trail reaches the Valley Trail, a bridle trail that connects Brecksville Reservation's system of bridle trails to those farther south in the national park. The BT and Valley Trail share the same path for a very short distance, then part again, the BT continuing south.

For the next two miles you will steeply climb and descend several side drainages for some very vigorous hiking. The woods vary from young stands of aspens to mature oaks, and lush fern gardens carpet areas along the creeks. Near the end of the two miles, you climb out of the last of this series of tributary valleys to reach an open meadow ridge near Riverview

Road. Cleveland Metroparks is currently managing this area for bluebird habitat. Follow the grassy lane south through the meadows.

Watch for the blue blazes which lead you back into the woods and steeply down to the next side creek. Cross this creek several times, working your way towards Snowville Road. You will come out into an old field with patches of dogbane, milkweed, and wild berries, just before reaching the road. White-tailed deer frequent this area, and if you're lucky you might also catch a glimpse of a red fox or coyote. This marks the end of this section of Buckeye Trail. A connector trail goes from Snowville Road to a small parking lot on Vaughn Road and to the Red Lock Trailhead. (The Buckeye Trail continues south from Snowville Road; the next road crossing is at Columbia Road, a little more than two miles away.)

Return on the Buckeye Trail, or if you left a car at Red Lock Trailhead—or wish to return via the Ohio & Erie Canal Towpath Trail—take the connector trail. At Snowville Road, turn to the left and walk along the shoulder, then cross Riverview Road. Follow the trail, which begins as a two-track, then narrows, over the railroad tracks and towards the power lines. A side trail goes north along the railroad tracks to a small parking lot on Vaughn Road. Alternatively, continue on the connector trail through the fields, along the river, then out to Vaughn Road. Follow the road across the river to the Red Lock Trailhead. If you have planned a round-trip using the Ohio & Erie Canal Towpath Trail, turn left to go back north (considerably flatter, faster, and shorter than your trip south). In two and a half miles you reach the Station Road Bridge Trailhead where you began.

Best Hikes for . . .
Fishing

- Tree Farm Trail, Oak Hill Area (p. 197)
- Oak Hill Trail, Oak Hill Area (p. 200)
- Hale Farm, Towpath Trail (p. 45)
- Lake Trail, Kendall Lake (p. 182)

Jaite and Red Lock Trailhead to Boston Store Trailhead

The Buckeye Trail in this section continues as a narrow footpath. From the Cuyahoga River valley, the trail climbs to the west rim, then, following a north-south course, it crosses several tributary valleys. These side valleys and intervening woodlands are typical of the rugged, forested terrain of the Cuyahoga Valley. Blue Hen Falls, towards the southern end of this section, is a good destination for lunch, additional exploring, or photography. You can return along the same trail, retracing your steps, or use the Ohio & Erie Canal Towpath Trail to make a loop hike of about eight miles.

This area is rich in local history. The northern trailhead is named after Lock 34 on the Ohio & Erie Canal, found next to the parking lot. More than one hundred years ago, the area would have been crowded and noisy, as farmers brought their products to a loading basin near here to be transported to markets via the canal. Just south of the lock, in the early 1900s, paper maker Charles Jaite built a mill along Brandywine Creek. In addition to the mill, he constructed a company town nearby to house workers and the company store. Most of the original buildings in the community of Jaite have survived through the years and have been faithfully restored to their original appearances, including their banana yellow color. They now house the Cuyahoga Valley National Park headquarters.

The Buckeye Trail also passes near the North District Ranger Station, which is housed in a restored brick home built in the 1800s by Jonas Coonrad, one of the early prominent citizens of Brecksville. In addition to farming, Coonrad had a cheese-making business at his farm.

To access this section of the Buckeye Trail, park at the Red Lock Trailhead on Highland Road, half a mile west of park headquarters. From Red Lock, an access trail connects to the Buckeye Trail, less than a mile away. Midway, another parking lot is located at Blue Hen Falls on Boston Mills Road, one mile west of Riverview Road. The parking at the south end is at the Boston Store Trailhead, located on the south side of Boston Mills Road alongside the Towpath Trail. There are restrooms at Red Lock Trailhead, and restrooms and a water fountain at the Boston Store. There are no facilities at Blue Hen Falls.

Directions: I-77 to SR 21 (Brecksville Road); north three-quarters of a mile to Snowville Road. East on Snowville Road to Riverview Road, then north on Riverview Road one quarter mile to Vaughn Road. East on Vaughn Road, across the Cuyahoga River, and left into the Red Lock Trailhead. Or on the east side of the park, take I-271 to the SR 8 exit. South on SR 8 one quarter mile to Highland Road. West on Highland, jogging right and left to go under I-271 about two and a half miles to Red Lock Trailhead.

Buckeye Trail

JAITE TO BOSTON

5.6 MILES
HIKING TIME – 3 HOURS
ELEVATION CHANGE – 250 FEET
RATING – DIFFICULT

Trail Description: Beginning from Red Lock Trailhead, take the access trail to the Buckeye Trail by following Highland Road west across the river. Cross over to the south side of the road, watching for the trail sign and path going away from the road. This connector trail follows the river, then swings west through fields. This part of the trail has been changed several times by floods and the river's changing course, so watch carefully for the trail signs. Follow the trail under a power line, across the Valley Railway, then across Riverview Road. Go about 200 yards up Snowville Road, then turn left, cross the road, and enter the woods. Watch for the trail sign marking this turn. You are once again on the Buckeye Trail.

Follow the blue blazes through the woods until you come to a set of steps built into the steep hillside. These steps were built in 1990 and 1991 by volunteers taking part in American Hiking Society's Volunteer Vacations. Imagine what the climb was like before the steps! This climb takes you about 140 feet above the valley floor.

At the top of the hill, turn to the right and follow an old farm road along the ridge. Massive oak trees line the trail, with beech trees on the slope off to the right. When the leaves are off the trees, there is a good view towards the south. There you can see the handsome, brick Coonrad house and its bright red barn. This historic house is home to CVNP's North District Ranger Station.

Just beyond a radio tower and block building, the trail comes out into the open, jogs left, then right. Watch for the blue blazes here when returning as it is easy to miss this jog.

This open area, created by utility corridors, is a couple hundred feet above the valley and is an especially good place for sighting hawks and turkey vultures soaring on thermals. Songbirds prefer the edge along the meadow and forest. It is worth it to have binoculars with you at this point. You can observe songbirds close by or enjoy the spectacular, long views.

After crossing the utility right-of-way, continue on an old one-lane road through the oaks and maples. Watch for the cutoff to the left, following the blue blazes. Beech trees become more prominent as you cross a small ravine, then a larger ravine, crossing a creek on stepping stones. Steps notched into the slope lead the way up the other side. The trail then widens again through fields and soon reaches Columbia Road. Cross Columbia Road. The trail now parallels Columbia Road for a short distance, just below the level of the road. A hemlock ravine slopes off to the right. Farther along, some foundation stones and large oak trees surrounding a clearing are all that remain of an old homestead.

Soon the trail begins to descend towards the ravine formed by Columbia Run. Thick, green moss and graceful, evergreen hemlocks framing a small clearing above Columbia Run make this an especially attractive spot. Hemlocks can be found in scattered locations throughout the state, but they need a moist, cool environment such as found here in this ravine.

Cross Columbia Run, then watch carefully for blue blazes pointing the way up out of the ravine. At the top, follow the ridge until you reach another utility right-of-way. Just after this right-of-way the trail drops down towards Spring Creek.

Boston Store Visitor Center

A side trail leads to Blue Hen Falls. These falls, like others in the valley, drop over Berea Sandstone to the less resistant Bedford Shale below, creating a much-photographed scene. Leaving Blue Hen Falls, and back on the Buckeye Trail, cross Spring Creek on a bridge, then follow the paved path uphill to a small parking area. Cross Boston Mills Road. Here the trail climbs gently towards I-271. Follow the blue blazes through woods paralleling I-271, into an open field, then back out to the road to get around the Summit County Engineer's Boston Mills Station. Walk the road shoulder past the facility and watch for the BT sign pointing back into the woods. The trail skirts the edge of the engineer's property, then goes down an old road and across a creek. After the creek, there is a set of eighty-seven steps to take you back up to the ridge. The trail comes off this ridge by switchbacks, ending the descent near the intersection of Boston Mills and Riverview roads.

Cross Riverview Road and follow the blue blazes along Boston Mills Road into Boston, situated alongside the Cuyahoga River. You reach the Ohio & Erie Canal Towpath Trail at the Boston Store, a National Park Service visitor center and canal boat building museum. From here the Buckeye Trail turns onto the Towpath Trail, continuing south. There is parking behind the Boston Store, and additional parking across the canal from the store. Return on the same route, or make a long loop hike by returning north on the level Towpath Trail. Via the Towpath Trail, it is less than two miles back to Red Lock Trailhead.

Boston Store Trailhead to Pine Lane Trailhead

This section of the Buckeye Trail is a narrow footpath on the east rim of the Cuyahoga Valley. It takes you through some terrain that has been altered by the construction of major highways, but also goes into less disturbed areas. Because of this, there is a wide variety of habitats along the trail, including old orchards, a borrow pit, mature oak woods, and the pristine Boston Run valley. Through these different areas, you can find an equally diverse collection of plants and animals.

Directions: I-77 to Exit 145, Brecksville Road. North one quarter of a mile to Boston Mills Road. East on Boston Mills Road, jogging left and right to go over I-80, about three miles to Riverview Road. Cross Riverview Road and the Cuyahoga River. Right into the Boston Store Trailhead. From the east side of the park, take I-271 to SR 8. South on SR 8 three and a half miles to Boston Mills Road. West on Boston Mills Road three and a quarter miles to the trailhead.

Trail Description: Starting from Boston Store Trailhead, get on the Ohio & Erie Canal Towpath Trail and go south, towards the I-271 highway bridges. After going under the bridges, look for the Buckeye Trail sign directing you left and uphill. You go along a wide field, then the trail turns left into the woods. Now the trail climbs more steeply, passing through an oak-hickory forest and an old apple orchard. Farther along, you go through a beech-maple woods, then come near the Ohio Turnpike. Follow the blue blazes as the trail goes away from the highway and descends to cross a creek on a bridge. The trail takes a switchback route up from the creek, then approaches and parallels Boston Mills Road.

Cross Boston Mills Road. The Buckeye Trail goes north a short ways, then swings southeast to follow a wooded ravine back towards Boston Mills Road. Turn left to cross the bridge over the Ohio Turnpike. At the end of the bridge, turn right and climb the short hill into the woods along the highway. The Valley Trail, a bridle trail, crosses the Buckeye Trail at this point. The Buckeye Trail swings south, entering a stand of white pines, once plentiful here in the Great Lakes region. White pines are easily identified by long, soft needles in bundles of five (five needles, five letters in w-h-i-t-e). On the whole, Ohio forests are mostly deciduous. Among the conifers, only white pines, Eastern hemlocks, and tamaracks are native to this area, and they only grow in specific habitats. These pines were undoubtedly planted here, judging from the straight rows they stand in.

Buckeye Trail

BOSTON TO PINE LANE

4 MILES
HIKING TIME – 2 HOURS
ELEVATION CHANGE – 240 FEET
RATING – MODERATE

When this country was first settled by Europeans, huge stands of white pines stretched for miles. An early pioneer saying declared that a squirrel could travel its lifetime without ever coming down from the pines. White pines, plentiful and useful, were cut and made into everything from giant masts of sailing ships to homes, bobsleds, covered bridges, and roof shingles. Soon the seemingly endless stands of pine were nearly all gone. The widespread decimation of the native pines contributed to the start of the forest conservation movement in the late 1800s and early 1900s. Now white and red pines, both tolerant of low moisture and nutrient levels in soils, are planted in disturbed areas to hasten the restoration of forest cover.

Along the trail and to the right of these pines is a depression that was made when soil was dug for the Ohio Turnpike bridge embankments. This is an interesting area to explore for unusual plants, such as the fringed gentian, which blooms in the fall. Deer browse this area, and in summer you can frequently hear field sparrows calling from the taller shrubs. Listen for the deliberate opening notes speeding to a trill. Some have likened the song to a coin spinning to a stop on a table.

At the end of the pines, turn right. The Buckeye Trail now passes through an oak woods along the south side of the borrow pit, then bears left and winds around the head of a side ravine, crossing two small drainages. A stand of young oaks is growing here on the uplands. Continuing on, a small pond marks a former home site to the right of the trail just before you reach Akron Peninsula Road (closed to vehicles in this section).

Turn to the left, walking east along the abandoned road, and watch for the blue blaze and sign marking the point where the trail leaves the road and reenters the woods. This last mile of trail goes in and out of the Boston Run valley. This rich, moist valley is full of ferns and wildflowers. Hepatica in delicate shades of pink or blue, trillium, toothwort, violets, and wild geranium are just a few of the flowers that can be found here in the spring. You might also hear the flutelike song of the wood thrush or the clear, musical song of the hooded warbler, both elusive birds of northern woodlands.

The BT crosses Boston Run at creek level (earlier bridges were washed out by floods). The trail then crosses a side creek on a log bridge and climbs out of the Boston Run valley. After the steep climb, follow the trail across a utility right-of-way, then through a pine planting, and finally into the parking area at Pine Lane Trailhead.

Buckeye Trail

Pine Lane Trailhead to Hunt House Trailhead

Here the Buckeye Trail allows you to leave the hills behind and enjoy an easy walk along the Ohio & Erie Canal Towpath Trail. By way of the trail you can visit the canal town of Peninsula and the farming hamlet of Everett, see two canal locks, and explore by a side trail an old stone quarry at Deep Lock. Another side trip could take you to the Everett Covered Bridge and Hale Farm & Village. There is enough to explore along the way to warrant allowing plenty of time for this hike, especially if you are interested in local history.

The Pine Lane Trailhead, located off State Route 303, seven-tenths of a mile east of Peninsula, serves the north end of this section of trail. This segment ends at Hunt House Trailhead on Bolanz Road, just west of Riverview Road. The Hunt House is open seasonally. There are restrooms at both ends of this section of Buckeye Trail, as well as midway at Deep Lock Quarry Metro Park. This is not a loop trail—you must return along the same route or arrange to leave a car at the end of your hike.

Directions: From I-77, exit at Wheatley Road. Take Wheatley Road to Riverview Road. North on Riverview Road to Peninsula and SR 303. Turn right (east) onto SR 303. Go about three-quarters of a mile outside Peninsula. Turn left onto Pine Lane and right into the trailhead.

From SR 8, exit at SR 303. Go west towards Peninsula. Turn right at Pine Lane just outside Peninsula.

Trail Description: To begin, look for the blue blazes directing you west out of the Pine Lane Trailhead parking lot and onto an old road (Pine Lane). Follow the road until it ends and the trail becomes a narrow path on a brick roadbed. This was an earlier roadbed of State Route 303; you can still find remnants of the old guardrail.

At the bottom of this road you join the present SR 303 and could take a short tour of Peninsula. There is much to see in this small canal town. In 1974, the Department of the Interior designated the entire village a national historic district. If you walk about two blocks off the Buckeye Trail, west up SR 303 to Riverview Road, you pass many historic homes and buildings. At the corner of SR 303 and Riverview Road is the restored Boston Township Hall and Cuyahoga Valley Historical Museum, open seasonally. South on Riverview Road is the Peninsula Library and Historical Society, which contains a good collection of local history. Here you can also enjoy the Mural of Transportation in the Cuyahoga Valley—a

Lock 28

stone mural on the face of the library giving a unique bird's-eye view of the area around Peninsula.

Peninsula has attracted artists since the early 1900s, and that tradition is continued today. Several shops and galleries in town offer the works of local artists. A bicycle shop, bookstore, and restaurants take care of other visitor needs. The Peninsula Depot is open seasonally and serves Cuyahoga Valley Scenic Railroad travelers, and other park and village visitors. Water fountains and public restrooms are available at the Lock 29 Trailhead one block north of SR 303. For a more complete tour of Peninsula, pick up the walking tour map available in any of the shops and the visitor center.

Back on the Buckeye Trail at the corner of SR 303 and Locust Street, near the Methodist Church, turn right (north) and go one block to Mill Street. Turn left (west) and go one block to the Peninsula Depot. From here you can cross the Valley Railway tracks and take the access trail along the river to the Lock 29 Trailhead and the Ohio & Erie Canal Towpath Trail. From the trailhead parking lot, climb the steps to Lock 29 and turn left to get on the Towpath Trail. Continue to follow the Ohio & Erie Canal Towpath Trail until you reach Everett, three miles south. Along the way you will pass Deep Lock (Lock 28), the deepest lock on the Ohio & Erie Canal. A side trail south of the lock leads uphill to Deep Lock Quarry Metro Park.

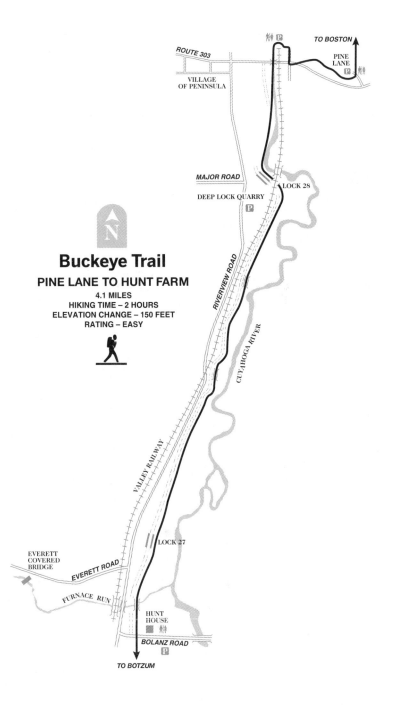

TO BOSTON

ROUTE 303

PINE LANE

VILLAGE OF PENINSULA

MAJOR ROAD

LOCK 28

DEEP LOCK QUARRY

RIVERVIEW ROAD

CUYAHOGA RIVER

Buckeye Trail

PINE LANE TO HUNT FARM

4.1 MILES
HIKING TIME – 2 HOURS
ELEVATION CHANGE – 150 FEET
RATING – EASY

VALLEY RAILWAY

LOCK 27

EVERETT COVERED BRIDGE

EVERETT ROAD

FURNACE RUN

HUNT HOUSE

BOLANZ ROAD

TO BOTZUM

(See Towpath Trail, page 37, and Deep Lock Quarry Metro Park, page 189, for more detail on this area.)

This section of Buckeye Trail ends at the Hunt House Trailhead, but an interesting side trip can be taken to visit the Everett Covered Bridge, following a former route of the BT. To reach the covered bridge, leave the Towpath Trail just south of Lock 27, and go west towards Riverview Road. Cross the road, then follow Everett Road west.

The National Park Service has restored the homes and commercial buildings in the crossroads of Everett for various uses. The Cuyahoga Valley Environmental Education Center oversees many of the homes as intern staff housing. Other buildings house park offices and facilities for several affiliated non-profit organizations. Proceed along the Everett Road berm to the Everett Covered Bridge (about half a mile). The covered bridge is a reconstruction of a bridge that was first built in the 1870s. The original bridge was destroyed by flood in 1975; in 1986, the National Park Service replaced it using new timbers, but in a design true to the original construction. A picnic table, restrooms, and small parking lot are located near the bridge.

If you are interested and have the time, you can go even farther on this side trip, and visit Hale Farm & Village. To get there, go across the Everett Covered Bridge and turn left on Oak Hill Road. The historic site is one mile away, reached via this very scenic and lightly traveled road. Hale Farm & Village is operated by the Western Reserve Historical Society. You can tour the homestead—one of the earliest brick houses in this area, dating to 1826—and other Western Reserve-style buildings in the village (fee charged). Craftsmen demonstrate skills used in the valley in the 1800s. The historic site also offers refreshments and a picnic area.

Hunt House Trailhead to Botzum Trailhead

The Buckeye Trail from Hunt House in Everett to the Botzum Trailhead near Bath Road uses the Ohio & Erie Canal Towpath Trail to Ira Road, then enters the woods at Ira Road and climbs steeply to O'Neil Woods Metro Park.

Park at the Hunt House Trailhead for the north end of this section of Buckeye Trail. The southern terminus of this section of trail is at Bath Road, near the intersection of Riverview Road. Park at Botzum Trailhead on Riverview Road, south of Bath Road. A short walk on the Ohio & Erie Canal Towpath Trail connects the trailhead to Bath Road and the Buckeye Trail.

Directions: From I-77, take Exit 143, Wheatley Road. East on Wheatley Road three miles to Riverview Road. South on Riverview one quarter mile to Bolanz Road. East on Bolanz Road to Hunt House Trailhead on the right.

Trail Description: From the parking lot, turn south (left) onto the trail. In a short distance you will pass behind a small trailer park. Just south of the trailer park is a connector trail to Hale Farm & Village, Western Reserve Historical Society's nineteenth-century farmstead and village. This mile-long trail will take you alongside Indigo Lake, then over a wooded ridge above Hale Farm, with an exceptional view into the pastoral setting below.

The Buckeye Trail continues south on the Towpath Trail into one of the most popular parts of Cuyahoga Valley National Park. Here the canal has been re-watered by nature's own engineer, the beaver. This large member of the rodent family has lived here since the late 1970s and has created prime wetland habitat for other species, including over 500 different plant and 65 nesting bird species. You might find signs of the beaver's work, including dams, trails, and chewed stumps, anywhere between the trailer park and Ira Road.

Before you reach the main part of the marsh, the trail passes a bend in the Cuyahoga River, another good spot from which to observe geese, ducks, and other birds. A wayside tells of the river's role as a pre-canal transportation route for Native Americans and how it failed to meet the needs of early settlers, leading to the building of the canal.

At the large beaver marsh on down the trail, a boardwalk built by the National Park Service takes you right out into the heart of the wetland, minimizing the human impact on the rich habitat. This is an excellent place to observe wildlife, so much so that the Ohio Department of Natural Resources has selected the marsh boardwalk as an official Watchable Wildlife site. From spring through summer you can see great blue herons, red-winged blackbirds, tree swallows, Canada geese, wood ducks, Baltimore orioles, yellow warblers, song sparrows, and many other species, depending on how quiet and observant you are. You might also catch a glimpse of a muskrat during the day, or beavers at dawn or dusk. (See Towpath Trail, page 42, for more information on this area.)

Next, beyond the end of the boardwalk, you reach Lock 26, or Pancake Lock, whose nickname came from a tale not unlike the one attributed to Lock 27 (Johnnycake Lock). The story goes that a flood caused the canal to be temporarily impassable, and the travelers were fed meals made from the freight on board—cornmeal. Another version, however, is that boatmen were fed corn cakes at these ports on the canal, and may also have enjoyed the juice of the corn—whiskey.

A side trail just north of Ira Road leads to the Ira Trailhead parking lot. The Buckeye Trail continues on the Towpath Trail out to Riverview Road. Cross Riverview Road and walk west on Ira Road, across the railroad tracks, and watch for the blue blazes that indicate where the BT leaves Ira Road and enters the woods, continuing south. The trail crosses a side creek and begins to climb, taking you into a large forested tract of land that the National Park Service acquired from Sherman O. and Mary Schumacher in 1991. Before that, from 1876 until 1963, the land was owned by Conrad Botzum and his descendents. The Botzums farmed here, and had a general store, warehouse, and depot on the Valley Railway, south of the farm, near the intersection of Riverview Road and Bath Road. When the Schumachers bought the property, Sherman Schumacher built miles of graveled jeep roads throughout the farm and steep hills up through the forest. He delighted in taking visitors on wild rides on these single-lane roads through the woods. The Buckeye Trail follows some of these jeep roads, and you will notice others intersecting along the way.

This tract of land has significance that relates to a time much earlier than the Botzums' farmstead era. Archaeological investigations have substantiated prehistoric Native American occupation of the land, not unusual considering the location of the farm on a terrace alongside the Cuyahoga River. The most recent chapter in the history of this land takes another interesting turn. A descendent of the Botzum family and her husband have leased the farm from the National Park Service and have developed rental facilities for special events.

Buckeye Trail

HUNT FARM TO BOTZUM

4 MILES
HIKING TIME – 2 HOURS
ELEVATION CHANGE – 160 FEET
RATING – MODERATE

When the Buckeye Trail reaches the ridge above the valley (a climb of about 200 feet), the trail follows above a small creek valley then swings east a bit to follow the edge of the forested hills above the Botzum farm. In some places you can get stunning views past the huge old beech trees to the far east rim of the valley, and down into the farmstead fields and meadows.

The trail takes a winding course, then leaves the Botzum farm property and enters O'Neil Woods Metro Park. Here, after crossing a bluebird meadow, the Buckeye Trail joins the Deer Run Trail. Turn right on Deer Run Trail and follow it to the right (north) towards the parking lot and Lone Pine picnic area. Continue through the picnic area and watch for where the trail again enters the woods at the opposite end of the parking lot. Descend the trail to Bath Road, cross, and continue on the Buckeye Trail as it follows Deer Run Trail across a stream and past another bluebird meadow, then along Yellow Creek. Some very large sycamore trees line the creek and trail. The trail returns to Bath Road a short ways southeast of where it crossed earlier. The Buckeye Trail turns right, leaving Deer Run Trail, and follows Bath Road east. You will cross a bridge over Yellow Creek, then reach the intersection of Bath and Yellow Creek roads. The historic Botzum cemetery is just off the trail, up Yellow Creek Road to the right. The Buckeye Trail bears left, continuing on Bath Road, to Riverview Road.

To reach the parking lot, turn south onto the Towpath Trail and go a short distance to the Botzum Trailhead. If you have time, however, an interesting side trip can be made to the Bath Road Heronry, located on Bath Road just a quarter mile east of the Riverview intersection. Great blue herons, which can stand four feet tall and have a wingspan of six feet, have been nesting at this site since the early 1990s, and have more than one hundred nests in the colony. People come from all around the area to enjoy watching the birds construct the nests and tend to the young. The birds can be seen here from February through July.

At Bath Road the Buckeye Trail leaves CVNP, turning south and following the remnants of the canal towpath along the Cuyahoga River. From here the BT next reaches Sand Run Metro Park, and then goes on around the state following canals, trails, and country roads. If you went on following the blue blazes, you could eventually return to this point!

Great Blue Heron

Bike & Hike Trail

The Bike & Hike Trail runs along the eastern rim of the Cuyahoga Valley, along the boundary of Cuyahoga Valley National Park. Metro Parks, Serving Summit County, maintains a total of thirty-three miles of Bike & Hike Trail, including a southern leg that makes a loop through Silver Lake, Munroe Falls, Kent, and Stow. Only the ten and a half miles of trail along the edge of CVNP are described here. Consult Metro Parks, Serving Summit County, for maps of the entire trail (see appendix).

The beauty of this trail is that the entire length, except for one mile, is separated from road traffic, allowing you a quiet and safe ride on even the busiest days. (Note: At the time of this publication, Metro Parks, Serving Summit County, was firming up plans to reroute this one mile of trail off the road, providing a continuously safe route.) The Bike & Hike Trail was one of the first "rails-to-trails" conversions in Ohio, utilizing abandoned railroad beds combined with utility rights-of-way. Following the railroad route, the trail takes you through some surprisingly remote areas, yet is never more than a mile or two from a cross road.

This trail is ideal for family bike rides. Grades are gentle at three percent or less. This trail tends to be less heavily used than the Ohio & Erie Canal Towpath Trail, which runs roughly parallel to the Bike & Hike Trail. If you wish to make a long loop ride, you can connect to the Towpath Trail by using one of the less-traveled cross roads or a portion of the Old Carriage Trail.

The Bike & Hike Trail and its adjacent parking areas are accessible at most road crossings. Please do not block the gates, as park vehicles need available access for maintenance and emergencies. Mileposts at these entry points note the distances to the next road crossing. The access points are noted on the accompanying map.

Some sections of the Bike & Hike Trail follow the abandoned rail bed of the New York Central Railroad, and the old "Alphabet Route" or Akron, Bedford, & Cleveland (ABC) Railroad, an electric interurban line that carried commuters between Akron and Public Square in Cleveland. That line merged with other electric railroads to form Northern Ohio Traction and Light Company, which later became Ohio Edison, and today is FirstEnergy. The Bike & Hike Trail in Summit County, which opened in 1972, is the result of a cooperative effort between FirstEnergy and Metro Parks, Serving Summit County. Cleveland Metroparks developed the northern section of trail in cooperation with The Illuminating Company, then in 2001 turned it over to Metro Parks, Serving Summit County, which made further improvements and now maintains the entire trail.

A mixture of woods, meadows, and wetlands borders the trail for its entire length. In July and August you can search for wild berries growing in the sunny patches between the woods and the trail. If you stop and look closely, you can find delicious wild strawberries in June, all the more delicious for their tiny size and the challenge in finding them. But watch out for poison ivy! It thrives along the edges. The ditches along the

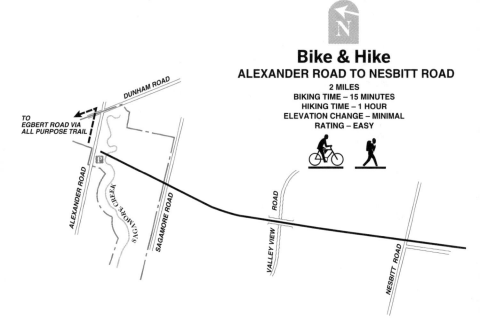

Bike & Hike
ALEXANDER ROAD TO NESBITT ROAD
2 MILES
BIKING TIME – 15 MINUTES
HIKING TIME – 1 HOUR
ELEVATION CHANGE – MINIMAL
RATING – EASY

route host cattails and other wetland plants, and one of our largest summer wildflowers, the common mullein, grows in the sunny borders of the trail. Common mullein can grow up to six feet tall and is recognized by its flannel-textured leaves and yellow flowers. It is not uncommon to find a goldfinch, matched in color to the flowers, perched on one of the mulleins.

Your chances of seeing wildlife along the trail are good, especially in the early morning or at dusk. Deer and rabbits might cross in front of you, and if you are extremely lucky, you might glimpse a fox or coyote. Birds such as song sparrows, chipping sparrows, yellow warblers, chickadees, and cardinals feed along the shrub edges, and in the summertime, colorful butterflies flutter about the trailside wildflowers.

Directions: To reach the northernmost end of the Bike & Hike Trail, exit from I-77 at Pleasant Valley Road and go east to Canal Road. At Canal Road, Pleasant Valley Road becomes Alexander Road. Continue east on Alexander Road to the trailhead, on the right side of the road.

To reach the southernmost end of the Bike & Hike Trail, take SR 8 to SR 303. Go west on SR 303 a quarter mile. The trailhead parking is on the south side of SR 303.

Bike & Hike
NESBITT ROAD TO BOYDEN ROAD

2.5 MILES
BIKING TIME – 20 MINUTES
HIKING TIME – 1.25 HOURS
ELEVATION CHANGE – MINIMAL
RATING – EASY

BOYDEN ROAD

AURORA ROAD · ROUTE 82

HOLZHAUER ROAD

NESBITT ROAD

CARTER ROAD

TO TOWPATH TRAIL
VIA OLD CARRIAGE TRAIL

Trail Description: Starting at the north end, you can access the Bike & Hike Trail on Alexander Road, just west of Dunham Road, where there is a small trailhead parking lot. Cleveland Metroparks' All Purpose Trail also begins here, offering you a paved hike/bike path heading north through Bedford Reservation. The Bike & Hike Trail goes south, following the New York Central Railroad right-of-way. The start of this trail is shared with the statewide Buckeye Trail. The Buckeye Trail leaves the Bike & Hike Trail a short distance south of the parking lot, dropping over the embankment to the right. The Buckeye Trail then follows the cliff edge above Sagamore Creek, an exceptionally scenic part of the BT that includes views of several small waterfalls.

At Sagamore Road the Bike & Hike Trail leaves Cuyahoga County and enters Summit County. The Bike & Hike Trail between Sagamore Road and State Route 82, about two and a half miles long, is less scenic than other parts of the trail, since it goes beneath high-voltage electric transmission lines. But even in this section, the surrounding vegetation provides pleasant scenery and wildlife habitat. At SR 82 there is trailhead parking. Use caution when crossing this busy highway.

The trail continues south on the railroad grade and soon crosses Holzhauer Road. Here there is an option for connecting to the Ohio & Erie Canal Towpath Trail if you wish to plan a side trip or round trip. To do so, follow Holzhauer Road south until it ends. Go onto the crushed stone path at the trail kiosk. This connector trail joins with the Old Carriage Trail, a hiking and cross-country skiing trail. Bicycles are permitted on the south leg of the Old Carriage Trail, which goes steeply downhill to the Ohio & Erie Canal Towpath Trail. Bicycles are not permitted on the rest of the Old Carriage Trail.

On a historic note, Holzhauer Road used to go all the way down this hill as well, ending at Red Lock on the Ohio & Erie Canal. It was a wagon road connecting the farms in Northfield Township to the canal loading dock.

Back on the Bike & Hike Trail, the next crossing is at Boyden Road, then shortly after that, you reach Highland Road. The trail then cuts diagonally over to Brandywine Road. Here the trail must leave the railroad right-of-way and use Brandywine Road for a mile in order to cross I-271. (Note: as of this publication, a reroute is being planned to get the trail off this road.) Turn right onto Brandywine Road to stay on the bike route. Midway along this one-mile stretch, you pass The Inn at Brandywine Falls, a popular bed and breakfast (see appendix). The innkeepers are George and Katie Hoy, regionally well-known for their gracious hospitality. Just

Bike & Hike

**HINES HILL ROAD
TO AKRON CLEVELAND ROAD**

**2.8 MILES
BIKING TIME – 25 MINUTES
HIKING TIME – 1.5 HOURS
ELEVATION CHANGE – MINIMAL
RATING – EASY**

beyond the inn is Stanford Road. You can leave the bike route here temporarily to reach the Brandywine Falls Trailhead, just around the corner on Stanford Road. The trailhead has restrooms and picnic tables, and is the start of the boardwalk leading to Brandywine Falls, a favorite destination for park visitors. Steps and viewing platforms allow you to get very close to the highest waterfall in Summit County, a beautiful sight any time of the year. The lush, cool creek valley is quite a contrast to the rail/trail bike route.

Back on Brandywine Road, continue on the Bike & Hike Trail route until you reach the sign directing you back onto the railroad grade. In less than a mile you cross Hines Hill Road, then cross the Ohio Turnpike on a bridge exclusively for the Bike & Hike Trail, just before reaching Boston Mills Road. West of the trail is the Bike & Hike Trailhead parking lot.

Continuing south, you finish the last couple miles of trail through the most beautiful section of the old railroad cut. Here the trail is deeply shaded and passes between huge sandstone outcrops and boulders, the remains of the Boston Ledges. These ledges were a popular spot for picnickers in the late 1800s and early 1900s, reached by some via the Akron, Bedford, and Cleveland interurban line. However, in the 1920s, the New York Central Railroad blasted right through the 100-foot-high ledges, destroying much of them. Some of the area was buried under tons of fill (probably made of the ledges themselves) used to level out the railroad grade as it traversed a deep ravine, but what remains gives you a sense of the nature of the Boston Ledges.

Today you can rest on a bench placed here near the huge, Sharon conglomerate sandstone rocks, a cool and especially welcome oasis on a hot summer day. Several species of ferns do well here, including common polypody and spinulose wood fern. Peterson's *A Field Guide to the Ferns* aptly describes the effect of the polypodies: "This small, evergreen, vigorous, and common fern, growing in matlike form, smooths and makes green and fresh the rugged contours of rocky woods." The spinulose wood fern is larger than the polypody. It has delicate, lacy-cut leaves that can grow to be thirty inches high. These ferns grow in rich, moist conditions such as you find here.

Continuing south, you soon go under State Route 303 and reach a ramp up to the Bike & Hike trailhead, where you will find restrooms and a small picnic area. From this point, the Bike & Hike Trail leaves CVNP and splits to make a big loop through Stow, Munroe Falls, Kent, and Silver Lake. This is a less rural route, but with some interesting sections, including a mile and a half or so along a scenic stretch of the Cuyahoga River. The entire loop would add another twenty-two miles to your trip. Contact Metro Parks, Serving Summit County, for further information on those sections.

Boston Ledges

Bedford Reservation and Viaduct Park

Bedford Reservation, a 2,206-acre park unit of Cleveland Metroparks, is famed for its main natural feature, the spectacular Tinkers Creek Gorge, a National Natural Landmark. The reservation protects the natural treasures in the gorge, and in turn creates a delightful place to picnic, hike, ride horseback, or explore for waterfalls. Viaduct Park is adjacent to Bedford Reservation and was created through a cooperative effort between Cleveland Metroparks and the city of Bedford. In contrast to the large Bedford Reservation, Viaduct Park is a small park of just a few acres. However, packed in those few acres are numerous remnants and relics of Bedford's earliest industrial history. Equally important, due to the development of this park, the public can now easily reach the legendary Great Falls of Tinkers Creek via a paved trail.

Tinkers Creek, the longest tributary of the Cuyahoga River, was named in memory of Captain Joseph Tinker, principal boatman of Moses Cleaveland's 1796 and 1797 surveying parties. Tinker was one of three men who died when their boat was capsized in a storm on Lake Erie. Tinkers Creek drops more than 200 feet in two miles, cutting a steep-walled gorge that is 140 to 190 feet deep. The inaccessibility of the gorge was a natural impediment to development in the 1800s, except for the more shallow upper gorge, where numerous mills were built around the Great Falls of Tinkers Creek in Bedford. While industry in Bedford flourished, the rest of the gorge largely escaped development or timbering, leaving it intact as a wild area to be explored and enjoyed.

As early as 1902, people began to visit Tinkers Creek Gorge for picnics and outings. A popular dance hall was the gem of Bedford Glens Park, on the north side of the gorge, from 1900 until 1944, when the hall burned to the ground, ending that romantic era. The gorge first achieved official park protection when Cleveland Metroparks acquired 1,300 acres in 1926. The park district later expanded the reservation to over 2,000 acres.

Bedford Reservation became a favorite haunt of local historian and artist, Joe Jesensky, who began exploring the area in 1923. He and his artist friends from Cleveland would come by train to Bedford and spend hours, sometimes days, exploring and sketching the nooks and crannies of the gorge. Jesensky's sketches and stories have preserved a special era of the park, when it was still a wild and largely unexplored place. Jesensky's *Tinkers Creek Valley Sketch Book: 1923–1933* is fascinating reading, and the sketches help conjure the sense of Bedford Reservation as a young, undeveloped park, when it was patrolled by one lone ranger on horseback.

This unique natural area has vast oak-hickory and beech-maple-hemlock forests, an unmatched spring wildflower display, and carpets of ferns, mosses, lichens, and liverworts. Here geology is clearly visible, as the water-cut gorge exposes the layers of bedrock found in the valley. Cleveland shale is bluish-black or brownish-black and is found at water level in the east end of the gorge. Delta-like deposits of red muds and offshore deposits of gray muds and silts constitute the Bedford Formation, a gray to bluish-gray shale found above the Cleveland shale. Berea sandstone, well known as a high-quality building stone, is found above the shales. Winter transforms this gorge into an icy wonderland. The park's more than seventy cascades and waterfalls freeze into ice formations, some 30 to 50 feet high. The vast and varied habitats in this park make it a refuge for birds, and has earned the park the designation of Important Bird Area from the National Audubon Society.

The scenic overlook on Gorge Parkway offers an expansive view of the forested gorge, a breathtaking vista that can be reached by all park visitors. Other attractions and facilities of this reservation include Bridal Veil Falls, Shawnee Hills Golf Course, scenic picnic areas and shelters, plus ballfields and playfields. Three long trails go from one end of Bedford Reservation to the other: the Bridle Trail, the All Purpose Trail, and the Buckeye Trail (described in the Buckeye Trail chapter). In addition, Cleveland Metroparks has created four loop hiking trails: Sagamore Creek Loop Trail, Hemlock Loop Trail, Egbert Loop Trail, and Viaduct Park Loop Trail. Some of these loops use and combine parts of the long, linear trails. Also, a physical fitness trail, less than a mile long, is located near the Egbert Trailhead.

Numerous other informal trails have appeared over the years, as more adventurous visitors explored along Tinkers Creek and its tributaries in search of Bedford Reservation's hidden treasures. In some areas, old roads and trails that were constructed years ago are no longer formally used or kept in repair. Detailed park maps that show all the official trails can be obtained from Cleveland Metroparks (see appendix).

There are picnic tables, grills, restrooms, water, and shelters at the major picnic areas, and a Cleveland Metroparks ranger station is located at the east end of the reservation. Lost Meadows Picnic Area is accessed by a gated drive and must be reserved in advance.

Directions: From I-77, exit at Pleasant Valley Road and go east to Canal Road. At Canal Road, Pleasant Valley Road becomes Alexander Road. Continue east on Alexander Road to Dunham Road. Turn left (north) on Dunham, then right onto Egbert Road. Take Egbert Road past Shawnee Hills Golf Course and turn left onto Gorge Parkway. The Egbert Picnic Area is on the right. To reach the west end of Gorge Parkway and Hemlock Creek Picnic Area, follow the above directions to Canal Road. From Pleasant Valley Road, take the ramp to Canal Road and turn north on Canal Road. Go about three-quarters of a mile to Tinkers Creek Road. Turn right and take Tinkers Creek Road to Dunham Road. Go straight into the entrance to Hemlock Creek Picnic Area.

From I-480 and I-271, exit at SR 14 (Broadway Road). Go northwest on Broadway to Union Street. Take Union to Egbert Road. Turn left on Egbert Road, then right on Gorge Parkway.

Directions to Viaduct Park: From I-77, follow the above directions to Bedford Reservation, to Egbert Road. Pass Shawnee Hills Golf Course and the east entrance to the reservation and continue to Union Street. Turn left on Union, then turn left on Taylor Street. The entrance is about 1,000 feet on the left. From I-480 and I-271, exit at SR 14 (Broadway Road). Go northwest on Broadway to Taylor Street. Turn left on Taylor. The entrance is about 1,000 feet on the left.

Best Hikes for . . .
Wildflowers

- Hemlock Loop Trail and Bridle Trail, Bedford Reservation (p. 98, p. 101)
- Sagamore Creek Loop, Bedford Reservation (p. 108)
- Wildflower Loop Trail, Brecksville Reservation (p. 118)
- Daffodil Trail, Furnace Run Metro Park (p. 156)
- Haskell Run Trail, Happy Days Lodge (p. 161)
- Buckeye Trail—Boston to Pine Lane (p. 70)
- Adam Run Trail, Hampton Hills Metro Park (p. 238)

All Purpose Trail

This paved, eight-foot-wide, multi-purpose trail offers access to Bedford Reservation's many attractions and accommodates a variety of uses including bicycling, walking, in-line skating, and jogging. In addition, a fitness trail is located along the All Purpose Trail near the Egbert Picnic Area.

From the All Purpose Trail, you can reach Tinkers Creek Gorge Scenic Overlook and Bridal Veil Falls. The trail crosses the three branches of Deerlick Creek and is bordered by hemlock ravines, and oak-hickory and beech-maple forests. The paved All Purpose Trail is easy to follow. It stays mostly within sight of the park roads and is accessible from many points along the way.

There are over seven miles of All Purpose Trail in Bedford Reservation, and at the south end of the trail, it links to the Bike & Hike Trail managed by Metro Parks, Serving Summit County. The Bike & Hike Trail continues another ten miles along the eastern edge of Cuyahoga Valley National Park, then extends east into Kent and Stow. At the north end, the All Purpose Trail goes beyond the Egbert Picnic Area for one mile to Broadway Avenue in Bedford, then parallels Hawthorn Parkway, and eventually links to South Chagrin Reservation.

Within Bedford Reservation, long loop hikes can be made by using the All Purpose Trail in one direction and the Buckeye Trail in the other direction. Bicycles are not permitted on the Buckeye Trail.

Trail Description: Starting at the east end, at Egbert Picnic Area, begin by paralleling Gorge Parkway on the north side of the road. After about one mile, cross over to the south side before the entrance road to Lost Meadows Picnic Area, which can be reserved. A side trip could be made down to Lost Meadows, a plateau perched on a very steep bluff overlooking the gorge.

Continue along the south side of Gorge Parkway. The trail will cross three branches of Deerlick Creek, a side creek that drains into Tinkers Creek and in many ways is a miniature version of Tinkers Creek. At the second creek crossing is a small parking area for Bridal Veil Falls. Another side trip can be made here, but by foot only: a ten- to fifteen-minute walk brings you to the waterfall, formed by this branch of Deerlick Creek etching its way through bedrock towards its confluence with Tinkers Creek.

The next major feature you reach is the Tinkers Creek Gorge Scenic Overlook, about two and a half miles from where you began. From here you can get a great view of the National Natural Landmark. There is a small

All Purpose
BEDFORD RESERVATION
5.25 MILES
HIKING TIME – 2.25 HOURS
BIKING TIME – 45 MINUTES
ELEVATION CHANGE – 120 FEET
RATING – MODERATE

parking lot here near the observation platform. Just past the overlook, the trail leaves Gorge Parkway and turns south to follow along Overlook Lane. In one mile, the All Purpose Trail crosses Egbert Road, veers to the west to parallel the curve on Egbert Road, where it crosses the bridle trail, then descends towards the intersection of Egbert and Dunham Roads. The trail bears left to parallel Dunham Road on the north side.

At the next intersection, where Dunham Road crosses Alexander Road, there is a small trailhead parking lot. You can continue on the All Purpose Trail by crossing Dunham Road and paralleling Alexander Road for a short distance, reaching the terminus at the Alexander Trailhead. The Bike & Hike Trail starts from here, going south on an abandoned railroad grade (see Bike & Hike Trail, page 83).

Bridal Veil Falls

This short trail is located off the Bridal Veil Falls parking area on Gorge Parkway, just east of Overlook Lane. A footpath and stairs lead you to overlooks from which you can view the falls on this middle branch of Deerlick Creek.

Trail Description: To begin the trail, cross Gorge Parkway and descend the steps. Follow along the shale-bottomed stream, then cross the stream on a footbridge. Walk a short ways to the last observation platform. From here you can absorb the beauty of the falls and surrounding hemlock ravines. From this point, Deerlick Creek winds downstream through its own gorge-like ravine, entering Tinkers Creek in a little more than half a mile, as the crow flies.

Part of the Buckeye Trail follows this trail and continues on to the Tinkers Creek Gorge Scenic Overlook to the west and Lost Meadows Picnic Area to the east. From Bridal Veil Falls, you can return to the parking lot via the same route you came on, or follow the Buckeye Trail as your time and

Bridal Veil Falls

wanderlust permit. The hike to the Tinkers Creek Gorge Scenic Overlook passes through a mixed hardwood forest with a spectacular spring wildflower display. Round-trip distance to the gorge overlook and back is about three miles.

Tinkers Creek Gorge Scenic Overlook

Hemlock Loop Trail

This short hiking loop from Hemlock Creek Picnic Area offers you entrée into the Tinkers Creek valley at the point where the stream comes rushing out of its narrow, cliff-lined gorge. In spring, you can find a lush display of eastern forest wildflowers, typical of what grows throughout the forested streamsides of this reservation. Virginia bluebells, wild geraniums, dog-toothed violets (including an unusual white variety), phlox, trillium, blood-root, and hepatica carpet the floodplain soils, delighting amateur botanists. If your interest is geology, you can study the layered history of the valley exposed in the cliff walls and the stream bed. This is also an excellent spot for the birder. Bring binoculars and a field guide!

Trail Description: Park at the Hemlock Creek Picnic Area, and walk towards the kiosk in front of the picnic shelter. The loop trail begins to the left of the shelter, following a wide, stone-surfaced bridle trail. The trail starts upstream along Tinkers Creek, and soon you can see an old stone and concrete wall that lines the stream. Floodplain forest is to either side of the trail. You can get some nice views of the stream, and might see a great blue heron or kingfisher looking for a good fish dinner. In places along the opposite bank of the stream, evergreen hemlock groves come right down to the water level. In contrast, on some south-facing slopes and in the upland, drier woodlands, you will find a mixture of oaks and hickories.

Tinkers Creek

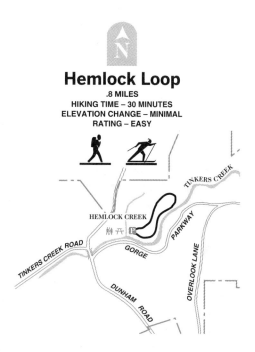

Hemlock Loop
.8 MILES
HIKING TIME – 30 MINUTES
ELEVATION CHANGE – MINIMAL
RATING – EASY

Near the end of the stone wall along Tinkers Creek, the trail turns left (west), away from the creek, and reaches an intersection. Here, the Bridle Trail goes to the right (north), and the Hemlock Loop Trail turns back south, towards the picnic area. You have reached an old road—Button Road. The entrance to Hemlock Creek Picnic Area is on Button Road, and Button Road still exists on the hill above, in Bedford, but here it was abandoned and is now part of the trail system. If you have time, a walk upstream on the old Button Road can be interesting, especially in the springtime. Here you find a wider expanse of woodland and wildflowers to either side of the trail. If you do take this side trip, in about five minutes you will reach another intersection. The Bridle Trail continues straight on the abandoned section of Button Road, and a side trail goes downhill towards Tinkers Creek. Button Road at this point begins a very steep climb, and the reason for this climb is obvious if you take the side trail towards the creek—a sheer cliff on the north side of the creek forces the old road to climb above the precipitous bluff.

After you have explored as much of Button Road as you'd like, return to the junction of the loop trail and the Bridle Trail and go south on the level trail to reach the picnic area. This was where Button Road leveled out and approached a bridge over Hemlock Creek. In the 1800s, Button Road was used by farmers bringing goods from the upland farms to the valley. From here travelers could reach Tinkers Creek Road, and in another one and a half miles they would be at the Ohio & Erie Canal.

As you approach the picnic area and look out across the creek you might be able to see the remains of supports for the old Pittsburgh and Lake Erie Railroad (later New York Central, then Penn Central) trestle which crossed Tinkers Creek. High above, on the south side of the valley, you can see the promontory formed by the railroad embankments. Built in 1911, the steel trestle stretched 150 feet above the creek and measured nearly a quarter of a mile long. It was used until the 1960s, then dismantled in 1974. Imagine the scary thrill that many kids must have had, daring each other to cross The Trestle.

Hemlock Ravines

For those whose impression of Ohio is one of flat cornfields, the rocky, waterfall-filled ravines of northeast Ohio come as quite a surprise. And most surprising—and to some, the most beautiful—are the hemlock groves and ravines tucked into the folds of northeast Ohio's valleys. Hemlocks, and the associated yellow birch and wildflowers such as partridge-berry, are a special gift left to Ohio by the receding glaciers. When you enter a hemlock grove, you know you are in a special place. Hemlocks grow where there is barely any soil at all—on rocks or steep slopes—and in the shade of the deep crevasses of creek ravines. In winter, their graceful, fluid branches droop with the weight of snow and brighten an otherwise black and white landscape. The cool, dense groves of hemlocks shelter special birds, as well, such as hermit thrush, winter wren, and magnolia warblers, usually found in more northern forests. Hemlocks grow very slowly and live to a great age—150 to 200 years or more. Unfortunately, they face danger from an imported pest called the hemlock woolly adelgid, which presents a threat comparable to the chestnut blight and Dutch elm disease. Aggressive programs are being implemented to try to find ways to control the aphid-like insect, and to conserve the genes of this irreplaceable tree species.

Bridle Trail—Bedford Reservation

The Bridle Trail makes a large loop through the reservation, going up one side of Tinkers Creek, across the creek, and down the other side, with much of the trail staying on the higher rims of the valley. A separate branch of the Bridle Trail leaves the big loop trail and goes south along Sagamore Creek. At the northeast end of the loop trail, the trail fords Tinkers Creek. (Note: At high water, this is not possible and you must return on the same trail.)

Some parts of the Bridle Trail were closed in the 1990s, but assistance from the Ohio Horsemen's Council helped reopen the trails in 1997. Trail riding has a long history in the reservation, dating back to the 1920s, when the park established the first bridle paths and began using a mounted ranger patrol. You can still find some of the original rock culverts and retaining walls along the trail.

Altogether, there are fourteen miles of Bridle Trail in Bedford Reservation. In some places, the Bridle Trail and the Buckeye Trail share the same path. Traveling the Bridle Trail, you can experience the best of what Bedford Reservation has to offer: deep woods, high ridges, hemlock ravines, Tinkers Creek valley, shallow cascades, and tumbling waterfalls.

South Rim Section:

The Bridle Trail begins on Button Road, the entrance road to Hemlock Creek Picnic Area. There is a parking area for horse trailers just south of the bridge over Hemlock Creek. Here you will find a picnic table or two and a small corral. Restrooms are across the bridge in the picnic area.

The Bridle Trail begins across the entrance road to Hemlock Creek Picnic Area, at the place where Hemlock Creek joins Tinkers Creek. Ford the creek to take the loop in a counterclockwise direction. (To stay on the north side of Tinkers Creek, ford Hemlock Creek and stay close to Tinkers Creek for a few yards until you reach the wide, gravel Bridle Trail.)

The ford across Tinkers Creek is not passable at high water, so in that case, go back out to Dunham Road and cross Tinkers Creek on the road bridge, then go up Gorge Parkway to where the trail fords Tinkers Creek.

Across Tinkers Creek, on the south bank, climb the short grassy slope onto the berm of Gorge Parkway. Follow the road to the left about 100 feet, then cross the road to where the trail is visible as it starts up a ridge. As you climb this ridge, you can see an old railroad embankment to the

Bridle Trail Ford

right, where the New York Central used to run; the creek valley lies below and to the left.

At the top of this climb, keep towards the edge of the ridge, bearing away from the embankment. The trail sweeps around to the north to follow the curve of the ridge, crossing a side drainage, allowing views of the Tinkers Creek valley when the trees are bare. Follow the trail as it curves, and in about three-quarters of a mile from where you left the road, you reach an intersection with the Buckeye Trail. The Bridle Trail splits north and south, sometimes sharing the path with the Buckeye Trail. Here you make a choice to either stay along the rim of Tinkers Creek Gorge or turn south to reach the Sagamore Creek valley. We'll first describe the section of trail that continues along Tinkers Creek Gorge.

At the intersection with the Buckeye Trail, turn to the left, along with the Buckeye Trail, continuing in a northerly direction through a scenic section along the steeply-sloped gorge. Near Overlook Lane, bear to the east, leaving the Buckeye Trail, and cross Overlook Lane and the All Purpose Trail, near the intersection with Gorge Parkway. The trail parallels the parkway, then crosses it beyond the Tinkers Creek Gorge Scenic Overlook. Now on the north side of Gorge Parkway, the trail rejoins the Buckeye Trail and moves away from the road into a mature woods of oaks, hickories, and beeches.

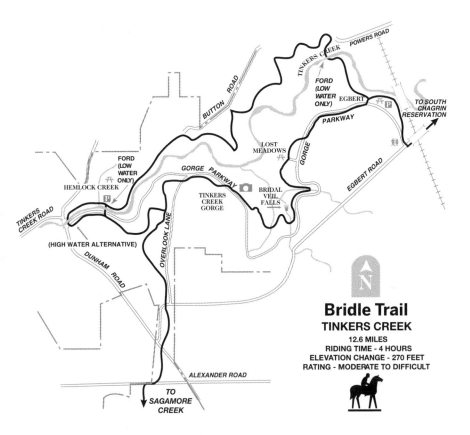

Bridle Trail

TINKERS CREEK

12.6 MILES
RIDING TIME - 4 HOURS
ELEVATION CHANGE - 270 FEET
RATING - MODERATE TO DIFFICULT

About one mile from the overlook is Bridal Veil Falls, on a branch of Deerlick Creek. To the left is the falls overlook; the trail bears to the right, crossing the creek by ford or footbridge. Steps to the right lead up to Gorge Parkway. The Bridle Trail and Buckeye Trail stay in the woods following the ravine of Deerlick Creek. Both skirt close to the road to get across to the other side of the ravine. This section is exceptionally beautiful, with hemlocks along the creek and waterfalls and rock tumbles below.

Cross the access road to Lost Meadows Picnic Area, go through another forested section, then cross the All Purpose Trail and Gorge Parkway. Here you follow along the south side of Gorge Parkway, with Shawnee Hills Golf Course to the right. Cross Gorge Parkway again, along with the Buckeye Trail, then cross the All Purpose Trail again, and reenter the woods. The Egbert Picnic Area is to the right. Bear right towards the picnic area, then left to start to descend to Tinkers Creek. (At the picnic area, the Bridle Trail leaves Bedford Reservation and continues to the east, towards South Chagrin Reservation.)

For several miles now you have been high above Tinkers Creek. To reach the creek, the Bridle Trail now descends to the bottom of the hill. (The Buckeye Trail leaves to the right partway down the hill.) There you reach the site of the old Powers Mill complex, a place that a century and a half ago would have been abuzz with activity. A sandstone slab dam was built here in 1842 to provide water power to run a woolen mill. Some of the stone dam is still there and is now covered with wildflowers. The mill buildings were located on the north side of the creek. About a mile upstream is the Great Falls of Tinkers Creek, the site of other nineteenth-century industrial mills, and downstream Tinkers Creek continues through its largely inaccessible gorge.

This section of trail ends at Tinkers Creek. There is a wide sand and stone beach alongside Tinkers Creek. If the creek is low enough, you can ford the stream to the north side and continue on the north rim section of trail. Otherwise, return on the same trail.

North Rim Section:

If the water level in Tinkers Creek is low enough, the south rim trail crosses Tinkers Creek near the site of the old mill dam. The trail continues along an old sandstone and mortar retaining wall, then turns to climb the hill. At a Y-shaped intersection, the trail splits. The section of trail straight ahead goes uphill on the old Powers Road, ending at a cul-de-sac where Powers Street now ends. To continue on the north rim of Tinkers Creek Gorge, turn left at the Y intersection and follow the switchbacks across a side creek and up the hill. In places you can see remains of old retaining walls dating to the early days of Bedford Reservation.

The Bridle Trail follows this old trail and road system for another mile and three-quarters or so, crossing side valleys and at times coming close to the steep cliffs along the gorge. The scenery is spectacular, and very typical of the gorge—hemlocks in narrow side ravines, hanging valleys dropping waterfalls over the edge, and upland woods full of deer. In places, side trails lead out to neighboring roads. About two miles from where the trail crossed Tinkers Creek, the Bridle Trail reaches and joins old Button Road (closed to vehicles). The trail comes steeply down Button Road, reminding you why the road is closed to traffic, and levels out at creek level, now closer to Tinkers Creek.

Close to the Hemlock Creek Picnic Area, the Bridle Trail intersects with a hiking trail. Bear left on the Bridle Trail, staying close to Tinkers Creek.

The trail skirts behind the picnic shelter, very close to Tinkers Creek, then fords Hemlock Creek, climbs a few feet to cross the entrance road, and ends at the Bridle Trail parking lot.

If you do not wish to do this whole loop, or if Tinkers Creek is too high to ford, you can still explore about three miles of this part of the Bridle Trail by coming up from the south at Hemlock Creek Picnic Area. If you take the trail all the way to the ford at Powers Mill, and return, you will go at least six miles. To begin from the Hemlock Creek Picnic Area, park as before at the parking area for horse trailers just south of the bridge over Hemlock Creek. Here you will find a picnic table or two and a small corral. Restrooms are across the bridge in the picnic area.

The Bridle Trail begins across the entrance road, at the place where Hemlock Creek joins Tinkers Creek. Ford Hemlock Creek and stay close to Tinkers Creek for a few yards until you reach the wide, gravel Bridle Trail. Follow the trail upstream along Tinkers Creek, then bear to the left, then right, to continue on up the valley. For a while you will follow the alignment of Button Road, now closed to vehicular traffic. The trail will climb very steeply to the top of a precipitous bluff and continue on a winding course high above the stream. It winds around some side ravines, and dips

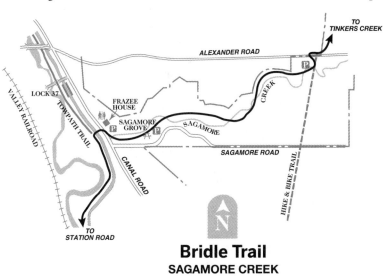

Bridle Trail
SAGAMORE CREEK
1.5 MILES
RIDING TIME - 30 MINUTES
ELEVATION CHANGE - 200 FEET
RATING - MODERATE

into other side valleys. Close to the north end, it makes a tight switchback down hill and intersects with the closed portion of Powers Road. A left turn takes you uphill to the Powers Street cul-de-sac. Going on downhill, you will reach the site of the historic Powers Mill complex. All that can be seen today are remains of the mill dam and a stone retaining wall.

Sagamore Creek Section:

To follow the southern spur of the Bridle Trail, take the south rim section of trail from Hemlock Creek Picnic Area, to where it intersects with the Buckeye Trail. Turn right (south) and follow this leg of the Bridle Trail about a mile, to Egbert Road. The Buckeye Trail shares the route for most of the way. Cross Egbert Road, continue south to Dunham Road, then to Alexander Road. The Bridle Trail crosses the All Purpose Trail, then crosses Alexander Road and the beginning of the Bike & Hike Trail near the Alexander Trailhead parking lot. Here the Bridle Trail and the Buckeye Trail separate, with the Bridle Trail going west to follow the north side of Sagamore Creek, and the Buckeye Trail going southwest along the south rim of Sagamore Creek.

This little creek valley has many of the attributes of the larger Tinkers Creek, but on an almost miniature scale. Here too you will find waterfalls, shale cliffs, and hemlock ravines. This section of Sagamore Creek is a mile and a half long, and at the end of the trail, the creek goes under Canal Road, then directly into the Cuyahoga River.

The Bridle Trail drops to creek level and crosses the creek several times. This trail can be very muddy, as well as quite beautiful with wildflowers. For about three-quarters of the way, the Bridle Trail and the Sagamore Creek Loop Trail share the same path. They split lower down the valley, where the Bridle Trail once again crosses and recrosses Sagamore Creek. This lower part of the creek valley is very prone to flooding, and both the Bridle Trail and hiking trails have been washed out in recent years. The path may be difficult to follow under these conditions.

At Canal Road, this section of Bridle Trail ends. However, the Bridle Trail continues south for three miles and connects to the system of bridle trails in Brecksville Reservation.

Bridle Trail—Pinery Narrows

Trail Description: The Sagamore Creek section of Bridle Trail emerges from the woods near the National Park Service's Frazee House on Canal Road. When you reach Canal Road, cross the road, then the canal and the Ohio & Erie Canal Towpath Trail. Follow the Bridle Trail into the woods. The Bridle Trail passes through Pinery Narrows by following closely along the Cuyahoga River. Where the space is too narrow for separate paths, the Bridle Trail uses the Towpath Trail.

At the southern end of Pinery Narrows (about three miles from Canal Road), the Bridle Trail turns west and crosses the Cuyahoga River via the Station Road Bridge. This wrought iron bridge was restored by the National Park Service for pedestrian and equestrian traffic in 1992 and reopened in June of that year. A large parking lot is just beyond the bridge. The Bridle Trail turns south to reach the parking lot, then crosses the entrance road and turns west, paralleling the entrance road, to reach Riverview Road. To enter Brecksville Reservation, cross Riverview Road. The Bridle Trail winds along Chippewa Creek then crosses the creek near the vehicle ford. From this point you can continue on the bridle trails that explore the scenic interior of Brecksville Reservation.

Bridle Trail
PINERY NARROWS
3 MILES
RIDING TIME – 1 HOUR
ELEVATION CHANGE – 8 FEET
RATING – EASY

FRAZEE HOUSE

SAGAMORE CREEK

TO BEDFORD RESERVATION

CANAL ROAD

DEVIL'S ELBOW

PINERY NARROWS

VALLEY RAILWAY

RIVERVIEW ROAD

ROUTE 82

LOCK 36

STATION ROAD BRIDGE

TO BRECKSVILLE RESERVATION

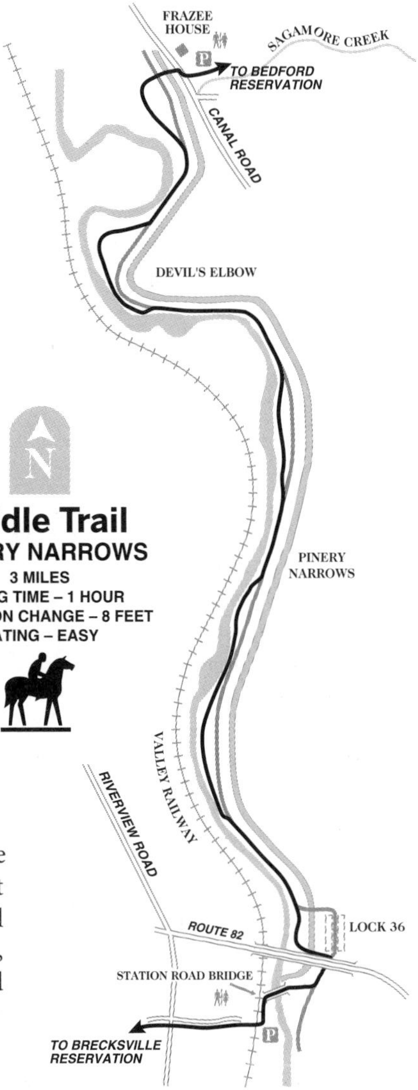

Sagamore Creek Loop and Egbert Loop Trails

Bedford Reservation has two hiking loops that were created by combining sections of other trails. The Sagamore Creek Loop Trail offers an adventurous hiking option. It is only three and a half miles long, but descends into and climbs out of the Sagamore Creek valley and has several creek crossings. These can be quite challenging in the spring when the water is high, although that is also when the wildflowers are at their peak. The Sagamore Creek loop uses the Buckeye Trail route on the south side of Sagamore Creek, and partly uses the Bridle Trail on the north side of the creek.

The Egbert Loop Trail is a much shorter, easier trail, and leaves from the opposite end of Bedford Reservation. It gives visitors a taste of the nature of the woodland surrounding Tinkers Creek Gorge and includes spectacular views into the gorge. It is described following the Sagamore Creek Loop description.

Trail Description: Begin the Sagamore Creek Loop at the Alexander Road trailhead. To go clockwise on the loop, start out on the wide and level Bike & Hike Trail. From the kiosk, turn right (south) on the rail/trail and go about a third of a mile, watching for the place where the Buckeye Trail drops off the railroad embankment and heads towards the rim of the Sagamore Creek valley. Follow the Buckeye Trail about one and a half miles along this beautiful gorge (see Buckeye Trail chapter) until you reach Canal Road. Cross Sagamore Creek to reach the Frazee House Trailhead.

At Frazee House, pick up the Bridle Trail which follows the north side of Sagamore Creek. In a short ways the Sagamore Creek Loop Trail and the Bridle Trail split—the hiking trail stays on the same side of the creek and swings up and away from the creek to explore the wooded hillside. The Bridle Trail crosses the creek then crosses back again upstream and the two trails once again follow the same route. Together they cross Sagamore Creek a couple more times, then switchback up from the creek bottomlands to the rim, ending just west of the Alexander Trailhead.

In comparison, the Egbert Loop Trail is a much easier and shorter loop—just a mile long, perfect if you have limited time to explore Bedford Reservation. It too links other trails in order to create a circular hiking route. The Egbert Loop stays on the drier upland, on the south rim of Tinkers Creek above the spectacular gorge. Part of the trail goes along sheer cliffs with good views of the gorge. (See the Buckeye Trail, page 53.)

Sagamore Creek Loop

3.6 MILES
HIKING TIME - 2 HOURS
ELEVATION CHANGE - 200 FEET
RATING - MODERATE

Begin the Egbert Loop Trail from the Egbert Picnic Area located on the parkway at the east end of Bedford Reservation, near Egbert Road. From the trail kiosk, go west across the grassy field and locate the Bridle Trail that parallels the paved All Purpose Trail. Go west into the woods. You will soon reach an intersection where the Bridle Trail goes right and left. Bear right on the Bridle Trail, which at this point is also the Buckeye Trail, marked with blue blazes on the trees. The trail starts to slope downhill. Midway on this hill watch for where the Buckeye Trail bears to the right, towards the gorge. Follow the Buckeye Trail uphill. It soon reaches the very edge of Tinkers Creek Gorge. Turn right and continue up along the rim, behind the Egbert Picnic Area. Here you can get some great views of the gorge; a split rail fence gives you some security. At one vantage point you can look up the creek gorge and get a glimpse of where Tinkers Creek emerges out of a large culvert. In 1901, the creek was routed through this culvert—and the surrounding gorge filled in—to carry a major railroad line across the gorge. The other end of the culvert, and the Great Falls of Tinkers Creek, can be seen from Viaduct Park, located on the north rim of the gorge in Bedford.

Continue along the gorge, past the picnic area, to where the hiking trail again joins the Bridle Trail. The hiking trail goes on just a short ways, then makes a little loop through the woods, between the gorge and the All Purpose Trail. Return to the picnic area via the Bridle Trail or the Buckeye Trail.

Viaduct Park Loop Trail

This short, scenic hiking trail, packed with history, was added in 2001 through a cooperative effort between Cleveland Metroparks and the city of Bedford. This trail now makes it possible for everyone to visit places that only the most adventuresome would scramble down to see in the past. Dramatic scenery, including the Great Falls of Tinkers Creek, and the early industrial history of Bedford are compacted within just a few acres in this park.

You access this trail from the Viaduct Park parking lot located at the intersection of Taylor and Willis Streets, and west of Broadway and Union Streets, in Bedford. A short ways up Willis Street is the Willis Picnic Area of Bedford Reservation, located on the site of the historic Bedford Glens Park.

Trail Description: Begin the Viaduct Park Trail from the parking lot. Several exhibits and maps help orient you to the area and point out numerous historic sites. An overlook is built upon part of an old railroad viaduct. Follow the paved trail down to creek level, where Tinkers Creek is making a big bend just before it drops over a fifteen-foot sandstone and shale ledge. The trail splits to make a small loop throughout the historic ruins. Signs and exhibits help identify various relics of the industrial past of this site.

Great Falls of Tinkers Creek

While waterfall enthusiasts can enjoy the view of the Great Falls of Tinkers Creek, history buffs will be drawn to the remnants of mills and mill-races. The focal point for many visitors is the locally famous Arch, the entrance into a 512-foot sandstone block tunnel built in 1901, through which Tinkers Creek disappears. It emerges from this artificial chute a short ways downstream, where it rushes into the natural and nearly inaccessible gorge. Above this arch is deep fill that partially buried an older 1864 stone viaduct built for the Pennsylvania Railroad. A couple of the older viaduct arches can still be seen above the great culvert. The other end of the culvert tunnel is just barely visible from a point along the Egbert Loop Trail on the south side of the gorge.

After visiting the many sites along Tinkers Creek, return to the parking lot via the same route.

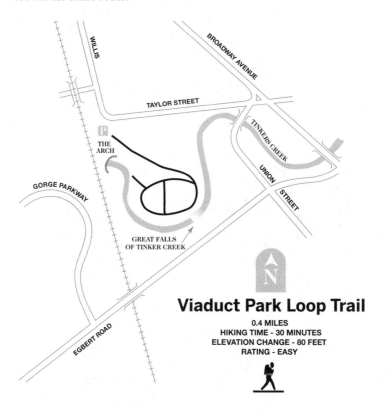

Viaduct Park Loop Trail

0.4 MILES
HIKING TIME - 30 MINUTES
ELEVATION CHANGE - 80 FEET
RATING - EASY

Brecksville Reservation

Brecksville Reservation is the largest reservation of Cleveland Metroparks, encompassing 3,494 acres of diverse parkland. Its exceptional beauty, extensive trail system, and abundant picnicking facilities make it an ideal destination for all-day family outings. Brecksville Reservation is located near the intersection of State Routes 82 and 21.

The first parcels of land were acquired for Brecksville Reservation in 1920, just three years after the establishment of the Cleveland Metropolitan Park District. In 1921, the park board passed a resolution to create the 300-acre Harriet L. Keeler Memorial Woods. In 1935, during the Great Depression, the Civilian Conservation Corps (CCC) established a camp in the reservation in order to construct trails and other facilities. The CCC camp operated through 1937, when it then moved to the Akron Metropolitan Park District's Sand Run park in Akron. The artful construction work of both the CCC and Works Progress Administration (WPA) crews—including trails, shelter houses, and the nature center—endures and has been enjoyed by many generations of park visitors.

Chippewa Creek cuts a deep gorge along the northern boundary of this reservation. Seven other ravines are formed by streams working their way to the Cuyahoga River. Therefore there are plenty of hills to climb, and streams to cross, when you explore Brecksville Reservation. Steep cliffs, huge boulders, and cascading water typify the gorge area. You will find a variety of other natural features throughout the rest of the reservation, including oak-hickory and beech-maple forests, shady hemlock ravines, floodplains, and a restored tallgrass prairie. Cleveland Metroparks is maintaining habitat diversity by managing old fields, reclaiming apple orchards, and enhancing wetlands. Deservedly, Brecksville Reservation is listed by the National Audubon Society as an Important Bird Area.

At several places in the reservation are clusters of often overlooked, but fascinating, trees. Located near the corner of SR 21 and Valley Parkway, at the entrance to Meadows Picnic Area, and near the intersection of Chippewa Creek Drive and Riverview Road, are groves of dawn redwoods. These trees are often called living fossils because they thrived 100 million years ago in the age of dinosaurs. During the 1940s they were discovered still growing in a remote valley in China. They have now been cultivated through seeds and cuttings.

These dawn redwoods are ancient relatives to our western giant

Chippewa Creek Falls

sequoias (thus the scientific name *Metasequoia glyptostroboides*). They differ, however, by being deciduous, dropping their lacy leaves in autumn. You can recognize them by their pyramidal shape, horizontal branches, and bark, which is deeply fissured and reddish.

Brecksville Nature Center, one of the oldest buildings in the park district, is a good place to begin your visit to the reservation. Its rustic architecture and woodland setting take one back to the beginnings of the metropolitan park district movement and the early days of conservation in northeast Ohio. Located on Chippewa Creek Drive, the small and cozy nature center is staffed by naturalists, offers scheduled programs, and has natural history exhibits. The bird-feeding station is especially popular with visitors. WPA craftsmen built the center in 1939, using local building materials—primarily wood from American chestnut trees killed by the chestnut blight in the 1920s and '30s, and Berea sandstone quarried in the reservation. The center is listed on the National Register of Historic Places.

Most of the trails in Brecksville Reservation radiate out from the nature center. They include hiking trails ranging from half a mile to four miles in length, a paved all purpose trail, twenty miles of bridle trails, and seven miles of the Buckeye Trail. Brecksville Reservation also offers golfing at the 18-hole Sleepy Hollow Golf Course. In the winter, good snow permits cross-country skiing on the golf course and trails. The reservation also includes the Squire Rich Historical Museum, operated by the Brecksville Historical Society. Brecksville Reservation has six picnic areas—five with shelter houses. All of the picnic areas are open on a first-come, first-served basis, except for Ottawa Point Picnic Area, which must be reserved.

The various hiking trails in Brecksville Reservation are well marked by signposts, using a different symbol for each trail, keyed to the trail map. Although the trails are well marked, at times more than one trail shares the same path. Just watch and follow the signposts carefully to avoid getting confused. You can also connect several of the loop trails to create even longer hikes. All the trails are described in the following pages except for the Buckeye Trail, which is described in the Buckeye Trail chapter (see page 51). Detailed park maps can be found at orientation kiosks in the reservation.

Directions: From I-77, exit at State Route 82. Go east on SR 82 to SR 21 (Brecksville Road) in the center of Brecksville. Continue east across SR 21 two-tenths of a mile to the entrance to Brecksville Reservation, Chippewa Creek Drive. The Chippewa Creek Gorge Scenic Overlook is located just inside the park. Brecksville Nature Center is located three-tenths of a mile down Chippewa Creek Drive. Alternately, from the intersection of SR 82 and SR 21, turn south on SR 21 and go one and a quarter miles. Turn left into the park on Valley Parkway. Valley Parkway intersects with Meadows Drive and Chippewa Creek Drive within the reservation. Yet a third entrance can be reached from Riverview Road. Take SR 82 to Riverview Road. Turn south and go down the hill to Chippewa Creek Drive. Turn right into the reservation.

Best Hikes for . . .
Geology

- Buckeye Trail—Egbert Rd. to Alexander Rd. (p. 53)
- Towpath Trail—Frazee House to Station Rd. (p. 24)
- Deer Lick Cave Trail, Brecksville Reservation (p. 120)
- Bike & Hike Trail—Hines Hill Rd. to Akron-Cleveland Rd. (p. 83)
- Brandywine Gorge Trail, Jaite/Boston Area (p. 145)
- Ledges Trail, The Ledges (p. 169)
- Quarry Trail, Deep Lock Quarry Metro Park (p. 191)

All Purpose Trail

The All Purpose Trail in Brecksville Reservation is an asphalt-paved, multi-use trail. It has several access points and two branches, and is suitable for hiking, cycling, jogging, or in-line skating. The northern branch (about one and three quarter miles) basically follows along Chippewa Creek Drive from Riverview Road to the Chippewa Gorge Scenic Overlook parking lot. The southern leg (about two miles) leaves Chippewa Creek Drive just west of the vehicle ford across Chippewa Creek. It follows Valley Parkway to the western boundary of the reservation, at SR 21. Part of the All Purpose Trail includes a physical fitness trail, located near the Chippewa Creek ford in the northeast corner of the reservation.

All Purpose Trail

Trail Description: To begin from the north entrance into the reservation, start at the Chippewa Creek Gorge parking area, located on Chippewa Creek Drive just south of SR 82. The paved path leaves from this parking area. As you begin, you pass the scenic overlook on the left, then a hiking path to the Harriet Keeler Memorial on the right. Shortly past this, you reach the Harriet Keeler Picnic Area and the Brecksville Nature Center Trailhead. Continue east along the road, going up and down several hills along the way, down to the floodplain of Chippewa Creek and the intersection with Valley Parkway. The Chippewa Picnic Area is on the right on the south side of the road. You can continue on the All Purpose Trail across Chippewa Creek, past a parking area and playfields, to finish at Riverview Road. It is here that you also find a physical fitness trail complete with exercise stations. Across Riverview Road, a paved trail leads to the Station Road Bridge Trailhead. From there you can access the Ohio & Erie Canal Towpath Trail, a multi-purpose trail surfaced with crushed limestone.

The southern leg of the All Purpose Trail climbs the hill alongside Plateau Picnic Area, paralleling Valley Parkway, and crosses the Buckeye Trail near the entrance to Oak Grove Picnic Area. Farther along, heading southwest, it intersects with the Bridle Trail and again with the Buckeye Trail, as you approach the Deer Lick Cave area.

Cross Meadows Drive and continue along Valley Parkway; Sleepy Hollow Golf Course is to the north. You come to the end of the All Purpose Trail in Brecksville Reservation at State Route 21.

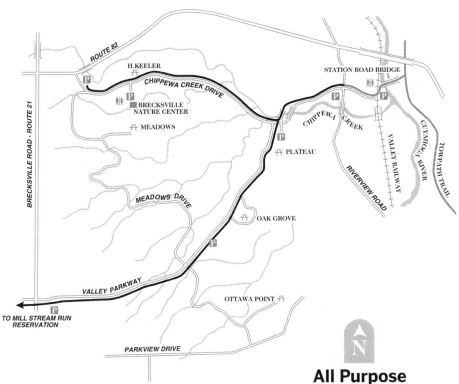

All Purpose
BRECKSVILLE RESERVATION
4.5 MILES
HIKING TIME – 2.25 HOURS
BICYCLING TIME – 40 MINUTES
ELEVATION CHANGE – 410 FEET
RATING – EASY TO MODERATE

Wildflower Loop Trail

The Wildflower Loop Trail starts from Brecksville Nature Center and passes through several habitats: coniferous and deciduous woods, a tallgrass prairie, and stream ravine. As the name would suggest, this trail is most beautiful in the spring when the woodland wildflowers are in bloom, and through the summer when the prairie flowers are in bloom. To help with identification, many of the wildflowers are labeled by name. The Wildflower Loop Trail is marked with a flower symbol on a blue background.

Trail Description: From the nature center, begin on the paved trail to the west (right) of the center. Small signs on the trees along this path have the names of the trees and some information about the species. At the first intersection, turn right, staying on the paved path, to reach the Tallgrass Prairie. (The trail straight ahead also connects with the continuation of the Wildflower Trail.) This prairie restoration project was developed by now-retired senior naturalist Karl Smith and his staff. An elevated deck to the right allows you to get a better look down upon the prairie. The Wildflower Trail turns left and goes along the south side of the prairie as you approach the Harriet Keeler Memorial. (See the Hemlock Trail description for more information on the memorial.)

Go around the memorial and exit on a narrow path to the left. Descend the trail to the stream valley. This stream flows into Chippewa Creek, entering it more than a mile downstream. Here in the low, moist woods along this tributary creek, you begin to find the wildflowers. The trail crosses the stream and wet places on bridges and boardwalks, then climbs back up out of the small ravine, heading back east now. A bench at a trail intersection at the top of the hill gives you a place to rest. Meadows Picnic Area can be seen in the distance.

Bear left, staying on the Wildflower Trail, above the creek valley. After a short distance it descends down a set of steps to the creek level again and intersects with the Deer Lick Cave and Hemlock Trails. Cross the creek on a boardwalk and go up the steps towards the nature center. Some evergreen Eastern hemlock trees are mixed in among the hardwoods in this creek valley so typical of those found in Brecksville Reservation. At the top of the hill you reach the nature center once again.

Prairie Loop Trail

This very short trail is entirely flat and paved, making it accessible to all. It leaves from the Brecksville Nature Center, goes through a small prairie and the Harriet Keeler Memorial Woods, returning on the All Purpose Trail. Trees and plants are labeled, making this a good trail for leisurely family walks or for learning about nature. It is marked with a coneflower symbol on a pink background placed on signposts.

Trail Description: Begin the Prairie Loop Trail at the Brecksville Nature Center or from the nature center parking lot. Follow the paved path to the intersection near the restroom building. Turn west towards the restored Tallgrass Prairie. This prairie is burned from time to time to help maintain the mix of prairie plants. Paths weave around the prairie, allowing you to enjoy the interesting flowers and grasses up close. The Prairie Trail continues west to the Harriet Keeler Memorial.

Go around the memorial and exit on a paved path to the right. Cross Chippewa Creek Drive at the crosswalk and reach the All Purpose Trail. Turn right on the All Purpose Trail. You soon reach the Harriet Keeler Memorial Picnic Area and an historic, rustic shelter house. This was the first shelter house to be built in Brecksville Reservation, dating to 1928. An exhibit explains its history.

Go back across Chippewa Creek Drive to reach the start of this trail. If you have the time, you can combine this trail with any of the other trails intersecting at the Brecksville Nature Center.

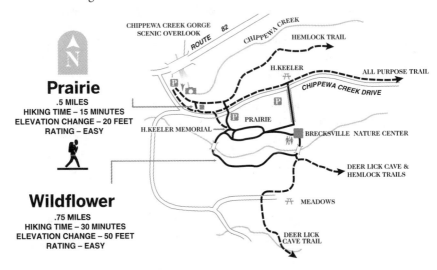

Prairie
.5 MILES
HIKING TIME – 15 MINUTES
ELEVATION CHANGE – 20 FEET
RATING – EASY

Wildflower
.75 MILES
HIKING TIME – 30 MINUTES
ELEVATION CHANGE – 50 FEET
RATING – EASY

Deer Lick Cave Trail

The Deer Lick Cave Trail is one of the longer loop trails in Brecksville Reservation. It crosses at least six stream valleys formed by tributaries flowing to Chippewa Creek, and reaches high ridges with views into these valleys. The trail's destination is a sandstone formation called Deer Lick Cave, reached halfway around the loop. The Deer Lick Cave Trail is a good choice for a long, rugged, and scenic hike.

Trail Description: The Deer Lick Cave Trail begins at Brecksville Nature Center, on Chippewa Creek Drive. The Deer Lick Cave Trail can also be reached from its southern end, beginning at Deer Lick Cave itself, off Valley Parkway. The trail is marked with an oak leaf symbol on signposts. It is described in a counterclockwise direction.

Begin the Deer Lick Cave Trail at the Brecksville Nature Center. Facing the center, take the trail to the left, between the bird feeding station and the small outside amphitheater. Descend through the forest, then cross the stream on a wooden bridge and take the steps to the left. (The Wildflower Trail branches off to the right.) The Hemlock Trail also shares this path.

At the top of the steps you will reach another intersection. Turn right to begin the loop. (The Hemlock Trail goes to the left.) The stream ravine is to your right. Continue towards Meadows Picnic Area. Cross the entrance drive, then cross through the picnic area to the other leg of the entrance drive, and you will come to the Bridle Trail. Turn right on the Bridle Trail for a short distance. The Bridle Trail splits—one leg goes out to Meadows Drive. To stay on the Deer Lick Cave Trail, turn left on the other leg of the Bridle Trail and descend to a beautiful bowl-shaped stream valley. The trail is wide and surfaced with well-packed stone. The trail crosses the stream on a footbridge next to the Bridle Trail ford. A very large white oak on the left of the trail has stood for many years but may nearing the end of its life. Many oaks in this forest were damaged by gypsy moths in the late 1990s. The oak-hickory forest is changing now, and other species may become more dominant over time. Cross another tributary stream; the trail now climbs out of this creek valley and turns east. You can see back into the valley on your left and to Meadows Picnic Area in the distance, as the trail skirts the edge of a large meadow on your right.

At the end of the meadow, you again reach woods and the beginning of another stream valley. Stay on the stone horse trail, again heading down-

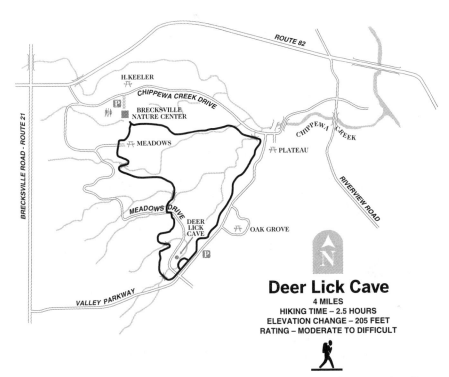

ROUTE 82

H.KEELER

CHIPPEWA CREEK DRIVE

BRECKSVILLE
NATURE CENTER

BRECKSVILLE ROAD - ROUTE 21

MEADOWS

CHIPPEWA CREEK

PLATEAU

RIVERVIEW ROAD

MEADOWS DRIVE

DEER
LICK
CAVE

OAK GROVE

VALLEY PARKWAY

Deer Lick Cave
4 MILES
HIKING TIME – 2.5 HOURS
ELEVATION CHANGE – 205 FEET
RATING – MODERATE TO DIFFICULT

hill. Along this trail, and in many other places throughout Brecksville Reservation, you will see stone work in retaining walls, culverts, and bridge abutments that dates back to the CCC and WPA days. At the bottom of this valley you reach another Bridle Trail intersection. Bear right to cross the stream on a bridge. There are several bridges like this on the trail: underneath are old CCC-era foundations, while the bridge itself is newer, built by late twentieth-century crews from the Ohio Department of Natural Resources Division of Civilian Conservation. Upstream of the bridge two streams converge around a pointed ridge of land. The nearest stream forms some beautiful cascades as it descends over shale ledges. The trail climbs out of this valley to Meadows Drive.

Turn left at Meadows Drive and walk along the wide shoulder for 100 yards, then cross and enter a red pine planting. Sleepy Hollow Golf Course begins to come into view on the right. The next small stream valley is also crossed via a bridge; this is a lovely sight in winter, when you can clearly see the trail curving down and around to cross the creek. Climb from this valley, with the golf course to your right. The trail again drops to cross another stream, this one with a miniature waterfall over sandstone ledges underneath the bridge. The Buckeye Trail now joins from the right

Deer Lick Cave

(marked by blue blazes). Follow the Deer Lick Cave Trail and Buckeye Trail to the left, now again on a narrow footpath (leaving the Bridle Trail behind), as you approach Meadows Drive and cross it again.

You are now approaching Deer Lick Cave. Follow the trail to the left, then descend stone steps to the sandstone formation for which the trail is named. The scene includes sandstone ledges, shelter caves, and miniature waterfalls, all with abundant mosses, wildflowers, and scattered large boulders. Cross the stream three times on footbridges to reach the main cave.

The trail climbs up from the cave, back to the main trail paralleling Valley Parkway. A short connector trail leads to the right, to an overlook of the Deer Lick Cave area where an exhibit explains how the cave got its name.

Continuing on the Deer Lick Cave Trail, shared with the Buckeye Trail, you soon reach a three-way intersection of the Buckeye Trail. One leg goes west towards Medina, the second leg goes south to Akron, and the third leg goes north to Headlands Beach State Park. This is about the half-way point of the Deer Lick Cave Trail hike. (You can find water fountains and restrooms a little farther on, off the trail and across Valley Parkway at the Oak Grove Picnic Area.)

Deer Lick Cave Trail continues north now, generally paralleling Valley Parkway. At one point the Buckeye Trail leaves the Deer Lick Trail briefly, then rejoins it. Next, both trails cross the Bridle Trail. Stay on the Deer Lick Cave Trail, following the edge of the ridge, where you get views back down to the horse trail in the valley to the left. At the next intersection, very near Valley Parkway, the Buckeye Trail parts from the Deer Lick Cave Trail and crosses the road. Stay on the Deer Lick Cave Trail as it curves around a side drainage, hugs the edge of the steep slope, then gradually begins a descent down a narrow hogback. Pass through groves of American beech trees and tall, straight, tulip trees to reach the intersection of Chippewa Creek Drive and Valley Parkway.

You now again join a bridle trail. Turn left, just south of Chippewa Creek Drive. Immediately you cross the entrance drive to Chippewa Picnic Area. The Hemlock Trail joins you here. Continue on the south side of the road. The trail continues into the woods and across a small stream on stepping stones. One branch of the bridle trail turns left. You bear right on the Deer Lick Cave Trail, Hemlock Trail, and bridle trail combined. At the next intersection you leave the horse trail altogether, before beginning a climb out of the valley. The Bridle Trail splits off to the right as you bear to the left, following the edge of the ridge, with views of the stream below. Cinnamon ferns and hemlocks do well here in the cooler microclimate of the stream ravine. Large white and red oaks line the trail, now again joined by American beech trees. In early spring, wild leeks, one of the first plants to come up in spring, cover this hillside in green.

At the top of this climb, the Deer Lick Cave Trail joins, then leaves, the Bridle Trail near Meadows Picnic Area. Shortly after leaving the Bridle Trail, you reach the end of the loop. Bear right and descend into the valley behind the nature center. Bear right again and retrace the route you started on, crossing over the stream one last time, then climbing the hill to finish the trail.

Hemlock Loop Trail

Hemlock Loop Trail begins by following the southern edge of the gorge formed by Chippewa Creek, then crosses Chippewa Creek Drive and shares a return route with the Deer Lick Cave Trail. Chippewa Creek has cut a remarkable gorge in the twelve thousand years since the retreat of the last glaciers. The bedrock geology of the Cuyahoga Valley is easily visible here, exposed in the cliffs of the gorge.

Chippewa Falls, located under the SR 82 bridge, is formed as the creek falls over Berea Sandstone onto the more easily eroded Bedford Shale. The creek itself is littered with huge blocks of stone, eroded off the walls of the valley. You can view the falls by taking a short side trip off the main trail. A parking lot just south of SR 82 allows close access to the falls viewing area.

Trail Description: We suggest that you begin the Hemlock Trail from Brecksville Nature Center, located on Chippewa Creek Drive. Hemlock Trail is marked on signposts with a white-on-green-background hemlock tree symbol. Here the trail is described in a clockwise direction.

Several trails begin together at the Brecksville Nature Center. Start this hike by following the paved path west of the center. Bear right, staying on the paved path as it turns north to reach the Tallgrass Prairie. Turn left along the prairie and follow the pavement to the Harriet Keeler Memorial. In a shady grove within the 370-acre Harriet Keeler Memorial Woods is a bronze plaque on a large glacial boulder. The inscription reads: "Harriet Keeler, 1846-1921, Teacher- Educator-Citizen. She liveth as do the continuing generations of the woods she loved." It is a beautiful little spot, with narrow paths radiating out beyond the memorial boulder.

Born in Kortright, New York, Harriet Louise Keeler graduated from Oberlin College in 1870. She moved to Cleveland where she was both teacher and administrator in the Cleveland Public Schools. She began in the primary grades, then taught high school English and history until her retirement in 1908. She was called back in 1912 to serve several months as superintendent. It was the first time that a woman had held the position in the school system. Keeler was also active in the suffrage movement and served as president of the Cuyahoga County Suffrage Association. She wrote her first book, *Studies in English Composition,* in 1892, and continued writing until near the time of her death. She published eleven books, mostly on nature topics. A facsimile reproduction of her 1900 guide, *Our Native Trees,* with an excellent introduction by Carol Poh Miller, was printed by Kent State University Press in 2005, making Keeler's work accessible to today's readers.

The Cleveland Metropolitan Park Board, in a resolution passed in 1921 to commemorate the life and services of Harriet Keeler, stated, ". . . the interest in the great outdoors and its woods and fields, so encouraged and promoted by the books of that gifted writer and educator, is so in keeping with the spirit and purpose of the Cleveland Metropolitan Park Plan" [that] "a suitable tract. . . shall be set aside to be known as The Harriet L. Keeler Memorial Woods" [to be] "planted with native trees, shrubs and flowers described in the writings." The memorial was erected in 1923 and was rededicated in 1990.

Leave the memorial, go north, and cross Chippewa Creek Drive to reach the All Purpose Trail. Turn left onto the All Purpose Trail and follow it a short distance to where the Hemlock Trail leaves the paved trail and goes downhill to the right on an unpaved footpath. This leads directly to the Chippewa Creek Gorge Scenic Overlook, a rustic shelter from which you can view the gorge. From here, turn right on the foot path above the creek. A wooden fence lines the edge of the steep banks above the creek. From here you can safely view Chippewa Creek, cascading over huge boulders far below.

Continue on Hemlock Trail through a hemlock woods that gives this trail its name. Hemlocks are evergreens that are fond of rocky, cool, shady areas. You can recognize them by their pyramid shape, small cones, and flat needles which have two white lines on their undersides. There are several benches spaced out along this scenic section of trail.

A little farther on, the shelter house at the Harriet Keeler Memorial Picnic Area is visible through the woods to your right. A side trail leads out to the shelter. The original part of the structure was built by the WPA in 1928, from materials found locally, including sandstone for foundations, steps, and flooring, and oak and pine timbers for the framing. It is a good example of the rustic style of park architecture that was being promoted at the time.

On the Hemlock Trail, you now begin a gradual descent along the edge of the gorge. Continue downhill through a forest of tulip trees, oaks, and beeches. Continue this descent to the floodplain of Chippewa Creek. At the end of this descent you reach a section of boardwalk that ends at a trail intersection. Here you reach the Chippewa Creek Trail that makes a one-and-a-half-mile loop through the floodplain and across the creek. To the left, it goes towards Chippewa Creek; ahead it shares the same path with the Hemlock Trail. You are paralleling the All Purpose Trail, which is sometimes visible to your right. A former bridle trail goes off towards the All Purpose Trail and parkway—it now serves as an access trail to the All Purpose Trail. Be careful to stay on the Hemlock Trail at this point.

Cross a branch of Chippewa Creek on a wooden footbridge; the main channel of Chippewa Creek is soon visible on the left. Cross another tributary of Chippewa Creek on a swinging suspension bridge. This bridge was built by the 26th Engineering Company of the Ohio National Guard from Brook Park in April 1981. At this point you are very close to Chippewa Creek.

Next the hiking trail reaches the All Purpose Trail just opposite the entrance to Chippewa Picnic Area, situated along a tributary of Chippewa Creek. Cross Chippewa Creek Drive, heading towards the picnic area. The trail now turns right (west) and shares a return route with the Deer Lick Cave Trail (marked with an oak leaf symbol), and for a while both trails join the Bridle Trail as well. Cross the bridge at the picnic area, then cross a small stream on stepping stones. One branch of the Bridle Trail goes south. Stay on the Hemlock and Deer Lick Cave Trails. Soon you begin a climb up out of the valley. Another branch of the Bridle Trail splits off to the right and the hiking trails bear left, following the edge of the ridge, with views of the stream below. The presence of cinnamon ferns and hemlocks suggests a cooler microclimate as you approach a cascade in the stream below. The trail continues into a more upland forest, passing some huge white and red oaks and American beech trees. Many of the oaks, unfortunately, have succumbed to damage caused by gypsy moth infestations in the late 1990s.

The Hemlock and Deer Lick Cave Trails again join the Bridle Trail for a short distance, near Meadows Picnic Area. Then the horse trail turns left and the hiking trail goes right. At the next Hemlock and Deer Lick Cave Trail intersection, descend steps to the creek behind the nature center. The Wildflower Loop intersects here. Bear right, cross a foot bridge, and go up the steps to end the hike at the Brecksville Nature Center.

Chippewa Creek Loop Trail

This one-and-a-half-mile trail is the latest addition to the Brecksville Reservation's trail system. It is the only trail that explores the north side of the Chippewa Creek drainage. It is almost entirely level and stays in the floodplain of Chippewa Creek. Because of one particular creek crossing within the floodplain, the loop can be completed only in times of low water. Nonetheless, you can still do half the trail any time of the year. The best place to begin this trail is at the Chippewa Picnic Area on Chippewa Creek Drive. The Chippewa Creek Trail is marked with signposts bearing the symbol of a songbird on a brownish background.

Trail Description: From the Chippewa Picnic Area, begin the trail by crossing Chippewa Creek Drive and reach the All Purpose Trail. Bear left. The Chippewa Creek Trail goes into the woods here at the intersection with the All Purpose Trail. The trail bears northwest, generally paralleling the park road and the All Purpose Trail. On this leg of the trail, the route is shared with the Hemlock Trail, marked with a tree symbol on a green background.

Here you are in the floodplain forest surrounding Chippewa Creek. It can be muddy in the spring, but also can be filled with wildflowers, including the bright yellow marsh marigolds. The trail angles towards Chippewa Creek and comes very close where you cross a fun, swinging suspension bridge. Farther on you cross another bridge, then reach a Y intersection. Here Hemlock Trail and Chippewa Creek Trail split. Bear right to stay

Swinging Bridge

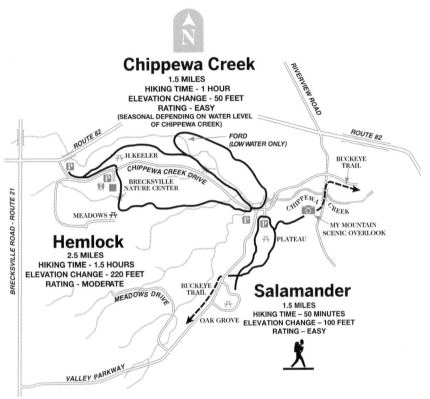

on Chippewa Creek Trail. Now the trails swings north towards the creek, reaching the place where you must cross. In the summer the water is usually shallow enough that you can follow the gravel bars and use stepping stones to get across.

On the north side of Chippewa Creek, the trail now swings back downstream. This is an enjoyable part of the creek to explore, however, and you might want to go upstream a ways. There the creek is emerging from a deep gorge, and you can see the very steep shale cliffs on the south side of the creek. Eastern hemlock trees cling to those cliffs, while sycamores, willows, and other wet-tolerant species populate the floodplain area.

Continue on the trail on the north side of the creek, now going southeast and downstream. You will come to several places where the creek is quite braided and has left oxbows. This segment of trail comes out to the All Purpose Trail just north of where the All Purpose Trail bridge crosses Chippewa Creek. Turn right onto the All Purpose Trail, cross the bridge, and finish the loop near the Chippewa Picnic Area.

Salamander Loop Trail

The Salamander Loop Trail climbs one of the many ridges in Brecksville Reservation, providing views of the beautiful surrounding hills and valleys. On the high ground are found some very special wetland areas—during the first warm spring rain, salamanders emerge from their damp, dark wintering places and migrate to these vernal pools in which they then lay their eggs. This Salamander Trail makes a one and a half mile loop around the breeding pond area.

Access this trail from the Plateau Picnic Area, off Chippewa Creek Drive, or from the Oak Grove Picnic Area on Valley Parkway. Both picnic areas have shelters.

Trail Description: To begin the trail from the Plateau Picnic Area, go to the shelter and look for the steps to the right of the shelter. The trail starts going uphill, heading south, up a steep ridge paralleling Valley Parkway. The ridge levels out to a plateau; a vernal pool lies to the left of the trail. Mature hardwoods and an occasional hemlock, make up the woods along the way up the hill. To the right is a nice vista of the next ridge; here you get a sense of the rugged topography formed by the side creeks cutting valleys towards Chippewa Creek and the Cuyahoga River.

On this high, level ground, the Salamander Trail enters a study area, where natural resource specialists are working to improve the habitat for wildflowers and the oak-hickory forest. In this study area, the Salamander Trail reaches an intersection with the Buckeye Trail , the Buckeye Trail going both right and left. An access trail goes straight, ending at the Oak Grove Picnic Area. To continue around the loop, turn left on the combined Salamander and Buckeye Trails. The trail will swing east, then north. Now you will have views of the forested ridges to the south and east.

At the next intersection, the Salamander Trail leaves the Buckeye Trail to return downhill to the Plateau Picnic Area. You can get some good views by taking a side trip out along a steep-sloped hogback ridge to My Mountain Scenic Overlook. It is a short walk along the oak ridge, ending at a vista point with benches. Return on the same spur trail to the Salamander Trail, then turn right and descend off the plateau alongside the picnic area. The Salamander Trail descends some steps, then after reaching the bottom of the hill turns left for a few yards on the Bridle Trail. Continue past the Plateau Picnic Area entrance drive, then leave the Bridle Trail and turn left (south) on the continuation of the loop Salamander Trail. Go south a short ways back uphill into the picnic area to finish the hike.

Bridle Trail—Brecksville

Brecksville Reservation has one of the finest bridle trail systems in north-east Ohio and is the hub for many miles of bridle trail within Cuyahoga Valley National Park. An interconnected web of trails winds through some of the most scenic and remote areas in the reservation. The main trail consists of a large figure-eight loop, with smaller loops around the Brecksville Stables. Bridle trail connectors go east, west, and south from the main loops. The trail to the west parallels Valley Parkway, heading towards Mill Stream Run Reservation. Another bridle trail connection goes east from Brecksville Reservation along Chippewa Creek Drive to Riverview Road and on into CVNP's Station Road Bridge Trailhead. From here one can ride north to Bedford Reservation. The Valley Trail goes south from Brecksville Reservation, connecting to the Wetmore and Riding Run bridle trails in CVNP.

The bridle trails in Brecksville Reservation are wide, well graded, and have a packed stone treadway. Much of this trail system dates back to the beginning of this reservation, and all along the trails you can see the Civilian Conservation Corps' fine stonework on culverts, bridge abutments, and retaining walls. All the bridle trails are marked with a horse-and-rider symbol on signposts. Various loops, ranging from eight-tenths of a mile to five and a half miles in length, are indicated by the shorthand "BK1," "BK2," "BK3," and "BK4." Connector trails are marked simply as "BK."

The trails can be reached from the stables located on Meadows Drive off Valley Parkway. The stables provide boarding and lessons, but no rental horses. There is parking for cars and trailers at the stables. A second, smaller parking lot is located on Chippewa Creek Drive just west of Riverview Road.

Trail Description: The short loops (BK1 and BK2) near the stables and the longer loops can all be reached from the stable parking lot. One short loop simply makes a circle around and behind the stable area, in the woods, and is mostly level. It skirts near private property on the west edge. BK2 makes a slightly larger loop, including some of the trail on the opposite side of Meadows Drive.

To take a longer ride (BK3 and BK4), start out on the trail just south of the stables driveway and turn and ride towards Meadows Drive. Cross the parkway and follow the trail to the left (BK3). Here you are sharing the trail with the Buckeye Trail (marked with blue blazes on trees). The trail parallels Meadows Drive; a branch of the bridle trail (BK2) intersects on the left. Descend to cross a creek. Meadows Drive can be glimpsed to the left, crossing the creek on an arched sandstone bridge.

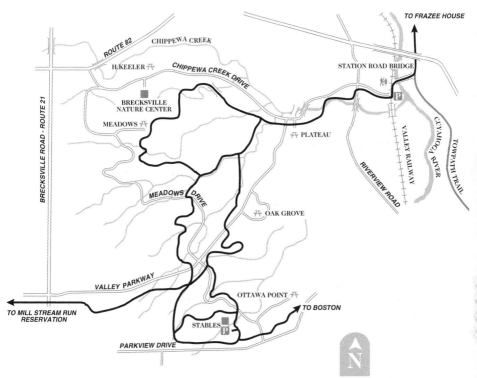

Bridle Trail
BRECKSVILLE RESERVATION
9 MILES
RIDING TIME – 3 HOURS
ELEVATION CHANGE – 260 FEET
RATING – MODERATE TO DIFFICULT

As the bridle trail approaches Valley Parkway, bear to the right to parallel the All Purpose Trail and the road. Here the Buckeye Trail leaves and crosses the road. Staying on the bridle trail, swing away from the road into a woods of tall oaks and hickories. A large ravine appears on the right. The trail follows this ravine edge around, then comes back out to the All Purpose Trail. Cross the All Purpose Trail, then the road, and intersect with the Buckeye Trail and Deer Lick Cave Trail on the far side of the road.

While the Buckeye Trail stays near the road, the bridle trail goes away from the road and begins a steep descent into a beautiful, wide creek valley. At the bottom, ford the creek and continue in the valley. The steep wooded hills to either side give a secluded feel to this lush, dished valley. It is in this bottom land that you come to an intersection, the middle of the figure-eight: the outer loop of the bridle trail (BK4) goes straight ahead in the valley, while to the left (west) the BK3 trail follows a creek upstream to join the western side of the BK4 loop. You can take the BK3 route for a shorter ride back to the stables (three and a half miles round-trip).

To continue on the longer loop (five and a half miles round-trip), stay in the creek valley following the BK 4 trail to the point where it meets the Deer Lick Cave and Hemlock hiking trails (marked with an oak leaf and a tree, respectively). Bear left. For a short way, all three trails share the same path. (Note that here the east connector bridle trail goes east out to Riverview Road. It continues across Riverview Road and into Pinery Narrows, linking Brecksville Reservation to the Bridle Trail in Bedford Reservation.) Going west, begin a gradual climb along with the hiking trails. At the next intersection, the hiking trails split off to the left, while the BK4 bridle trail bears to the right. Cross another creek, go straight ahead, then wind out around a knoll and up onto a ridge. Another scenic creek valley is now on your left. This is the stream that runs behind the Brecksville Nature Center. Hemlock trees intermingled with tall oaks and hickories are especially attractive in the winter.

Follow the bridle trail down to the left, across the creek, then back up. Again the bridle trail meets up with the hiking trails, as all go out towards the fields at Meadows Picnic Area. When the hiking trails and bridle trail split again, go left along the fields, then follow the field edge around to the right, still following BK4. You again join up with the Deer Lick Cave Trail. The bridle trail going straight ahead goes out to Meadows Drive. To stay on BK4, turn and descend into a ravine where you can cross the creeks via footbridges or fords. Climb out of this valley; at the top you find the trail bordered by a ravine to the left and an extensive meadow on the right.

At the end of the meadow, an unofficial trail takes off to the left. Both the bridle and hiking routes go to the right and take you back down to the creek bottom. Along the way the trail is edged by an old stone retaining wall. At the bottom you reach the intersection with the leg of BK3 that connects the east and west sides of the bigger loop.

Now bear right on BK3 and cross another creek. Look to the right to see the rocky confluence of two branches of the creek. Climb out of this valley towards Meadows Drive. Turn left at Meadows Drive to follow it 100 yards, then cross. On the opposite side you go immediately into a planting of red pines.

Just beyond, the trail winds in graceful curves as it drops to cross a creek, then climbs again to within sight of Sleepy Hollow Golf Course. Beyond the golf course, as you approach Valley Parkway, you again cross the Buckeye Trail. The Deer Lick Cave Trail turns left with the Buckeye Trail, but you proceed straight ahead to cross the parkway, then the All Purpose Trail. In a short distance, you reach an intersection: the crossing trail is a bridle path leading to State Route 21 to the west and on towards Mill Stream Run Reservation. The trail going east (BK2) crosses Meadows Drive and connects to the trail near where you began. Go straight ahead (south) on BK2 to return to the stables. Before reaching the stables, you will come to another intersection where BK2 and BK1 meet. Bear left on BK1 for the shorter route to the parking lot. The BK2 loop behind the stables is short, level, and goes through an attractive fantasy-land spruce woods. It intersects with the Valley Trail, then ends at the southeast end of the stables area, near Meadows Drive.

Brecksville Bridle Trail

Jaite/Boston Area

The Jaite/Boston area is, in more ways than one, the heart of the 33,000-acre Cuyahoga Valley National Park. Here public and private lands intertwine. Three park agencies have jurisdiction here—Cleveland Metroparks, Metro Parks, Serving Summit County, and the National Park Service. In addition to the publicly owned land, there are two privately owned downhill ski areas in the vicinity.

Cuyahoga Valley National Park's headquarters is housed in the former company town of Jaite. From 1907 to 1924, the town's buildings were built to house mill workers who worked at the Jaite Paper Mill. The buildings have since been adaptively restored for use as offices. Located near park headquarters in the main parking lot is an interpretive wayside exhibit that tells the story of Jaite.

Boston, the neighboring community south of Jaite, is a small village that during its canal heyday was reported to be larger than Cleveland. It was from a boatyard in Boston that the *Allen Trimble* was launched on July 3, 1827, joining a flotilla of boats that were celebrating the opening of the Ohio & Erie Canal. Boston also gained a certain notoriety in the 1800s as being the home of Jim Brown, described in 1890 as "the leader of the greatest gang of counterfeiters of his day." Brown was arrested, acquitted, and later elected justice of the peace. He is buried in the cemetery west of the canal towpath.

Most of the buildings in Boston are private, except for the Boston Store, a National Park Service visitor center, and a store across from the Boston Store, operated by the Cuyahoga Valley National Park Association. The Boston Store houses a canal boat building exhibit, a small bookstore, and a meeting room. The visitor center, with its long porch next to the Ohio & Erie Canal Towpath Trail, is a popular gathering spot for park visitors. Trails in the Jaite/Boston area offer something for everyone who loves the outdoors: scenic hemlock ravines, waterfalls, mature forests, cool creek-side bowers, steep terrain with scenic views, and numerous options for creating long hikes by combining various trails.

Old Carriage Trail

Winding stretches of trail that border deep, wooded ravines make up most of the three and a half miles of the Old Carriage Trail. The upland portions of trail are mostly level. However, to reach that part of the loop, you must first climb the trail from the Cuyahoga River to the top of the valley's eastern rim. On the high section of trail, three bridges ranging in length from 150 to 166 feet carry you across three deep ravines. The entire trail is surrounded by mature forest that now shades barely visible signs of this area's wealth of history and prehistory. These features, along with beautiful vistas across the Cuyahoga River valley, make this trail one of the most enjoyable and challenging for hiking or skiing.

The Old Carriage Trail is located on the eastern side of the valley between State Route 82 and Highland Road. This area has had a significant history in the Cuyahoga Valley, from the time of Native Americans to the present. In 1847, Charles Whittlesey, assistant geologist for the state of Ohio, surveyed and reported on ancient Indian earthworks and mounds in this area. Archaeological investigations conducted here in the 1980s gleaned more information on the ancient hilltop enclosure and dated it to the Late Woodland period, AD 750. There was also evidence of much earlier use by natives, as well as an 1830-1889 Euro-American occupation.

Settlers began arriving in this area in the early 1800s. Then, with the coming of the canal, rough roads were built from the high farmlands down to the canal boat loading areas. At one time, Holzhauer Road extended farther south than it does now, connecting the Northfield Township farms to a canal boat landing at the foot of Red Lock Hill.

In the late 1800s, Wentworth Goodson Marshall and his wife Louise purchased one thousand acres of farmland in this area, bordered generally by Northfield Road, Holzhauer Road, and the canal. At that time Marshall, a Canadian-born and educated chemist, was establishing himself in Cleveland as a drug store merchant. He bought an interest in a store on the site of the present Terminal Tower in 1876, then established a store at the corner of Superior Avenue and Public Square. He went on to create a successful chain of forty-six Marshall Drug Stores. Marshall and his two sons all had beautiful homes built in Shaker Heights, but for the summers W.G. Marshall moved his family to their summer home built on his farm called Rocky Run.

Both Wentworth and his son George enjoyed botany and invested much energy into developing an arboretum on the farm. There they conducted botanical experiments to determine which plants were best suited for the northeast Ohio climate. They also planned and built carriage roads throughout the wooded acres, designing them to take advantage of the ridgetops.

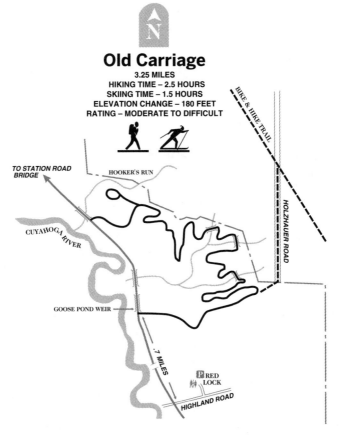

Old Carriage

3.25 MILES
HIKING TIME – 2.5 HOURS
SKIING TIME – 1.5 HOURS
ELEVATION CHANGE – 180 FEET
RATING – MODERATE TO DIFFICULT

Large culverts were placed in ravines and covered with fill to eliminate steep grades. The Marshalls also encouraged a summer camp here, affiliated with the Friendly Inn social settlement of Cleveland, which gave city youngsters opportunities for country experiences.

After the Marshalls sold their farm, developers in Northfield began building an open-space development known as Greenwood Village. It was partially completed when it encountered financial troubles. During the early 1980s, a new owner decided to continue the development. However, in the meanwhile the remaining undeveloped acreage had been included within the boundary of the new Cuyahoga Valley National Recreation Area (now Cuyahoga Valley National Park). Just in time, in 1983 the National Park Service purchased 518 acres inside the park boundary, and the builder proceeded with development outside the park boundary.

When the park acquired this property, it also acquired a ready-made trail, the old carriage roads which the Marshalls had built throughout their land. Much of the road system was still in excellent condition. However, in several places the park boundary was drawn across ravines, cutting off portions of the carriage roads that crossed farther upstream. This resulted in the necessity of building the beautiful steel box truss bridges that the trail is now known for.

Exploring this trail is like time travel—going from the canal days of the mid-1800s, to prehistoric times when elk and bear still inhabited this land, to the early 1900s when urban youngsters came to the country for fun and fresh air. As you explore this trail, keep an eye out for clues to the land's history, from the waysides describing Native Americans' hilltop enclosures, to old posts or foundations from the Marshalls' Rocky Run Farm, which they loved and shared.

The Old Carriage Trail, plus a section of the Ohio & Erie Canal Towpath Trail, together make a three-and-a-half-mile loop. To reach the loop, you must start either at Red Lock Trailhead or Station Road Bridge Trailhead. A round trip from Red Lock Trailhead is five miles, and from Station Road Bridge Trailhead is six miles. Please note that the Towpath Trail is a multi-use trail, but the Old Carriage Trail is reserved for hiking and skiing only, except for the southern leg, which is designated as a multi-use connector between the Towpath and the Bike & Hike Trail. The Old Carriage Trail is described here from the southern entrance at Red Lock Trailhead, where there are parking and restroom facilities. The Station Road Bridge Trailhead is larger, with a Cuyahoga Valley Scenic Railroad shelter that has restrooms, and picnic tables near the historic Station Road Bridge.

Directions: I-77 to SR 21 (Brecksville Road). North three-quarters of a mile to Snowville Road. East on Snowville Road to Riverview Road, then north on Riverview Road one quarter mile to Vaughn Road. East on Vaughn Road, across the Cuyahoga River, and left into the Red Lock Trailhead. Or, on the east side of the park, take I-271 to the SR 8 exit. South on SR 8 one quarter mile to Highland Road. West on Highland, jogging right and left to go under I-271, about two and a half miles, to Red Lock Trailhead.

Trail Description: From Red Lock Trailhead, follow the Ohio & Erie Canal Towpath Trail north. The canal basin is on your right. This low-lying area provides excellent habitat for wildlife. In the spring, you can hear spring peepers and toads, and possibly spot wood ducks and mallards before they spot you. You can also watch for various warblers, Baltimore orioles, indigo buntings, several species of woodpeckers, flycatchers, and many other birds, as well as signs of deer, muskrat, and beaver.

Follow the Towpath Trail into a more forested section, where the overarching trees create a tunnel effect. About seven-tenths of a mile from the start, you reach the intersection of the Towpath Trail and the Old Car-

Old Carriage Trail at Towpath Connector

riage Trail. Turn right to follow the Old Carriage Trail counterclockwise. (You can also go straight ahead on the Towpath Trail for four-tenths of a mile to pick up the northern end of Old Carriage Trail if you wish to do the trail clockwise.)

Turning to the right, cross the canal bed via a wooden bridge. A bench on the bridge provides a pleasant spot for a break. From this point, the trail climbs steeply up a section of one of the old roads which has been resurfaced for bicycle traffic as well as foot traffic. Follow this for six-tenths of a mile to reach the top of the ridge, a gain in elevation of 150 feet. This section of trail connects the Towpath Trail to the Bike & Hike Trail. For a short span, you are on a narrow hogback with views to either side. Along this trail you will find exhibits regarding the Native American earthworks that were mapped here in 1847.

At the top of the ridge you reach a trail intersection. Turn left to continue on the Old Carriage Trail. (The bike connector trail goes straight to Holzhauer Road.)

Now the trail begins a winding course along the fingers of land projecting between the side ravines, following along the east rim of the Cuyahoga Valley. Park geologists have compared this intricately-carved landscape to the badlands of the American West—both were caused by natural erosion, and both are difficult to traverse.

You come near the boundary of the park in several places and can see the homes of Greenwood Village and subsequent developments. About one mile from the start of the Old Carriage Trail loop, you descend to the first of three single-span steel bridges, this one named Rocky Run Bridge, after the Marshalls' farm. From here you can see the small stream below rippling over a bed of shale.

After another half mile of winding trail, you reach the second bridge, this one crossing a ravine lined with oaks, maples, and beeches. Two mature oaks at the north end gave this bridge its name, Twin Oaks Bridge. These trees were damaged by the gypsy moth infestation in the 1990s, and one has succumbed to the damage. Other oaks in the vicinity are surviving, however, and another might eventually take its place. Shortly after this, you reach the third bridge—Hemlock Bridge—spanning a particularly scenic hemlock ravine. As you can see from the way all three bridges are nestled between the trees, the National Park Service made sure that these bridges were carefully installed in a manner that did not damage the surrounding forest.

Continue to follow the Old Carriage Trail along the edges of ravines, and then south along a long narrow point of land. Turn back north, then, on a switchback that descends to cross a short wooden bridge. Past this bridge, you once again come close to the park boundary, then reach the start of the 170-foot descent to the Towpath Trail. Just after you begin your descent, a side trail branches off to the right. (For skiers this serves as an emergency runaway ramp!) This short trail makes a loop at the end of a point of land overlooking the Cuyahoga Valley. A bench placed here allows you to rest in comfort. Back on the main trail, it's all downhill from here, and challenging enough for most skiers.

At the bottom of the hill, the Old Carriage Trail rejoins the Towpath Trail. Turn left (south) to complete the loop. The canal is now on your left; the Cuyahoga River is to the right, at one point coming close to the trail. Just before you reach the point where you first left the Towpath Trail, you cross a bridge built upon the old abutments of a canal structure known as Goose Pond Weir. This was one of many such structures on the canal that helped regulate the water level in the canal basin.

Continue straight ahead to finish your ski or hike (unless you'd like to go around a second time!). In seven-tenths of a mile you return to Red Lock Trailhead.

Stanford Trail

The Stanford Trail connects the Stanford House to the Brandywine Gorge Trail and Brandywine Falls. Although relatively short, the trail has several steep sections, making it more challenging than it may first appear. Allow plenty of time for this trail as there is much to discover. The gorge and falls of Brandywine Creek provide a dramatic scenic reward at the upper end of the trail. Midway on the trail a short spur trail leads to a woodland pond, and nearly the entire trail is surrounded by a mature hardwood forest. This is not a loop trail—double the time allotted for this hike if you do not leave a car at Brandywine Falls.

There is also a short trail from the Stanford House to the Ohio & Erie Canal Towpath Trail. Find this trail just opposite the lower end of the drive-way. From the Towpath Trail you can go north or south and make connections to other trails, including the Buckeye Trail, making the Stanford House an excellent hub from which to explore the valley.

The name of the house and trail is derived from an early settler named James Stanford. In 1806, Stanford arrived as part of a surveying crew from the Connecticut Land Company. He settled in the Cuyahoga Valley and became a prosperous farmer and community leader in Boston Township. His son George built the home which is now the Stanford House.

The Stanford Trail goes through both federally owned land and property owned by Metro Parks, Serving Summit County. The metro park land you cross on the Stanford Trail once belonged to Waldo L. Semon. Dr. Semon, a surveyor himself as well as a noted inventor and future park commissioner, became interested in the history of the land that he owned. He reported in a monograph that this area is transected by David Hudson's trail, one of the earliest roads in this part of the valley. In 1799, David Hudson left Connecticut for the wilderness of Ohio, traveling mostly by water, as over-land routes were plagued with difficulties. Going from Lake Ontario to Lake Erie, he eventually reached the mouth of the Cuyahoga River. Hudson traveled upstream until his way was blocked by shallow water and rapids. This "Hudson's Landing" is located near the confluence of Brandywine Creek and the Cuyahoga River. From this point he set out over land to locate his West-ern Reserve holdings, an area which is now Hudson. He most likely followed Indian trails southeast towards the high ground in Hudson Township, pass-ing through the area that you now can visit via the Stanford Trail. In 1974, Dr. Semon and his wife donated 121 acres to Metro Parks, Serving Summit County. It is now known as the Waldo Semon Woods Conservation Area.

The Stanford Trail was cleared by the Cleveland Hiking Club (CHC), which has since adopted this trail. Further improvements, including the con-struction of several bridges, have been made by CHC, the Cuyahoga Valley

Trails Council, and several Eagle Scouts. There are picnic tables near the house, and picnic tables, grills, and restrooms at Brandywine Falls.

Directions: I-77 to Exit 145, Brecksville Road. North one quarter mile to Boston Mills Road. East on Boston Mills Road, jogging left and right to go over I-80, about three miles to Riverview Road. Cross Riverview Road and the Cuyahoga River, entering Boston. Turn left onto Stanford Road and go half a mile. The Stanford House is on the right. You will find a small parking lot behind the barn for trail users.

From the east side of the park, take I-271 to SR 8. South on SR 8 three and a half miles to Boston Mills Road. West on Boston Mills Road three and a quarter miles to Boston. Right on Stanford Road to the Stanford House.

Trail Description: Start the Stanford Trail at the National Park Service kiosk located behind the Stanford House, at the northeast corner of the parking lot. Follow the mowed path through an old field, towards Stanford Run. The trail crosses the creek on a bridge, then winds through the woods, away from Stanford Run. Fairly soon after, bear to the left to climb the hill out of the creek valley. Some of the larger, older trees here—many of them oaks—were killed by the gypsy moth infestation between 1996 and 2000. Other species fared better, and are filling in where the fallen oaks have created holes in the forest.

Partway up the hill, the trail crosses a saddle between two small drainages, then later follows the edge of a shallow ravine. Some of this route follows long-established trails that were used by former landowners. Daffodils, planted by Waldo Semon's family, mix in with the native spring wildflowers along the route here.

Cross the top of the ravine on a small boardwalk. Soon after this boardwalk you reach the historic David Hudson trail. You are about halfway to Brandywine Falls. Turn to the left along the historic route for about fifty yards, then turn to the right.

For a side trip, you can stay on the David Hudson trail and go north to reach Averill Pond. Stu Averill, son-in-law of Waldo Semon, owned a farmstead on Stanford Road just north of the Stanford house. Mr. Averill constructed the pond in the early 1950s and stocked it with bass and bluegill. The Averills enjoyed many family picnics along the pond's shores, and over the years documented the great variety of wildflowers growing throughout the surrounding woods. There is a bench here, at the edge of the pond, where you can take some time to enjoy this tranquil spot.

Brandywine Gorge

1.5 MILES
HIKING TIME – 1 HOUR
ELEVATION CHANGE – 160 FEET
RATING – MODERATE

THE INN AT
BRANDYWINE FALLS

BRANDYWINE
FALLS

AVERILL POND

STANFORD ROAD

BRANDYWINE ROAD

BRANDYWINE CREEK

271

TOWPATH TRAIL

STANFORD RUN

STANFORD
HOUSE

Stanford

1.5 MILES
HIKING TIME – 1 HOUR
ELEVATION CHANGE – 190 FEET
RATING – MODERATE

You won't be entirely alone, however. Green frogs, red-winged blackbirds, violet dancer damselflies, painted turtles, beaver, and deer are just a few of the animals that live in and around the pond.

Follow this Averill Pond side trail back to the intersection with the Stanford Trail to continue on to Brandywine Falls. Continue on the Stanford Trail, now lined with large beech trees, descending towards another creek valley. Steps help you down the steep slopes, and bridges make the creek crossings easy.

Just before the climb back out of this creek valley, the Stanford Trail intersects with the Brandywine Gorge Trail. (You can follow the Brandywine Gorge Trail to the left as an alternate route to reach Brandywine Falls, if Brandywine Creek is not too high.) At this intersection, the Stanford Trail continues up a steep slope, the climb made easier by a long set of steps constructed by Cuyahoga Valley Trails Council (CVTC) volunteers. At the top of the hill, the trail goes from the more mature forest into younger growth, and then into a utility right-of-way. Cross the right-of-way and go onto Stanford Road. (The road is closed to vehicles.) Walk along the road for about 200 yards until you reach the Brandywine Falls boardwalk. The scenic reward for your efforts lies just beyond.

The National Park Service built a series of stairs and observation platforms here to provide a close-up view of 65-foot Brandywine Falls. Hemlock, maple, and black locust trees surround the walkways which incorporate two observation decks and benches. The upper part of the boardwalk, the picnic area, and restrooms are all accessible.

The upper walkway (750 feet long) is poised along the rim of the gorge and leads to the remains of a grist mill and factory. It is beautiful here in any season: In spring and summer the boardwalk is shaded by mature trees, including evergreen hemlocks. Sugar maples light the gorge in gold and yellow in fall, and in winter, ice formations along the gorge are spectacular. (Parts of the boardwalk may be closed at times in winter if icy conditions make the footing hazardous.)

The lower walkway and stairs—measuring 300 feet long and hugging the rock ledges—lead to a lower observation deck where you might get showered by waterfall mist. This spot has become a favorite of artists and photographers, as well as many wedding parties looking for a romantic backdrop for their photographs. The rock ledges—often dripping with moisture—and the steep wooded slopes harbor mosses, lichens, and many wildflowers. If you are in the area in the latter part of May, you will also be treated to the heavenly scent of the black locust trees in bloom.

On the north side of Brandywine Creek is the Wallace farm, circa 1848, which is now the Inn at Brandywine Falls. This bed and breakfast, operated by innkeepers George and Katie Hoy, is a delightful place to stay while exploring CVNP. The Hoys lease the buildings from the National Park Service through the Historic Property Leasing Program. They have restored the farmhouse and barn and filled the rooms with nineteenth-century-style furnishings, many of them made in Ohio.

After visiting the falls, return to the start of the Stanford Trail using the same route, or continue across the top of the falls and along the north side of Brandywine Creek, following the Brandywine Gorge Trail. One mile from the falls, the gorge trail rejoins the Stanford Trail.

Brandywine Gorge Trail

This beautiful trail begins at Brandywine Falls, descends the Brandy-wine Creek gorge on the north side of the creek, crosses the creek and Stan-ford Road, then joins the Stanford Trail to complete a loop back to the falls. Delicate wildflowers in the spring, cool shade in summer, dramatic fall color, and winter ice formations make this gorge a great destination at any time.

The Brandywine Gorge Trail was built almost entirely by Cuyahoga Val-ley Trails Council volunteers during 1992 and 1993, and was dedicated on National Trails Day, June 5, 1993. The beginning of the trail route partially follows an old farm road cut into the side of the hill, on the north side of the creek. Undoubtedly there is much history hidden here, dating back to the heyday of the village of Brandywine, when the mills at the falls were the center of local activity. The village no longer exists, most of the buildings having been removed when I-271 was built through the site of the original settlement.

Directions: From I-77, exit at SR 21. North on SR 21 to Snowville Road. East on Snowville Road to Riverview Road. North on Riverview one quarter mile to Vaughn/Highland Road. Right on Vaughn to Brandywine Road. Right on Bran-dywine Road two and a half miles to the Brandywine Falls Trailhead. From SR 8, take Hines Hill Road to Olde Eight Road. Right on Olde Eight and an immediate left on Brandywine Road. Take Brandywine Road one and a half miles to the trailhead.

Trail Description: Begin the Brandywine Gorge Trail by following the path from the parking lot to the start of the boardwalk. The National Park Service built the boardwalk, stairs, and observation platforms to provide views of the beautiful gorge and spectacular 65-foot Brandywine Falls. An exhibit on the lowest observation deck explains the geology of the water-fall and helps you identify the various rock layers. Use the upper deck to reach the old mill foundations at the lip of the falls. Cross over the top of the falls on an old road bridge, then follow the north side of the gorge for a short distance, watching for the trail sign behind the Inn at Brandywine Falls. The trail continues on a stone path between the inn and the edge of the ravine.

From this point, the Brandywine Gorge Trail enters the cool shade of the woods. Dramatic views of the gorge can be seen to the left, especially in winter and spring. Even when foliage obscures the view, you can hear the sound of rushing water far below. Along the rocky rim of the gorge,

Brandywine Falls

a few large hemlock trees are mixed in with the hardwoods. These grace-fully shaped evergreens grow in moist ravines throughout the Cuyahoga Valley.

Chunks of sandstone of varying sizes line the trail. In a number of places, volunteer trail crews have arranged sandstone pieces into rock waterbars to keep the trail well drained as it descends towards the bottom lands. Near the bottom of the hill, descend a few steps and cross a low area on stepping stones. To the right is a small woodland pond formed at the base of a rock ledge. In the spring, amphibians migrate here to breed, and it can be quite lively with frogs and salamanders. After going up a few more steps, you will come to a spur trail that goes to the left. It ends at a bench overlooking a small, picturesque cascade on Brandywine Creek.

On the main trail, continue in the bottom lands for a short distance, past the rock ledge edging the small breeding pond. A mix of hardwood trees, including a number of white oaks, form the extensive forest here below the waterfall. After the trail winds closer to the stream, it turns sharply to the left and descends to Brandywine Creek. Cross the creek using the footbridge. This bridge, built in 2009 by volunteers, replaces a series of sandstone stepping stones, making crossing Brandywine Creek much easier and safer.

Across the creek, follow the trail a short distance to Stanford Road. Stan-

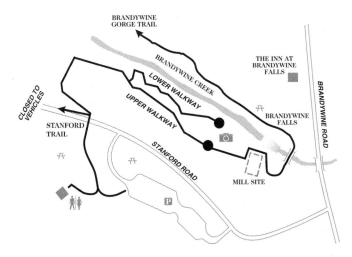

BRANDYWINE
GORGE TRAIL

BRANDYWINE CREEK

THE INN AT
BRANDYWINE
FALLS

LOWER WALKWAY

UPPER WALKWAY

CLOSED TO
VEHICLES

STANFORD
TRAIL

BRANDYWINE
FALLS

BRANDYWINE ROAD

STANFORD ROAD

MILL SITE

Brandywine Falls Detail

ford Road is closed to vehicles from here to Brandywine Falls. The trail continues on the other side of Stanford Road, crossing a utility right-of-way before reentering the woods. A single old oak tree is growing among younger trees along the east side of the trail.

About 250 yards from Stanford Road, the Brandywine Gorge Trail intersects with the Stanford Trail. To complete the loop and return to Brandywine Falls, the Brandywine Gorge Trail joins the Stanford Trail and goes up a long set of steps to the top of the hill. At the top, the trail veers to the left and goes onto Stanford Road. Turn right for the short walk back to the Brandywine Falls parking lot.

Blue Hen Falls Trail

The Blue Hen Falls Trail is one of the shorter trails in CVNP, yet it offers some beautiful scenery and is a favorite of many visitors with limited time in the park. Blue Hen Falls is formed when Spring Creek makes a clean fifteen-foot drop over erosion-resistant Berea Sandstone to a layer of Bedford Shale, the same bedrocks that Brandywine Falls spills over, on the opposite side of the Cuyahoga Valley.

Directions: From I-77, exit at SR 21. Take SR 21 to Boston Mills Road. East on Boston Mills Road, jogging over I-80, to the trailhead. Watch for a sign and narrow drive to the left (north). At the end of the short drive is parking for four to five cars.

Trail Description: To follow the trail, start out on the paved path, an old driveway. The trail descends from the parking lot and winds down quickly to stream level, where it crosses Spring Creek, so-called because a spring just upstream from here feeds this creek year-round. Looking down from the bridge that crosses this creek, you can clearly see the Berea Sandstone creek bottom, including fractures in the rock and a pothole formed by rock particles swirling around in the pools.

Blue Hen Falls

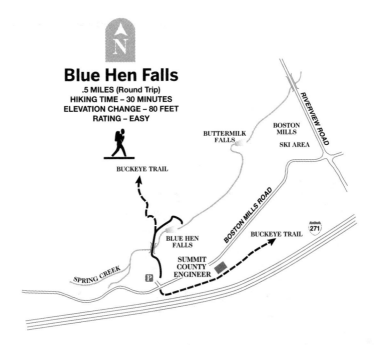

Blue Hen Falls

.5 MILES (Round Trip)
HIKING TIME – 30 MINUTES
ELEVATION CHANGE – 80 FEET
RATING – EASY

Just past the bridge, the long-distance Buckeye Trail (marked by blue blazes) splits to the left for destinations to the north. Follow Blue Hen Falls Trail to the right to reach the view of the waterfall.

From here you can see the capstone of sandstone at the head of the falls. This is the result of water eroding the softer shale underneath, forming an undercut. At the base of the falls is a plunge pool, a large cavity formed from the force of falling water striking the Bedford Shale below. Mineral deposits under the falls seep from, and stain, the surrounding rock. In winter, ice sculptures form along the falls. This is a favorite spot for artists, photographers, or anyone who enjoys the serenity of a woodland waterfall.

A split-rail fence is here to protect the easily-damaged habitat around Blue Hen Falls. Please stay on the trail to minimize damage to the area.

Return to the parking area via the same trail, or hike for a while on the Buckeye Trail, as your time allows. About a mile north on the Buckeye Trail, you would reach Columbia Run and a scenic hemlock gorge. A mile to the south and east on the Buckeye Trail would bring you down a steep slope into the village of Boston.

Furnace Run Metro Park

One of the oldest park areas in Summit County, Furnace Run is owned and operated by Metro Parks, Serving Summit County. The beginning of this 890-acre park dates to 1929, when the widow of Charles Brush, Jr. donated in his memory 272 acres of the Brush farm to the metropolitan park district. Charles Brush, Jr. was the son of Charles Francis Brush, a distinguished Cleveland inventor best known for his arc light. The park district developed the family's donated acreage into a park in the 1930s, employing work relief crews to do the construction. Brushwood Lake, originally built as a swimming lake, was closed to swimming in the 1950s and is now enjoyed by fishermen, wildlife, and wildlife watchers. Metro Parks, Serving Summit County, more recently has restored a section of Furnace Run downstream of the lake, creating improved habitat for aquatic life.

Two place names—Furnace Run and Bog Iron Pond—suggest a history of iron ore in this area. Bog iron is a hydrous iron oxide that was found in wet areas in Summit County. An early history of the area states that iron ore was discovered along the Furnace Run valley, and that there was probably an iron furnace in the area.

Two major highways near this park make it easy to reach, but have had negative environmental effects on this once-remote area. Nonetheless, Furnace Run Metro Park retains a special beauty and charm, especially in autumn when the many sugar maples turn gold.

The park system remodeled and expanded the original bathhouse into an attractive pavilion. Brushwood Pavilion, on the edge of Brushwood Lake, is enclosed, heated, and fully accessible, and has a food service area and restrooms. (The pavilion can be reserved for a fee.) There are picnic tables and grills along the playing field, in the woods at the start of the trails, and in a grove of trees near the end of the Rock Creek Trail. Weather permitting, you can also go sledding and ice skating here.

Two easy trails are located in the Brushwood area. They can be hiked separately or intertwined to create a pleasant two-mile hike. A third short walk goes along a section of restored stream to the right of Brushwood Shelter (return on the same trail).

The H.S. Wagner area of Furnace Run Metro Park is about two miles southeast of the Brushwood area. The metro parks' first director, Harold S. Wagner, owned this land and planted it with over 150,000 daffodil bulbs, now a great local attraction.

Old Mill Trail

Old Mill Trail, in the Brushwood area of Furnace Run Metro Park, provides an easy walk along Furnace Run and the ridge above it. American beeches, sugar maples, and red maples surround the trail, with wildflowers at your feet in the spring and the sunshine of golden leaves overhead in the fall. The trail is marked with the symbol of a deer hoof print.

Directions: From I-77, take exit 143, Wheatley Road. West on Wheatley Road one-half mile to Brecksville Road. North on Brecksville Road two and one-half miles to Townsend Road. Left on Townsend Road one mile to the park entrance on the right.

Trail Description: Begin Old Mill Trail from the parking lot of the Brushwood area. Go past the pavilion, across a bridge, and into the picnic grove. Turn to the right. Fairly soon you come to the point where the return loop of Old Mill Trail comes in from the left; continue straight here.

In about a half mile, you reach a bench and a turn in the trail; go to the left and climb a short, steep slope to reach the ridge above. You are going north, paralleling I-77. American beech trees, identified by their smooth, blue-gray bark, are mixed in with cherry trees, other hardwoods, and red pines, in this woods above Furnace Run. The trail dips and curves to get across side drainages on bridges and boardwalks.

Charles Brush Memorial Rock

Just before the trail descends again, you come to a large boulder commemorating Charles Francis Brush, Jr. From here, in the winter time, you get a view of Brushwood Lake to the west.

Complete the trail by descending the hill and turning right, returning to your starting point in the picnic grove. You can continue onto the Rock Creek Trail for a longer hike.

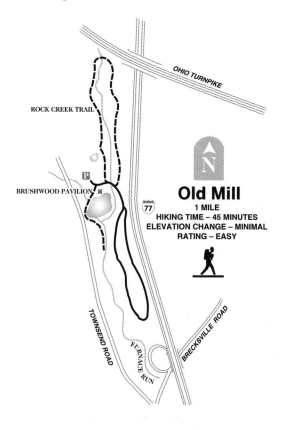

OHIO TURNPIKE

ROCK CREEK TRAIL

BRUSHWOOD PAVILION

Old Mill
1 MILE
HIKING TIME – 45 MINUTES
ELEVATION CHANGE – MINIMAL
RATING – EASY

77

TOWNSEND ROAD

FURNACE RUN

BRECKSVILLE ROAD

Rock Creek Trail

The Rock Creek Trail, another easy trail in the Brushwood area, follows a narrow, shallow section of Furnace Run upstream of Brushwood Lake. Below the lake, Furnace Run flows several miles downstream, eventually passing under the Everett Covered Bridge and the Ohio & Erie Canal Towpath Trail before reaching the Cuyahoga River at Everett. The Rock Creek Trail is good for family hikes, even with small children, as they love to toddle along next to the creek, picking up stones and surprising frogs. This streamside area is also great for spring wildflowers. The Rock Creek Trail is marked with signposts bearing an oak leaf symbol. It begins from the picnic grove near Brushwood Shelter.

Directions: From I-77, take exit 143, Wheatley Road. West on Wheatley Road half a mile to Brecksville Road. North on Brecksville Road two and a half miles to Townsend Road. Left on Townsend Road one mile to the park entrance on the right.

Trail Description: Begin the Rock Creek Trail by following the walkway past the pavilion and towards the creek. Cross the creek and enter the picnic grove. Straight ahead, a trail sign directs you to turn left to begin the loop. As you begin the Rock Creek Trail, you will likely hear the traffic

Picnic Area at Furnace Run

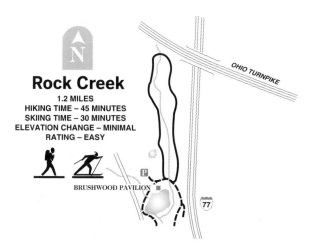

Rock Creek

1.2 MILES
HIKING TIME – 45 MINUTES
SKIING TIME – 30 MINUTES
ELEVATION CHANGE – MINIMAL
RATING – EASY

on I-77, but the creek here takes your attention away from the highway. The trail stays close to the creek, winding this way and that, hemmed in by short, forested hills between the trail and the highway. Mature sugar maples, American beeches, and other deciduous trees line the trail. The trail crosses the creek a couple times, on bridges, and there are plenty of places where you can get quite close to the water.

Patches of the ancient plant *Equisetum*, commonly called scouring rush or horsetail, help anchor the sandy soil along the stream banks. Several species of this genus grow in North America and are the last plants in a long line of plant ancestors dating back 300 million years. Children are intrigued by their unusual appearance and hollow, segmented stems. The stems contain silica, and the plants were sometimes used to smooth or polish wood, bone, or fingernails, or to scour pots and pans.

More than halfway around, you cross the stream and change direction, now heading south. On the return side of the loop, you go through deciduous woods, then reach a stand of older pines and younger evergreens which have been planted in a grassy area alongside the creek. Picnic tables are scattered throughout this scenic grove. Leaving the picnic area, you pass Bog Iron Pond, now a small marsh. It was probably dug sometime in the nineteenth century by bog iron miners for charcoal furnaces in the area.

Complete the Rock Creek Trail by following the path out into the playing field above Brushwood Pavilion. There are more picnic spots here along the field. The parking lot is directly ahead.

H. S. Wagner Daffodil Trail

The H. S. Wagner Daffodil Trail is a favorite of many hikers of all ages, especially in the springtime. You may find yourself returning year after year to enjoy the welcome color of thousands of daffodils along the six-tenths-mile trail. Harold S. Wagner, the Akron Metropolitan Park District's first director, planted the flowers on this property which he had bought for a home site. Wagner came to Akron from Boston, having had experience working with both the Olmsted Brothers landscape architects and Warren Manning, a well-known Boston landscape architect. Wagner served as Director-Secretary of the park district from 1926 to 1958. He never built a home here on Brush Road, and later sold the land to the park district (now Metro Parks, Serving Summit County), allowing it to be enjoyed by all. From time to time the park district renews and adds to the daffodil beds, keeping this trail cheerfully yellow in the spring.

Directions: From I-77, take exit 143, Wheatley Road. West on Wheatley Road half a mile to Brecksville Road. North on Brecksville Road two miles to Brush Road. Right on Brush Road one mile to the H.S. Wagner Area. There is a small parking lot on the right.

Daffodil Trail

Trail Description: Begin the Daffodil Trail at the parking lot. The trail starts off wide and level, with hardwoods to either side, passes a row of lovely hemlock trees, then opens out into a grassy area. A bench and a tall old oak tree invite you to rest awhile in this peaceful setting.

From the clearing, the trail begins to make a loop through a relatively level area bounded by two stream ravines. Keep going straight ahead to take the loop in a clockwise direction. Large oak trees and beeches line the ravine that is now visible to your left, while at your feet are the beginning of the many clusters of planted daffodils. The bottomland forest is a perfect habitat for red-shouldered hawks, sometimes seen or heard near the trail.

The tributary to your left empties into Furnace Run; the trail stays on the high ground above these streams. Where the trail begins to curve around, you may be able to glimpse Furnace Run flowing through the wide valley below. This is about the halfway point. Continuing on around you come to the other tributary valley which bounds this trail. Again, large, older trees line the trail and slopes, including some tall shagbark hickories, obvious by their loose, "shaggy" bark. The hickories, oaks, and beeches that you see through here are all indicative of a mature woods. The area to the right, however, has much younger trees, indicating the area was a clearing not long ago.

To complete the loop, follow the path back into the grassy clearing. A couple of American holly trees stand out among the plants edging the grass. Bear to the left to follow the trail back to the parking lot.

Daffodil

.6 MILE
HIKING TIME – 45 MINUTES
SKIING TIME – 30 MINIUTES
ELEVATION CHANGE – MINIMAL
RATING – EASY

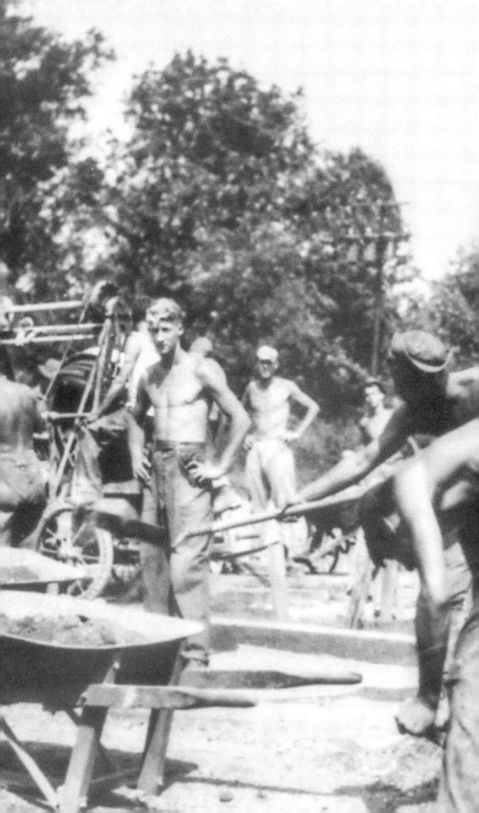

Happy Days Lodge

Two trails are located in the immediate vicinity of Happy Days Lodge: the Haskell Run Trail, just to the south of the center, and the Boston Run Trail, to the north. The Haskell Run Trail is only half a mile long but connects to the Ledges and Kendall Lake trails, giving you the opportunity to hike for a half hour or all day.

Before starting on the trails, you may want to get acquainted with the interesting history of the Happy Days Lodge, which has served the public throughout its history. The area around the center was a Civilian Conservation Corps (CCC) camp during the 1930s. At that time, the CCC was constructing shelters and other facilities in Virginia Kendall Park, owned by the state of Ohio and managed by what was then called the Akron Metropolitan Park District (now Metro Parks, Serving Summit County). The CCC craftsmen constructed Happy Days to house a summer camp for children from the Akron public school system. The camp started in 1935 in an old farmhouse, and by 1938, when construction began on the Happy Days Shelter, nearly 2,000 children had already enjoyed the benefits of the camp. Happy Days Shelter was the last and largest building the CCC constructed in the area.

The name for the camp and building derives from the Roosevelt-era song, "Happy Days Are Here Again." The building itself was a joint project between the Akron Metropolitan Park Board and the National Park Service, with the National Park Service preparing the design and contract documents. Local money ran out before the project was completed, but the Metropolitan Park District's Director, H.S. Wagner, convinced the National Park Service to fund its completion. Little did the NPS know at that time that the fruit of their investments would be returned to them forty years later.

Happy Days Camp continued here until the mid 1940s. From then until 1976, the Akron Metropolitan Park District operated the building as a reservable shelter. In 1974, President Gerald Ford signed the law to create Cuyahoga Valley National Recreation Area, now called Cuyahoga Valley National Park. A few years later the metropolitan park district relinquished management of Virginia Kendall Park to the federal government. The National Park Service then made improvements to the building to allow for year-round use. In 1980, Happy Days became the first visitor center in CVNP.

Civilian Conservation Corps statue

The building is constructed of wormy chestnut wood and locally quarried sandstone. The many chestnut trees that had thrived in the surrounding forests were all killed in a fungal blight during the 1920s. Ironically, though the trees were dead, they provided excellent building material, for the wood has exceptional workability, resistance to decay, and a desired rustic appearance. Therefore, all the CCC buildings in Virginia Kendall were built of chestnut wood, including the privies! In this way, the chestnut trees live on.

Happy Days Lodge is located on State Route 303, between State Route 8 and Akron Peninsula Road. The Great Hall can be rented for special events. For more information, phone 330-650-4636 or 800-257-9477.

Directions to Happy Days Lodge: From I-271, exit at SR 303. Go east on SR 303 through Peninsula. Two miles east of Peninsula is Happy Days Lodge. Parking is on the left (north). Accessible parking is on the right (south). From SR 8, exit at SR 303. Go west on SR 303 one mile to Happy Days.

Haskell Run Trail

The Haskell Run Trail is a short footpath that guides you through a wooded ravine, typical of many such ravines in the Cuyahoga Valley.

The trail is located just outside Happy Days Lodge and makes a short loop beginning and ending near the lodge.

Trail Description: Begin the Haskell Run Trail at the trailhead bulletin board just behind the visitor center. The first part of the trail is perched on a narrow corridor of land between the edge of the Haskell Run ravine and the Mater Dolorosa cemetery. The Irish Catholic cemetery was established in 1869 as the burial grounds for the parishioners of The Mother of Sorrows Church in Peninsula. Twenty-three people were interred here in the late 1800s. There is a headstone for Thomas C. Coady, a Union soldier, but he might not be buried here. According to the Summit County Chapter of the Ohio Genealogical Society, he was aboard the ship *Sultana,* which was carrying Union soldiers freed from Confederate prison camps, when it exploded and sank in the Mississippi River on April 27, 1865.

At the junction with a service lane, turn to the right and descend towards the ravine, then continue downstream along Haskell Run. Water is the prominent feature here, and water-loving plants, such as mosses, skunk cabbages, and sycamore trees, thrive in the shaded glen. Especially in summer, you can notice the drop in temperature and increase in moisture along the creek. In the spring, it's a wildflower garden.

Cross the creek on a bridge. Just after this crossing is the intersection with a short trail connecting the Haskell Run Trail to the Ledges Trail (see page 169). Stay down by the creek to continue along the Haskell Run Trail. The stream runs year-round and descends from here 360 feet to the Cuyahoga River, two miles to the west. Frogs, salamanders, songbirds, chipmunks,

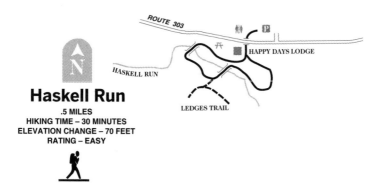

ROUTE 303

HAPPY DAYS LODGE

HASKELL RUN

LEDGES TRAIL

Haskell Run
.5 MILES
HIKING TIME – 30 MINUTES
ELEVATION CHANGE – 70 FEET
RATING – EASY

squirrels, raccoons, deer, and other animals all live in this creek valley. In the summer you might hear two of the most beautiful songsters of our deciduous woodlands: the hooded warbler, calling out a loud *weeta wee-tee-o*, and the veery, a thrush with a voice like a descending, liquid woodland flute.

After crossing the creek again, the trail climbs out of the ravine and brings you out of the woods at the west end of the large playfield near Happy Days Lodge. Cross the field to finish the hike.

Best Hikes for . . .
Kids

- Viaduct Park Trail, Bedford Reservation (p. 110)
- Hemlock Loop Trail, Bedford Reservation (p. 98)
- Wildflower Loop Trail, Brecksville Reservation (p. 118)
- Prairie Loop Trail, Brecksville Reservation (p. 119)
- Rock Creek Trail, Furnace Run Metro Park (p. 154)
- Haskell Run Trail, Happy Days Lodge (p. 161)
- Lake Trail, Kendall Lake (p. 182)
- Forest Point Trail, The Ledges (p. 174)
- Towpath Trail—Ira Rd. Trailhead to Beaver Marsh (p. 42)
- Bicycling with kids: Towpath Trail and Bike & Hike Trail (p. 17 and p. 83)

Boston Run Trail

The Boston Run Trail loops around the upper portion of Boston Run, one of the many tributaries of the Cuyahoga River. The trail is mostly in the woods. Stands of beech trees, with their silver-gray bark, and a rocky hemlock ravine add special beauty to this route.

The trail's length and several moderate hills make it a good one for skiers of intermediate skill level. Take extra caution here if the snow cover is marginal or icy—the hills are short and steep. When in doubt, sit it out!

The Boston Run Trail partially follows the route of an earlier motorbike trail which was opened in 1972 by the Akron Metropolitan Park District (now Metro Parks, Serving Summit County). In 1978, the park district transferred the entire Virginia Kendall Park area to the National Park Service, making the trail part of the new Cuyahoga Valley National Park. The badly eroded trail was closed and remained unused for several years until the National Park Service improved it, rerouted some sections, and reopened it as a cross-country ski trail. Subsequent improvements and reroutes have made this a premier skiing and hiking trail.

Trail Description: Begin the Boston Run Trail at the trailhead bulletin board located near the northeast corner of the large Happy Days Lodge parking lot on the north side of SR 303. The trail is marked with signs in a

Boston Run Trailhead

counterclockwise direction for the pleasure and safety of skiers, taking best advantage of the terrain. Follow the edge of the mowed field on the gravel path. Go past the exit of the loop trail to find the start of the trail. The trail veers to the left into a maple woods to begin the loop.

Very soon, the trail makes a steep, curving descent. After a short climb and another steep descent, the trail crosses a bridge and begins to climb alongside SR 303. At the top of this slope the trail winds away from the road through a woodland. There is another short descent, then a section heading north, away from the road, through a beech-cherry-maple woods. White pines to the right of the trail soften the scene and help buffer noise from the highway.

Your next downhill section of trail is a lovely curving descent that turns sharply at the bottom to cross a bridge over a branch of Boston Run. After the climb back up, you can enjoy over one and a half miles of level to gently rolling terrain. If you are skiing, this is one of the most enjoyable parts of this trail, as it has a very gentle downhill grade through a mature beech forest. At the northernmost point on the trail, you come to a hemlock ravine along the north branch of Boston Run. This is also the halfway point and a pleasant place to take a rest. Extensive woodland surrounds you, so the birds you are most likely to see and hear are those species that prefer deep, mature forest, such as wood thrushes or Eastern pewees.

Some of the water flowing into the creek comes from the Boston Ledges located northeast of here. Although partly destroyed by a railroad cut in the 1800s, they are still worth a visit and can be reached via Metro Parks, Serving Summit County's Hike & Bike Trail (see page 83). Downstream, the Boston Run valley is known for its spring wildflowers. It can be reached via the Buckeye Trail, from the Pine Lane Trailhead (see page 73).

The trail heads generally south now, with one section swinging west to take advantage of the terrain. Benches are strategically placed for rest and views. Older-growth hardwoods on the ravine slopes mix with younger aspens, dogwoods, and shrubs on the uplands. Some of the older oaks have died from gypsy moth damage, but there are still many mature hickories and maples filling the holes left by the old oaks.

Follow the trail as it winds along the plateau rim, then descend steeply into the valley of Boston Run one last time. Cross a bridge, then climb very steeply back to the field where you began. Turn right to return to the parking lot.

Best Hikes for . . .

Long Hikes, Vigorous Exercise

- Combine sections of the Towpath Trail (p. 17) with sections of the Valley Trail (p. 220)

- Combine sections of the Towpath Trail (p. 17) with sections of the Buckeye Trail (p. 51)

- Combine sections of the Buckeye Trail (p. 51) with sections of the Valley Trail (p. 220)

- Any of the Bridle Trails (p. 101, p. 107, p. 130)

- Old Carriage Trail (p. 136) and Towpath Trail (p. 28)

- Plateau Trail, Oak Hill Area (p. 203)

- Salt Run Trail (p. 184) combined with Cross Country Trail (p. 178)

The Ledges

For many generations, people have been coming to the Ritchie Ledges area to enjoy its unique natural beauty. The dramatic rock cliffs come as a surprise to someone new to northeast Ohio. The weathered rock, the graceful hemlocks, the cool water oozing from cracks in the rocks, and the abundant mosses and ferns all seem more like the Canadian north woods. This is understandable, because this habitat we enjoy today is related to the colder climate associated with the glaciers. Some northern plant species that migrated south before the advancing ice sheets still can be found in these forests. Two common examples are yellow birch trees and Eastern hemlocks.

There are three hiking trails in this immediate area, totaling about five miles, and connections to five other trails, totaling over ten miles, making this one of the best hiking destinations in the national park. The scenery, along with many picnic sites, reservable shelters, and a spacious playing field, makes the Ledges a popular group-picnic spot.

The Ledges, Pine Grove, and Forest Point Trails are all part of the Virginia Kendall Unit of Cuyahoga Valley National Park. This area was Cleveland industrialist Hayward Kendall's country retreat in the early part of the twentieth century. Upon his death in 1927, Kendall willed 390 acres to the State of Ohio for park purposes, and the park was named in memory of his mother. Later additions of acreage increased the size of the park. In 1933 a Civilian Conservation Corps (CCC) camp was established at Virginia Kendall Park. In order to get the Corps' assistance, the Akron Metropolitan Park District board, which managed the new park, had to agree to use rustic-style architecture in its park buildings. Harold S. Wagner, Director-Secretary of the district at the time, partnered with an Akron architect, Albert H. Good,

Ice Box Cave at the Ledges

who later became a consulting architect for the National Park Service. Good edited the now-classic manual, *Park and Recreation Structures*, establishing a style now known as "parkitecture." Virginia Kendall Park was managed by the Akron Metropolitan Park District (now called Metro Parks, Serving Summit County) until it was transferred to the National Park Service in January 1978, four years after the creation of Cuyahoga Valley National Park.

The CCC crews built park drives, parking areas, privies, shelters, trails, and benches, and planted thousands of trees and shrubs, all within a master landscape design. One of the pleasures of the Virginia Kendall trails is discovering these reminders of the early days of this park.

View from the Ledges

Ledges Trail

The Ledges Trail makes a loop around the base of the Ritchie Ledges. The ledges are rugged rock outcrops of a formation called Sharon Conglomerate. About 320 million years ago, a large, shallow sea covered this area. The Sharon Conglomerate was formed when fast-moving streams from the north carried sediment into the sea. In time, the sediment was compacted into conglomerate rock comprised of cemented sand and small quartz pebbles, rounded and smoothed by the action of the water.

This rock resists erosion and is often found exposed where other materials have eroded away. It usually occurs as the cap rock at elevations of 1,150 to 1,300 feet. That is the case here, where the forces of erosion have sculpted an oval-shaped island of rock. You can also find Sharon Conglomerate rock cliffs at Gorge Metro Park in Cuyahoga Falls, Nelson Ledges State Park in Portage County, and Lake Katherine State Nature Preserve in Jackson County, 150 miles south of here.

A moist, cool microclimate along the ledges encourages the growth of plants which are typical of more northern climes. You can find ferns, starflowers, Canada mayflowers, hemlocks (evergreens with flat needles, each with two white lines on the underside), and yellow birch trees along the trail. The birches snake their roots over the rock, clinging to whatever they can, creating interesting shapes and patterns. Recognize yellow birches by their yellowish, peeling bark. The birds you are likely to see around the ledges include woodpeckers, flycatchers, warblers, wood thrushes, wrens, and more rarely, the brilliantly colored scarlet tanager.

The Ledges Shelter and restroom buildings are excellent examples of the rustic style of architecture that flourished during the parks and conservation movement of the 1930s and influences park design to this day. The style emphasizes building designs that blend well with the environment and make use of natural materials—in this case, wood and stone. When Virginia Kendall was first being made into a park, a deadly fungal disease had ravaged the forests, killing thousands of American chestnut trees, praised by many as the grandest tree in Ohio. It is some small comfort that these trees remain a part of the park as the main building mate-

Ledges Trail

rial for many park buildings, including the Ledges Shelter. Worm holes give chestnut wood a distinctive patterning and reason for its common name, "wormy chestnut." Light-colored sandstone from nearby quarries was used for foundations, walls, and pavement, pleasantly complementing the wormy chestnut.

More recently, another invader attacked the woods around the Ledges Shelter, only this time it was not a disease, but an insect. Infestations of gypsy moths chewed their way through the forest from 1996 through 2000, defoliating mostly oaks, some of them the tallest and oldest trees in the woods. The worst damage was done in 1999, when aerial surveys determined that 4,372 acres of the national park had been defoliated. Application of biological insecticides, along with a naturally occurring fungus, succeeded in suppressing the gypsy moth population. Since 2000, the defoliated trees have died, and many of the trees were felled for safety reasons. Those left standing provide nest holes for cavity-dwelling birds and mammals.

CVTC volunteers help maintain and improve the Ledges Trail. Their work preserves the historical look and feel of the trail, since they make use of available rock for building material and replicate the trail building techniques and trail designs used by the CCC crews of the 1930s.

Directions: From I-77, exit at Wheatley Road (SR 176). East on Wheatley Road to Riverview Road. Right on Riverview Road a quarter mile, then left on Bolanz Road half a mile to Akron Peninsula Road. Left (north) on Akron Peninsula Road about two and a quarter miles to Truxell Road. Right on Truxell Road two miles to the Ledges entrance on the left.

From SR 8, exit at SR 303, then go south on Akron-Cleveland Road for one mile. Turn right (west) on Kendall Park Road (named Truxell Road at the west end), one mile to the Ledges entrance on the right.

Trail Description: Begin the Ledges Trail at the trailhead bulletin board at the northeast corner of the parking lot. From this corner, a trail to the right leads to picnic tables tucked into the woods. Follow the service road north alongside the shelter. The picnic table loop comes back to this road a hundred yards ahead. Just past that you will find a trail intersection, with a wayside illustrating the ledges area. Turn to the right to reach the Ledges Trail. Soon there is a noticeable change in the woods, from oaks and hickories to hemlocks. At this point you begin to see the fissured conglomerate rock and sense a subtle change as you move into the ledges' cooler environment.

Follow the trail as it drops alongside the ledges and reaches the Ledges Trail. You can walk it in either direction—it is described here in a counterclockwise direction. Turn to the left; in about 100 yards is Ice Box Cave. This narrow slit in the rock, not a true cave, reaches fifty feet into the dark dampness. A spring seeps from the rock near a wooden bridge just beyond Ice Box Cave. The temperature is noticeably cooler here, and a fern garden thrives on the rock above. Leaving Ice Box Cave, cross the bridge, climb the steps, and continue on. Informal trails to the left lead into the maze of ledges.

Continue on for a quarter of a mile to a set of stone steps. These steps lead back up to the top of the ledges, near where you turned off the service road. These graceful, curving, sandstone steps are one of the features built by the Civilian Conservation Corps in the 1930s. They have been in continuous use ever since. The Ledges Trail continues to follow the base of the ledges. Just beyond the steps you will find a trail to the right which leads to the Haskell Run Trail and Happy Days Lodge. To stay on the Ledges Trail, continue around the nose of exposed rock, via boardwalks and steps. You have rounded the northern end of the loop trail. A trail to the left leads back up to the Ledges Shelter, and shortly after this a trail to the right goes to the Octagon Shelter. Stay at the base of the rock if you wish to complete the loop.

Continue along the towering rock face for about half a mile. The ledges begin to diminish towards the southern point of the loop. At the trail intersection, turn to the left and climb the hill. (The trail to the right leads to the Lake Shelter, about one mile away.)

At the highest point on this short climb, a side trail leads west towards the edge of the ledges. From this popular overlook you can enjoy an expansive view of the Cuyahoga Valley. Since it faces west, it is a favorite sunset-watching spot. Past the overlook, bear to the right, skirt the south edge of the field, just inside the woods, then cross the Ledges area entrance drive. After a short walk through deciduous trees, you reach a wooden bridge. Across the bridge is a magical-looking grove of hemlocks. Complete the loop trail just before Ice Box Cave; watch for the trail leading up to the left to take you to the top of the ledges, then another left that leads back to the Ledges Shelter. A perimeter trail goes around the playing field, and along the west edge of the field other trails lead to picturesque picnic sites where you can get a closer look at the cracks and fissures and precipices of the Ritchie Ledges.

Pine Grove Trail

The Pine Grove Trail circles through the forests west of the Ritchie Ledges in the Virginia Kendall unit of CVNP. It is named after the pine plantation through which it passes. This trail can be combined with others in the Ledges and Kendall Lake areas for longer hikes. Near the start of the trail is the Octagon Shelter, a Civilian Conservation Corps structure, which is reservable (see appendix). Picnic sites with grills line the edges of a playing field near the shelter, and restrooms and water fountains are located in Octagon Shelter.

Directions: From I-77, exit at Wheatley Road (SR 176). East on Wheatley Road to Riverview Road. Right on Riverview Road one quarter mile, then left on Bolanz Road half a mile to Akron Peninsula Road. Left (north) on Akron Peninsula Road about two and a quarter miles to Truxell Road. Right on Truxell Road one and three quarter miles to the Octagon entrance on the left.

From SR 8, exit at SR 303, then go south on Akron-Cleveland Road for one mile. Turn right (west) on Kendall Park Road (named Truxell Road at the west end); one and a quarter miles to the Octagon entrance on the right.

Trail Description: Begin Pine Grove Trail at the trailhead bulletin board located at the upper, southeast corner of the Octagon parking lot. The first half mile is an access trail to the main loop trail. Follow the access trail south, cross the entrance drive, and continue up some steps and across a short boardwalk to reach the Pine Grove Trail. For many years there has been a trail in this part of the Virginia Kendall forest, but not always following the route that this one does. Earlier versions dipped into the ravines, but landslides and erosion made it necessary to reroute and shorten the trail.

The Pine Grove Trail can be followed in either direction. To follow the trail counterclockwise, turn to the right. You are in the midst of the red pines for which the trail is named. Pines were often planted in groves such as this during the reforestation efforts of the 1930s. Most of the pines here are red pines, identified by the reddish bark and needles, two to a bundle. Later on you will find some white pines mixed in—their needles are five to a bundle.

About one-fourth of the way around is a bench facing a triple confluence of creeks in the ravine to the north. This is the northernmost point of the trail. Across the ravine is the field behind the Octagon Shelter. The trail

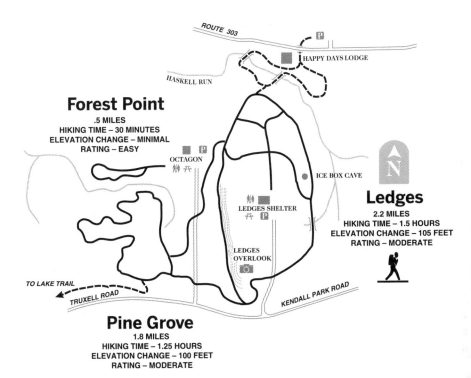

swings now to the south and west, with a couple of gentle dips and climbs. A little more than halfway around the loop, you reach a trail leading to the Boy Scouts' Camp Manatoc. At this point the Pine Grove Trail swings due east, then drops south where it meets a trail leading to the Kendall Lake area. Continuing on, at the next trail intersection bear to the left (the trail straight ahead leads up to the south end of Ritchie Ledges and the Ledges Overlook).

An aspen grove borders the pine woods along this portion of the trail. Aspens do well in cutover areas and probably established themselves here after the area was left to reforest. In one-tenth of a mile you have completed the loop; take the trail to the right back down the steps, across the road, and on to the Octagon Trailhead.

Forest Point Trail

This short, easy trail begins at the western edge of the playfield behind the Octagon Shelter. It provides a pleasant walk for people of all ages—perfect for after a holiday picnic! It can be combined with other nearby trails, such as the Ledges Trail and Pine Grove Trail, for much longer hikes.

Directions: From I-77, exit at Wheatley Road (SR 176). East on Wheatley Road to Riverview Road. Right on Riverview Road a quarter mile, then left on Bolanz Road half a mile to Akron Peninsula Road. Left (north) on Akron Peninsula Road about two and a quarter miles to Truxell Road. Right on Truxell Road one and three quarter miles to the Octagon entrance on the left.

From SR 8, exit at SR 303, then south at Akron-Cleveland Road for one mile. Turn right (west) on Kendall Park Road (named Truxell Road at the west end). A mile and a quarter to the Octagon entrance on the right.

Trail Description: Begin this trail at the Octagon Shelter. This shelter has seen countless family gatherings and church picnics, and is a great example of the rustic style of architecture that was spread across the country by the Civilian Conservation Corps in the 1930s. The shelter has been beautifully restored and maintained by the National Park Service. Note the unique weather vane on the center of the octagonal roof!

From the back of the shelter the land slopes gently towards the woods. Cross this open field and watch for the trail sign at the edge of the woods. Here and elsewhere along the edge are secluded picnic sites tucked in among the trees. Shortly after entering the woods, the trail splits to the right and left. Follow it in either direction to reach a point of land overlooking Ritchie Run. From the trail you can see how the many side creeks have created a broken, sculpted landscape of hogbacks and valleys.

The forest here is typical of upland deciduous woods of Cuyahoga Valley National Park. Until recently, the oldest and tallest trees were oaks and beeches. Successive years of gypsy moth infestations in the late 1990s left many of the oaks so denuded that they eventually died, completely changing the appearance of this forest. Dead oaks, both standing and fallen, have left openings in the woods where young trees, many of them beeches, are sprouting up. Time will tell what mixture of tree species will eventually dominate this part of the woods. In the meantime, the decaying trees may be a boost to woodpeckers, which nest in tree cavities. The largest of Ohio's woodpeckers, the pileated, makes its home in this forest, along with the smaller red-bellied woodpeckers and even smaller downy woodpeckers.

The Forest Point Trail circles back to where it split left and right. Follow the single path back out to the field to end your walk.

Octagon Shelter

Kendall Lake

Kendall Lake is located in the Virginia Kendall Unit of Cuyahoga Valley National Park. The lake and surrounding hills act like a magnet to fishermen, hikers, picnickers, and kite flyers, from spring through fall, and draw skiers, sledders, and snowshoers in the winter. There is challenging hiking and skiing here and plenty of wide open spaces. Over eight miles of trails lead into a variety of habitats: woodlands, hemlock ravines, fields, and wetlands. The Kendall Hills, above the lake, offer an excellent point from which to enjoy autumn's color show, or to launch a thrilling sled ride on a snowy winter's day.

The Kendall Lake area is part of what was formerly Virginia Kendall Metropolitan Park. In the early part of the twentieth century, Hayward H. Kendall, a wealthy Clevelander in the coal business, owned these acres of forest and farmland and made them his country retreat. Kendall died in 1927, willing his land to be used for public park purposes. The State of Ohio accepted his gift, and the Akron Metropolitan Park District lobbied the state to allow the park district to manage the park land, settling the matter in 1933. The park district gradually added more land to the nascent park, and in 1940, the state of Ohio provided $75,000 for more acreage, doubling the size of the park. The park was named Virginia Kendall, in honor of Kendall's mother.

The Civilian Conservation Corps (CCC) accomplished much of the early work of transforming the private retreat into a public park. Structures in the park built by the CCC in the 1930s include Kendall Lake itself, completed in 1935 and built primarily for swimming, toboggan chutes in 1936 (later removed by the National Park Service), the Lake Shelter in 1937, originally used as a swimmers' bathhouse and concession, and the unique chestnut wood privies.

Had Ohio declined Kendall's gift of land, his will stipulated that it be offered to the federal government as a national park. It would have been likely rejected at the time, but not in due course. In 1978, in an ironic turn of history, Virginia Kendall park was transferred to the National Park Service, making it the first federal unit of what was then called Cuyahoga Valley National Recreation Area.

Cross Country Trail

The Cross Country Trail was designed for skiing and is equally good for hiking. It winds through the area east of Kendall Lake bounded by Truxell and Quick Roads. The trail is mostly in the woods, but comes out onto Kendall Hills where there is a lot of room to practice downhill runs (and falling). Because of the hills, this trail requires at least intermediate skiing skills. The ski trail is separated from the sledding hills, where you can find hundreds of sledders on a snowy weekend.

Most of this area was farmed at one time, and even still you can see evidence of the fields, wood lots, farm lanes, and pastures. The mixture of woods, fields, hills, and streams, supports much wildlife. Beavers inhabit the lake and its environs, joining the fish, frogs, mallards, and Canada geese. Many species of birds reside in the area due to the diversity of habitats. Migratory waterfowl feed and rest on Kendall Lake, while migratory songbirds stop over in the surrounding forest.

You can reach this trail from the Kendall Lake Shelter off Truxell Road, or from Little Meadow Parking Area on Quick Road, just east of the sledding hills. A combination first aid station and all-season restroom facility is located at the sledding hills. The National Ski Patrol, operating out of the first aid station, patrols the trail during ski season.

The Lake Shelter operates as the Winter Sports Center in January and February, offering information, hot drinks, recreational programs, and snowshoe and cross-country ski rentals (216-524-1497). Buckeye Sports Center at 4610 State Road, just east of the Kendall Lake area, rents cross country ski equipment (330-929-3366). There are picnic tables near the Lake Shelter and restrooms in the lower level. When hiking this trail during the skiing season, please observe the multi-use trail etiquette: refrain from hiking in the ski tracks and yield to skiers, especially on hills.

Directions: From I-77, exit at Wheatley Road (SR 176). East on Wheatley Road to Riverview Road. Right on Riverview Road one quarter mile, then left on Bolanz Road half a mile to Akron Peninsula Road. Left (north) on Akron Peninsula Road about two and a quarter miles to Truxell Road. Right on Truxell Road one and a quarter miles to the lake entrance on the right.

From SR 8, exit at SR 303, then south at Akron-Cleveland Road for one mile. Turn right (west) on Kendall Park Road (named Truxell Road at the west end). One and three quarter miles to the lake entrance on the left.

Trail Description: Find the trail at the southeast corner of the Kendall Lake parking lot, just to the left of the trailhead bulletin board. A sign at

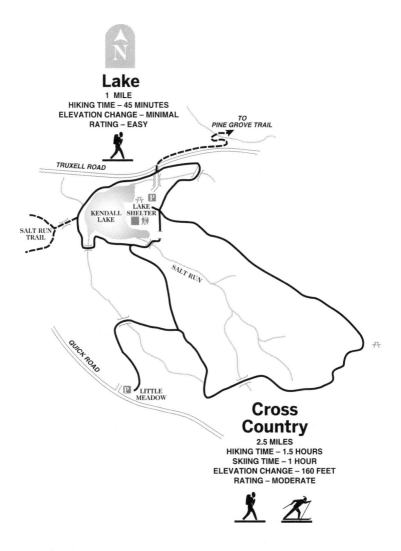

Lake
1 MILE
HIKING TIME – 45 MINUTES
ELEVATION CHANGE – MINIMAL
RATING – EASY

TO
PINE GROVE TRAIL

TRUXELL ROAD

KENDALL
LAKE

LAKE
SHELTER

SALT RUN
TRAIL

SALT RUN

QUICK ROAD

LITTLE
MEADOW

**Cross
Country**
2.5 MILES
HIKING TIME – 1.5 HOURS
SKIING TIME – 1 HOUR
ELEVATION CHANGE – 160 FEET
RATING – MODERATE

the edge of the drive marks the way to the Cross Country and Lake Trails. The Cross Country Trail is described in a clockwise direction. Begin to climb up an open slope lined by pine trees. Partway up this slope the Lake Trail crosses at right angles; the Cross Country Trail continues straight up the slope. At the top of this slope the trail narrows and continues to climb more gradually. Pines and hardwoods make up the surrounding woods. Sweetgum trees, with their star-shaped leaves, are particularly attractive here in the autumn when the leaves turn yellow, orange, and red. In pioneer days the resin from these trees was used medicinally and for chewing gum. To the right of the trail is a stand of tulip trees recognized by their tall, straight trunks and tulip-shaped leaves. You will also see some stands of aspens, a species that is often the first to thrive in old fields or cleared areas. Aspen seeds can take hold in disturbed or burned soils and the seedlings grow rapidly, helping to stabilize the soil and begin the process of forest regeneration.

In about three-quarters of a mile from the start you reach the location of a former farmstead. Looking around, you can deduce a bit of this area's history by reading the landscape. A couple of large old white oaks can still be found here—their size, in comparison to surrounding trees, indicates that they grew singly, in the open, with lots of sunshine. The surrounding area was probably pasture or crop land. You can find remains of foundations for perhaps a house and a barn, with silo. In the spring, some clusters of daffodils mark the homestead area.

The trail curves and dips slightly to cross a tributary of Salt Run, the creek which feeds Kendall Lake. You then come to where the trail emerges from the woods and continues straight ahead bordered by a mature woods on the left and a meadow on the right. There's a picnic table here, for those ready for a rest. Follow the trail a short distance beyond the table; it veers to the right to cross through the meadow. Bear to the right to stay on the Cross Country Trail. The fields to the left are being used for agriculture. A smaller patch of old field is a mix of goldenrod, large ant hills, and small shrubs. The trail wanders in and out of the shrubs and along the agriculture fields, then bears right and reenters the woods. A big, old oak stands sentinel at this spot.

Soon you begin the steep descent to Salt Run, crossing the creek on a bridge. This narrow descent can be tricky on skis. The trail then uses an old roadbed to climb out of the creek valley.

At the top of this hill, make a hairpin turn to the right (a service road straight ahead goes to Quick Road). Now once again high on a plateau, you pass through young forests that were old fields just decades ago. Here also, aspens are a dominant tree. Soon the trail splits at a Y intersection. The branch to the left leads down a hill, across a stream, then up and across a field to the Little Meadow parking area. The branch to the right is the continuation of the Cross Country Trail. Following it, you soon reach the top of the Kendall Hills. From here you get a good view of the lake shining in the distance at the foot of the hills. The trail is routed down the right edge of the nearest hill, but the whole open slope is a good place for skiers to practice downhill techniques.

Cross Country Trail

As you approach the lake, the Cross Country Trail jogs left, then right, and joins with the Lake Trail. Watch for the trail sign. At the intersection, turn to the right to complete the loop. (You can take the Lake Trail to the left to circle the lake, but this is not suitable for skiing). The trail to the right drops down and across Salt Run on a boardwalk. After crossing Salt Run, you come to a small cove of Kendall Lake. Over the years, beavers have removed trees along this cove, and some of the beaver-chewed stumps remain.

Climb the hill along the cove to reach a tunnel that was constructed to go under toboggan chutes. From the 1930s into the 1980s, thousands of young people and adults experienced the heart-thumping thrill of racing down these chutes and spinning wildly out of control onto frozen Kendall Lake—and then trudging back up the hill to do it all over again. The old wooden chutes deteriorated over time and were removed in 1990, but the memories and stories linger on.

After passing through the tunnel, go straight ahead to rejoin the Cross Country loop near where you started. A turn to the left takes you back to the parking lot.

Lake Trail

The Lake Trail allows you close access to the entire circumference of Kendall Lake, beautiful in any season. The fairly level trail is suitable for a family stroll and offers good chances to see wildlife where forest, stream, and lake all come together. The most common wild inhabitants found here are Canada geese, and they share the lake and shores with many other bird species, insects, amphibians, and mammals. You might even see beavers, as they have returned to the Salt Run valley and taken up residence in and near the lake.

The Lake Shelter overlooks Kendall Lake, which was constructed by the Civilian Conservation Corps (CCC) as a swimming lake. In January and February, the Lake Shelter serves as a Winter Sports Center. In other seasons, the shelter is available for rental. The upper porch is particularly nice for picnics, with the lake view framed by the shelter's stone walls. There are more picnic tables and benches on the lawn along the lake. Restrooms are located in the lower level of the shelter and in historic CCC privies nearby. Fishing is permitted in the lake in the summertime, and the small pier is a good place for teaching children the fine art of placing the worm on the hook.

Directions: From I-77, exit at Wheatley Road (SR 176). East on Wheatley Road to Riverview Road. Right on Riverview Road one quarter mile, then left on Bolanz Road half a mile to Akron Peninsula Road. Left (north) on Akron Peninsula Road about two and a quarter miles to Truxell Road. Right on Truxell Road one and a quarter miles to the lake entrance on the right.

From SR 8, exit at SR 303, then south at Akron-Cleveland Road for one mile. Turn right (west) on Kendall Park Road (named Truxell Road at the west end). One and three-quarter miles to the lake entrance on the left.

Trail Description: Start the Lake Trail along with the Cross Country Trail; both leave from the southeast corner of the Kendall Lake parking lot, near the trailhead bulletin board. Begin to climb the open slope, then turn to the right at the trail intersection to go clockwise around the lake. The trail passes through a tunnel. An exhibit at the end of the tunnel tells the story of the toboggan chutes that used to give thousands of young people an exciting winter adventure. The trail drops down along a cove of the lake then turns left to cross Salt Run. Shortly after this, the Cross Country Trail leaves to the left. To stay on the Lake Trail, continue ahead along the shores of the lake. The trail winds through a narrow band of trees, bordered by the lake to your right and the Kendall Hills to your left. One of the most conspicuous trees here is the American hornbeam, a good example of how confusing common names can be. Its sinewy, gray trunk resembles muscles, suggesting one common name—muscle wood. American hornbeam is a member of the birch family, but is also called water beech because it prefers moist soil, and the bark resembles that of beech.

As you circle the lake, the view changes. The small, quiet coves are favorite spots for birds, and you may see the smaller of our common herons, the green heron. About halfway around, cross the earthen dam which forms Kendall Lake from the waters of Salt Run. (At the south end of the dam a trail to the left connects to the Salt Run Trail.) At the north end of the dam, follow the Lake Trail to the right and climb a set of steps to the hill above the shoreline. Mature beech trees frame a view of the Lake Shelter. Rattlesnake weed, identified by its striking purple-veined leaves, can be found clinging to these slopes in the summer, along with club mosses. The club mosses are notable as they are one of the most ancient plants on earth, dating back at least 400 million years.

Descend a short way, climb again, then descend steps to reach the back-waters of the lake. Here is one of the places along the shore where you might be able to spot signs of beaver activity, such as sharply-pointed, gnawed stumps of saplings. Continue across the Kendall Lake entrance drive. Across Truxell Road, opposite the entrance drive, a connector trail leads up the hill to Pine Grove Trail, Octagon Shelter, and the Ledges area. The Lake Trail enters a swamp east of the entrance road. Perched on the cattails and tree stumps, red-winged blackbirds and woodpeckers claim their territories. Sounds announce the seasons, with spring peepers proclaiming the return of spring and the dry rustle of cattails ushering in winter.

Leave the swamp by crossing the creek on a bridge, then climb steps into a planted pine forest. Rejoin the Cross Country Trail on the open slope where you began. Turn to the right to reach the parking lot.

Salt Run Trail

Salt Run Trail, west of Kendall Lake, takes a long route through the forested, rugged hills drained by Salt Run. The length and terrain make this trail more challenging than others in the area, and it can be combined with the Lake and Cross Country Trails for an even longer hike. The shortcut loop on the Salt Run Trail offers a less challenging alternative hike. Both the long and short routes take you through pine, oak, hickory, beech, and hemlock stands. A variety of ferns, including the evergreen Christmas fern, and wildflowers, border the trail.

You can reach the Salt Run Trail from the Kendall Lake parking lot or from the Pine Hollow parking area at Kendall Hills on Quick Road. There are picnic tables, grills, water fountains, and restrooms at both Kendall Lake and Pine Hollow.

Directions: From I-77, exit at Wheatley Road (SR 176). East on Wheatley Road to Riverview Road. Right on Riverview Road one quarter mile, then left on Bolanz Road half a mile to Akron Peninsula Road. Left (north) on Akron Peninsula Road about two and a quarter miles to Truxell Road. Right on Truxell Road one and a quarter miles to the lake entrance on the right.

From SR 8, exit at SR 303, then south at Akron-Cleveland Road for one mile. Turn right (west) on Kendall Park Road (named Truxell Road at the west end). One and three quarter miles to the lake entrance on the left.

Trail Description: To reach the Salt Run Trail from Kendall Lake, follow the Lake Trail to the far side of the lake; watch for the trail sign at the south end of the dam. Turn away from the lake and follow the trail a short distance west to a sign marking the beginning of the three-and-a-quarter-mile Salt Run Trail loop, described here in a clockwise direction. Go straight ahead, across the bottom of the sledding hills, and into the pine woods. Climb a short distance through the pines; you'll reach another trail sign that marks the trail for those entering from the Pine Hollow parking area on Quick Road.

Bear to the right and descend to cross a stream on a small bridge. Climbing out of this creek valley, continue through a mixed forest for less than a quarter mile, then out along Quick Road in order to get around the head of a narrow ravine. Walk parallel to the road for seventy yards, then follow the trail back into the woods.

About one mile from the start, you reach the shortcut trail. Follow this to

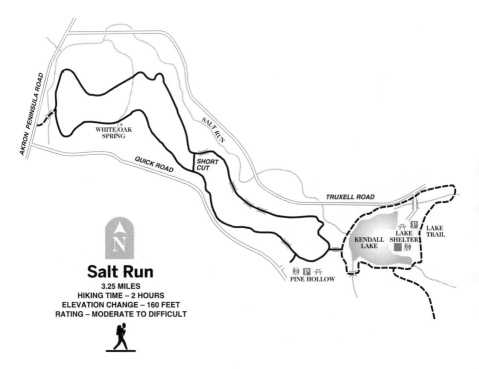

Salt Run
3.25 MILES
HIKING TIME – 2 HOURS
ELEVATION CHANGE – 160 FEET
RATING – MODERATE TO DIFFICULT

your right for a shorter loop (shortening the trail by about one mile). This area where the shortcut intersects was a clearing in the 1960s and is now a young forest. If you follow the shortcut, pick up the trail description a few paragraphs below.

On the main loop, and shortly past the shortcut intersection, you begin a steep drop to the lowlands. A large, old oak tree in the valley appears to have escaped the saw, and the aging fruit trees nearby provide food for wildlife. Next is a steady, short climb to White Oak Spring, a natural spring at the base of a white oak tree. Continuing on, you descend a steep slope on a gradual switchback to the valley floor. Now near Akron Peninsula Road, the trail follows the route of the older East River Road for a short way. A tributary of Salt Run is on the left, and a side trail (part of the Boy Scout's Order of the Arrow trail) joins in from Akron Peninsula Road.

Just before reaching Salt Run, the trail turns to the right and goes into a thicket of young deciduous trees. According to local historian Joe Jesensky, Salt Run gets its name from a salt works that was located here in pioneer times. Salt was a valuable commodity, especially as a meat pre-

Kendall Hills

servative, and was not easily found at ground level. Apparently salt was discovered here, and the settlers established a place where they could dig a shallow salt well, then boil the salty water to extract the salt. Jesensky, in his explorations, found what he believes are the depressions where the salt was collected and boiled down. Eventually the salt source must have petered out, or was supplanted by more easily obtained salt.

The trail can be very muddy here, but the surrounding wet habitat supports some interesting plants. Mosses, often producing the first green of spring, soften the rocks and tree trunks. Jewelweed thrives here in the summer, along with wild grapes, thistles, goldenrods, thorn apples, and walnut trees. Because of the food and cover, this is a good area for seeing birds and deer. After this section, you climb up a steep, narrow ridge, and come to where the shortcut trail rejoins the main trail.

Past the shortcut, drop down a steep slope and cross a long bridge. You are again in the floodplain of Salt Run. In this creek valley, you come to an area of hemlocks and beeches on an island of land separated by drainage cuts in the landscape. Here you can often see remnants of mud slides, exposing clay soils. Many of the slopes in the valley are unstable, and you can find evidence of their movements where slumps like these occur. Cross a side creek via a bridge, follow along the hemlock island, then cross two more bridges placed close together. Some of the evergreen hemlocks here reach heights of thirty to fifty feet.

Kendall Lake

Climb out of the creek valley, leaving the hemlocks behind. You'll reach some white pines mixed in with deciduous trees. Climb some more to reach a white pine grove. A severe storm in 1995 blew down many trees throughout this area. Follow the trail as it winds along, then begin the last climb. From this height, and when the leaves are off the trees, you can see Kendall Lake down below.

Descend towards the base of the sledding hills to complete the loop. Turn left to return to Kendall Lake, or right to return to the Pine Hollow parking lot.

Deep Lock Quarry Metro Park

Deep Lock Quarry Metro Park, as its name implies, contains remnants of the Cuyahoga Valley's canal and quarrying history. Berea Sandstone was quarried here at various times, beginning in the early 1800s and ending in the 1930s. This sandstone is durable and can be split or sawn into blocks, making it very valuable as a building stone. The stone's location so near to the canal was advantageous as well. An 1888 report on the geology of Summit County noted that by then Berea Sandstone had already been quarried for decades in Peninsula and shipped via the canal to points near and far. The Deep Lock part of the park's name refers to Lock 28, which was the deepest lock on the canal and is in good condition to this day.

In 1879, Akron cereal king Ferdinand Schumacher owned a part of Deep Lock Quarry. He found that the sandstone made good millstones for his American Cereal Works (later called Quaker Oats). You can find discarded millstones along the trail leading to the quarry. Deep Lock Quarry became a metro park in 1934, following the donation of forty-one acres by the Cleveland Quarries Company. Later on, the state of Ohio donated the canal lands to Metro Parks, Serving Summit County, bringing the total size of the park to over seventy acres. The last stones cut from this quarry were used by the Civilian Conservation Corps as building stones for several facilities in other metro parks.

During the heyday of the canal and quarrying era, pioneers stripped this area of its trees. It is now mostly reforested and has more Ohio buckeye trees than any other metro park in the county. The buckeye, Ohio's state tree, is most conspicuous in the spring when it displays six-inch-long, upright flower clusters. In the fall, children, as well as many adults, enjoy picking up the large, smooth, glossy brown seed that resembles a buck's eye.

The old canal lock still holds shallow water. On warm spring days, turtles sun themselves on floating logs, while the croaking of bullfrogs echoes off the lock walls. A fast-flowing stretch of the Cuyahoga River is nearby. A shallow marsh on the floor of the quarry features some wetland plants, including rose pink, a summer wildflower. The quarry and canal area is also a popular spot for birders, especially in the spring. On a relatively short walk, birdwatchers might spot orioles, finches, hawks, several species of flycatchers, vireos, warblers, woodpeckers, and sparrows, and perhaps a wood thrush or a brilliant scarlet tanager. Along the river they might see great blue herons, geese, kingfishers, and on rare occasions, a bald eagle. This is a small area, but with much to see!

There is one trail that loops through Deep Lock Quarry Metro Park, and an access trail to the Ohio & Erie Canal Towpath Trail. Bicycles are allowed on the access trail and the Towpath Trail, but not on the Quarry Trail. There is a bicycle rack at the trail junction where visitors can leave their bikes while they explore the quarry on foot. The Buckeye Trail (a 1,400-mile hiking trail) uses the Ohio & Erie Canal Towpath Trail as it passes through the Deep Lock area. It is marked with a blue BT in a directional arrow. A picnic area and restrooms are located near the park's parking lot.

Sandstone at Deep Lock Quarry

Quarry Trail

The Quarry Trail makes a loop through the remains of the Berea Sandstone quarry that furnished much of the stone for local foundations, millstones, and canal locks. It's fun to look for the many pieces of quarry history that are scattered throughout the park.

Directions: From I-77 and I-271, take I-77 north to I-271. Exit at SR 303, then east on SR 303 one and three quarter miles to Riverview Road. South on Riverview Road less than a mile to the park entrance on the left.

From SR 8, exit at SR 303. Go west about three and a quarter miles to Riverview Road. South on Riverview Road less than a mile to the park entrance on the left.

Trail Description: Begin this trail from the Deep Lock Quarry Metro Park parking lot. Descend to the bottom of the hill. At this junction, the Quarry Trail goes straight and the access to the Towpath Trail bears to the right. The Cuyahoga Valley Scenic Railroad tracks are also to your right. (A short walk or ride on the access trail will bring you to the historic towpath and Deep Lock, or Lock 38, on the Ohio & Erie Canal. You can see other canal remnants there as well, including the lock's spillway structure.) Staying on the Quarry Trail, go straight, passing discarded millstones that rest along the trail like outdoor sculptures commemorating a bygone technology. Continue straight on the Quarry Trail into the quarry. Be careful —here, as the stones are often wet and slippery.

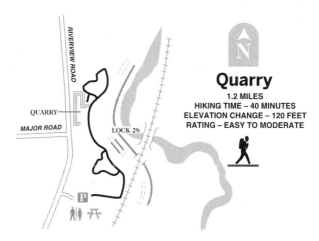

Quarry

1.2 MILES
HIKING TIME – 40 MINUTES
ELEVATION CHANGE – 120 FEET
RATING – EASY TO MODERATE

Deep Lock Quarry

This quarry provided sandstone for many regional structures including the first section of Akron City Hospital. The stone was also used in building the breakwall in Cleveland, along with the intake crib in Lake Erie where Cleveland's water supply inlet is located. After 1879, Ferdinand Schumacher began quarrying stone here. He had them shaped into huge millstones on-site, then shipped to his American Cereal Works in Akron, where they were used to hull oats. Schumacher is credited with introducing oatmeal to America, so these stones deserve a place of honor in America's breakfast history!

Early quarrying was slow, difficult work performed with hand tools. Workers risked their health as they faced occupational hazards, including lung damage from inhaling the fine stone grit. Small sponges tied under the noses of quarry workers were the precursors of today's masks. Late in the 1880s, the introduction of mechanization altered the quarrying process. One of the new machines was a channeling machine driven by a steam engine. It traveled on a portable track, driving bits against the stone, cutting a channel about three inches wide. By cutting such channels at right angles, the stone could be "cubed," and the bottom side loosened by wedges or a small blast. You can still see the channel marks in the remaining exposed sandstone of the quarry.

After exploring the quarry bottom, leave via the Quarry Trail by turning to the right of the sandstone walls. Follow the Quarry Trail around the base of a hill, then go left, uphill. After some ups and downs over the rough quarry hillside, you reach a junction. Turn to the left to go to the rim of the quarry, from which you gain an impressive view. Please be careful while exploring around the steep-walled quarry. Return to the junction and continue to follow the Quarry Trail away from the rim. It now makes a short loop through the north part of the park, then swings south again to rejoin the trail you left earlier. For a while you are following the route of a railroad that operated in the quarry. You might still find pieces of old rail poking out of the ground near the trail.

Back at the quarry, exit it the way you came in, going south on the wide trail. At the next junction, turn to the right and go up a small hill past other old quarry-related foundations. Follow this short section until it rejoins the main trail just at the foot of the first hill. Turn right to climb the hill to the parking lot.

Millstones

Oak Hill Area

This upland region of Cuyahoga Valley National Park contains one of the largest roadless areas of federally owned land in the national park. The area is dotted with numerous small ponds and contains extensive stands of deciduous trees, plus meadows, pine plantations, and a Christmas tree farm. The Oak Hill and Horseshoe Pond trailheads serve the area. There are picnic tables at Oak Hill and picnic tables under a pavilion at Horseshoe Pond; neither area has running water, but both have restrooms.

The Cuyahoga Valley Environmental Education Center is just south of the Oak Hill Trailhead. The center is operated by the National Park Service and the Cuyahoga Valley National Park Association, and offers programs year-round to area school children and adults. The use of the campus area is reserved for groups using the environmental education center (see appendix); signs are posted marking the entrances to the campus area.

Much of the Oak Hill area was farmed in earlier times. One of the oldest farmhouses in the vicinity, the John Gilson home, now serves as a dormitory for the environmental education center, while the handsome barn also has a new use—housing a dining hall and classroom. In local lore, Gilson is linked to the history of the Everett Covered Bridge. One night in the winter of 1877, John Gilson and his wife were swept into icy waters while attempting to ford Furnace Run. Mrs. Gilson survived, but Mr. Gilson lost his life in the rapidly flowing stream. In his memory the local residents pressed to have the Everett Covered Bridge erected to provide a safe crossing. The bridge served travelers for nearly a century, then suffered a series of hard times. Severely damaged by a careless truck driver, then destroyed by a flood in 1975, it lay in ruins. Strong public support for the bridge, including monetary donations from school children, led to the National Park Service rebuilding and reopening the Everett Covered Bridge to non-motorized traffic in 1986.

Fishing in the three small ponds behind the environmental education center is reserved for wildlife. However, fishermen can try their luck at one of four other public ponds in the Oak Hill area—Meadowedge, Sylvan, Goosefeather, and Horseshoe.

There are three different hiking trails in the Oak Hill Road area. Oak Hill Trail and Plateau Trail leave from the Oak Hill Trailhead, and the Tree Farm Trail is accessed from the Horseshoe Pond Trailhead. The Plateau Trail and the Tree Farm Trail are both designed specifically for cross-country skiing, and the Oak Hill Trail is also skiable. The Tree Farm Trail crosses gently rolling terrain and is a good trail for beginning skiers. Both the Oak Hill and Plateau Trails have steeper hills and more challenging turns.

Best Hikes for . . .

Birds

- Hemlock Loop Trail, Bedford Reservation (p. 98)
- Chippewa Creek Trail, Brecksville Reservation (p. 127)
- Towpath Trail—Frazee House to Station Rd. (p. 24)
- Towpath Trail—Station Rd. to Red Lock (p. 28)
- Towpath Trail—from Lock 29, Peninsula north and south (p. 37)
- Towpath Trail—Hunt House to Ira (p. 42)
- Ledges Trail, The Ledges (p. 169)
- Quarry Trail, Deep Lock Quarry Metro Park (p. 191)
- Towpath Trail—Hale Farm Connector (p. 45)
- Deer Run Trail, O'Neil Woods Metro Park (p. 232)

Tree Farm Trail

The Tree Farm Trail traverses what was part of the Robert Bishop family's Christmas tree farm. This was a "cut-your-own" tree farm. In December, cars would line Major Road as each family hunted for their special Christmas tree. The Bishops have roots far back into Peninsula history, and Robert Bishop's daughter and son-in-law continue family tradition by operating Heritage Farms tree farm and daylily business on their property adjacent to the national park. Although the Tree Farm Trail is entirely on public land, it comes near the Bishops' private property. Please respect these property lines when exploring this lovely trail.

The topography here is gently rolling, and the ski trail is wide with generally good sight lines, making this an excellent novice- to intermediate-level trail. Some stands of hardwoods and a large open field with a good view to the east interrupt the now mature rows of evergreen trees. In the winter, snow-laden evergreen tunnels add to the appeal of this trail. Though the trail is bordered by two roads and the village of Peninsula, you will usually find there a feeling of quiet and remoteness.

Wildlife is abundant here, and it is possible to see deer, fox, rabbits, and coyotes, or at least their tracks. This is also a good bird habitat, and a keen eye may spot several species of warblers and many other songbirds, plus waterfowl on the pond, a hawk soaring overhead, and perhaps even an owl resting in the evergreens. In the summertime, bring a picnic and enjoy idling on the banks of the pond, watching the colorful damselflies and dragonflies darting about over the water.

Horseshoe Pond is a popular fishing pond, where lucky anglers catch bass or bluegill. From the parking lot, a short trail leads around the pond to the left, reaching a picnic pavilion with a pleasant view of the pond. This fishing trail incorporates an accessible fishing pier, a casting platform, and a boardwalk. Volunteers with the Cuyahoga Valley Trails Council partnered with the National Park Service to fund and build these improvements. Other funds came from the Cuyahoga Valley Association's March for Parks, the Telephone Pioneers of America, and the National Park Foundation.

Directions: From I-77 and I-271, take I-77 north to I-271. Exit at SR 303, then east on SR 303 less than a quarter mile to Major Road (very near an exit ramp). Turn right on Major Road and go about one and three quarter miles to the Horseshoe Pond Trailhead on the left.

From SR 8, exit at SR 303. Go west about three and a quarter miles to Riverview Road. South on Riverview Road half a mile to Major Road. Right on Major Road three-quarters of a mile to the Horseshoe Pond Trailhead on the right.

Tree Farm Trail

Trail Description: The Tree Farm Trail begins at the north edge of the trailhead parking lot, about fifty feet east of the trailhead bulletin board. To go clockwise around the loop, begin the trail from the trail sign and go north, towards the pond. The trail drops a few feet to cross the pond's emergency spillway, then goes up onto the pond dam. At the end of the dam, watch for the trail sign indicating a turn into the woods to the right. This begins a gently rolling section of trail heading east that uses some of the old tree farm lanes. After a gentle downhill grade, the trail swings north, then west, through a more open area edged with brambles and multiflora roses. Soon after this, the trail turns east again, follows an aisle through the trees, then breaks out into an open field. Follow the path to the top of the open knoll, now at an elevation of 890 feet. Here you can see across the valley to the east. The high points on the opposite rim are at the Ledges Area. Closer by and just below, you can see the neatly planted rows of evergreens at Heritage Farms.

Descend the hill and cross a former farm lane lined with trees. Continue on through a young woods, then drop down a small hill to cross a stream via a bridge. There is a short climb up from the bridge, then the trail continues at a mostly level plane, with easy, gentle ups and downs. A bench at the top of an easy climb is a good spot to sit and watch for deer.

You are about halfway around the trail at this point. The latter half of the trail continues a winding course through evergreens and along sumac and dogwood shrub thickets. For a short while you parallel Riverview Road, then turn west to parallel Major Road. After a straight stretch of a couple thousand feet, between the straight rows of trees, the trail makes a series of S-turns, in and out of evergreens again, using old farm lanes.

Near the end of the trail you come out of one of these lanes towards an open field; turn sharply to the right. The trail descends a slope and turns left to go back into the evergreens one last time. Once again it emerges into the open, then bears right and drops to cross a small intermittent steam via a bridge. At the top of a short slope you reach the parking lot where you began.

Tree Farm
2.75 MILES
HIKING TIME – 1.5 HOURS
SKIING TIME – 45 MINUTES
ELEVATION CHANGE – 80 FEET
RATING – EASY TO MODERATE

Oak Hill Trail

The National Park Service opened the Oak Hill area in 1983. It offers a small picnic area under a shagbark hickory tree, fishing ponds, hiking and cross-country skiing trails, and restrooms. The western part of this area was farmed in the past and is now covered with shrubs; the eastern section is forested and hilly. Historically, this woods was primarily a mixed oak-chestnut forest. Early in the twentieth century, chestnut blight, an introduced fungal disease, spread into Ohio and killed most of the American chestnut trees. A few rare chestnut stumps endure in the woods, a testament to the loss of a beautiful species. Young chestnuts sprout and live a few years before succumbing to the disease. Researchers continue to try to find a strain of chestnut that can survive the blight. More recent invaders—gypsy moths—have killed many of the old oak trees, robbing this hill of its namesake. You might see some of these oaks still standing, and many fallen ones as well. This forest continues to change, and only time will tell which species will dominate the woods next.

The Oak Hill Trail is designed for easy hiking or cross-country skiing and provides access to fishing ponds. The trail makes a one-and-a-half-mile loop, while a longer trail, the Plateau Trail, leaves from the same parking lot and makes a four-and-a-half-mile loop. Sometimes the two trails overlap, so follow the trail signs carefully.

A Youth Conservation Corps crew cleared this trail originally, then when the Cuyahoga Valley Trails Council was established, the council adopted this trail. Cuyahoga Valley Trails Council volunteers have made many improvements to this trail over the years, including building bridges and boardwalks, and hardening the trail.

The loop trail starts from the eastern edge of the parking lot at the trailhead bulletin board. About a half-mile walk in either direction will bring you to Sylvan Pond. From the Oak Hill Trail you can also reach Meadowedge Pond and Chestnut Pond via the Plateau Trail. Goosefeather Pond is also nearby, reached by going north on Oak Hill Road, then west on Scobie Road. All these ponds are good for fishing and ideal for introducing young people to the beauty and delight of pond life.

Directions: From I-77 and I-271, take I-77 north to I-271. Exit at SR 303, then east on SR 303 less than a quarter mile to Major Road (very near an exit ramp). Turn right on Major Road and go one mile to Oak Hill Road. Right on Oak Hill Road one mile to the trailhead entrance on the left. Or take I-77 to the Wheatley Road exit. East on Wheatley Road to Oak Hill Road. Left on Oak Hill Road one mile to the trailhead entrance on the right.

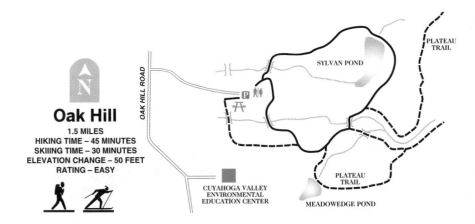

Oak Hill
1.5 MILES
HIKING TIME – 45 MINUTES
SKIIING TIME – 30 MINUTES
ELEVATION CHANGE – 50 FEET
RATING – EASY

From SR 8, exit at SR 303. Go west about three and a quarter miles to Riverview Road. South on Riverview Road half a mile to Major Road. Right on Major Road one and a half miles to Oak Hill Road. Left on Oak Hill Road one mile to the trailhead entrance on the left.

Trail Description: Leaving from the information kiosk, take the trail to the right to go in a counterclockwise direction. An old farm field on your left is naturally revegetating in a process called succession. Grasses, wildflowers, and shrubs, such as gray dogwood, provide a habitat for butterflies, birds, small mammals, and many other creatures. These shrubs will eventually be replaced by larger trees as the fields revert to forest. Huge ant hills dot the old field, and can sometimes be seen near the trail. Other insects, such as grasshoppers and praying mantises, find plentiful shelter and food throughout the field.

Continuing on the trail, you reach a young forest of oaks and hawthorns, where you turn left and drop down to cross a small stream via a bridge. At the top of the next slope you come to a trail intersection. Here the Plateau Trail joins from the right and continues with the Oak Hill Trail for the next two-tenths of a mile. Both trails bear to the left and pass through a young woods; the Cuyahoga Valley Environmental Education Center campus is to the right, but out of sight. Continue one-tenth of a mile through hawthorns and black cherries until you reach the next trail junction. The Oak Hill Trail turns to the left.

A side trip on the Plateau Trail to the right leads to Meadowedge Pond. This little pond is typical of man-made farm ponds and is a pleasant spot any time of year. In the warm months, you can try to spot bullfrogs and

Sylvan Pond

green frogs before they spot you, and listen for the *chickaree* of red-winged blackbirds perched in the cattails. Follow the same trail to return to the Oak Hill Trail.

The Oak Hill Trail swings northeast through the woods then descends to cross the same creek you crossed earlier. The Plateau Trail rejoins the Oak Hill Trail to cross this creek then leaves again, going east. Stay on the Oak Hill Trail, going straight ahead, where it enters an older woods of oak, hickory, and maple trees, and climbs very gently to the highest point along the trail, a small pine-forested knoll. Leaving the pines, bear to the left and go towards Sylvan Pond, which is about twice the size of Meadowedge Pond. The trail leads across the pond's dam then reenters the woods at the far end. In a few yards a connector trail to the right leads to the Plateau Trail. Keeping straight ahead, a short walk of ten to fifteen minutes on the Oak Hill Trail takes you through a mixed woods, past another trail intersection, and back to the parking lot.

Plateau Trail

This four-and-a-half-mile loop trail around the Oak Hill plateau was designed and graded as a cross-country ski trail. The Oak Hill Trail is a smaller one-and-a-half-mile loop trail that intersects with the Plateau Trail at several places. Together these trails present many options for hiking and skiing. There is also the option of adding four-tenths of a mile of trail to the loop by taking a spur trail to Hemlock Point and back. Watch the junction trail signs carefully to avoid getting lost. The Plateau Trail is a challenging ski trail with two steep hills. It has also become a favorite with hikers, due to its variety and challenge. If you do the whole loop, you will see ponds, fields, stream valleys, a hemlock ravine, and acres of uninterrupted forest.

Directions: From I-77 and I-271, take I-77 north to I-271. Exit at SR 303, then east on SR 303 less than a quarter mile to Major Road (very near an exit ramp). Turn right on Major Road and go one mile to Oak Hill Road. Right on Oak Hill Road one mile to the trailhead entrance on the left. Or take I-77 to the Wheatley Road exit. East on Wheatley Road to Oak Hill Road. Left on Oak Hill Road one mile to the trailhead entrance on the right.

From SR 8, exit at SR 303. Go west about three and a quarter miles to Riverview Road. South on Riverview Road half a mile to Major Road. Right on Major Road one and a half miles to Oak Hill Road. Left on Oak Hill Road one mile to the trailhead entrance on the left.

To access the trail from the Valley Picnic Area, go south out of Peninsula on Riverview Road one and a quarter miles. Turn right into the Valley Picnic Area. The loop trail begins a short ways up the old driveway out of the picnic area.

Trail Description: The Plateau Trail begins at the lone shagbark hickory tree which shades the picnic tables south of the Oak Hill Trailhead parking lot, and ends at the trailhead kiosk. We describe it here in a counterclockwise direction. Start the trail at the picnic tables and go west through the field. Bear left just after you enter a spruce plantation beyond the field. Head south, crossing a small headwater drainage. The trail swings east, through a stand of young red maples, then continues through a young beech-maple woods. Half a mile from the start of the trail, you join the Oak Hill Trail. Bear right, and soon reach an old lane lined with hawthorns and black cherries. The Plateau Trail then leaves the Oak Hill Trail, turning south (right) toward Meadowedge Pond. At the pond, turn left onto the dam to follow the trail along the edge of the pond. The Cuyahoga

Meadowedge Pond

Valley Environmental Education Center is west of the pond. The center is reserved for students or others who are staying on campus; please do not enter the area without permission. For more information, see the appendix.

At the end of the dam, turn left and enter the woods. The trail winds along for another half mile and comes to a T intersection. A spur trail leaves to the right and parallels a beautiful hemlock ravine, ending in two-tenths of a mile at Hemlock Point. Return by the same trail. On the main trail you now head west and descend to cross a bridge shortly before the Plateau Trail joins the Oak Hill Trail again. Together both trails turn right and cross another bridge. Soon the Plateau Trail leaves the Oak Hill Trail again, and does not rejoin it for three miles. A well-placed bench provides an opportunity to observe the hemlock ravine from the opposite side of the creek. Small waterfalls cascade over shale ledges thirty to forty feet below the overlook.

The trail then bears northeast, crosses a bridge, then passes around a small knoll. You then reach a stand of evergreens and soon cross an old driveway. The trail continues through a thick conifer woods before turning to the right to begin a long descent. At the bottom of the steepest part, the trail turns sharply to the west (left). If you are on skis, enjoy this wonderful downhill run, but remember: what goes down, must come up! At the end of this half-mile downhill, the trail reaches another intersection.

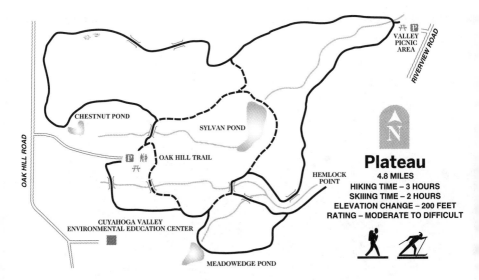

The lane to the right leads to the Valley Picnic Area on Riverview Road. The Plateau Trail turns west (left) and begins a long, steady climb back up to the elevation from which you began.

At the top of the climb, a connector trail leads to the Oak Hill Trail and Sylvan Pond. Just past the connector, the Plateau Trail swings north, then west, and winds through the woods along a scenic stream valley. Another bench invites you to rest and enjoy the view. The trail continues, crossing two bridges, then passes a delightful little round pond edged in cattails. Soon the trail swings south through old fields, then heads east down a straight lane with a cathedral-like feel, aimed directly at Chestnut Pond. A single row of oak trees lines each side of the trail. Beyond them, evergreens spread out to the right and left. Surely a previous owner planted this lane with purpose and design.

Chestnut Pond is quite secluded and often has many frogs floating in the thick duck weed along the shallow edges. But beware in the summer—the mosquitoes are ferocious.

Turn left at Chestnut Pond and continue generally north, then east, through a shrubby area, then back into the woods again. In the springtime you might hear wood frogs and spring peepers in a small vernal pond north of the trail. Follow the trail until it joins the Oak Hill Trail. Turn right and cross a boardwalk, and in a few yards you reach the parking lot where you began.

Wetmore & Riding Run Bridle Trails

The Wetmore Trailhead is the starting place for seven interconnected trails designed for horseback riding. The four trails in the Wetmore area, located on the east side of the Cuyahoga River, cross the wooded ridges and stream bottoms of Dickerson Run and Langes Run, through acreage once used for raising horses. Scattered throughout the area are old barns, shelters, and horse pastures, all reminders of the earlier farming days. Across the valley, on the western side of the river, the Riding Run area offers two trails: the Riding Run Trail and the Perkins Trail. The Valley Trail links the two clusters of trails, then continues north from the Wetmore Trailhead, linking all these bridle trails with Cleveland Metroparks' bridle trails in Brecksville and Bedford Reservations. The Wetmore and Riding Run Trails can also be accessed from the Everett Covered Bridge Trailhead on Everett Road, west of Riverview Road. Selecting different combinations of routes allows you to plan rides of any length.

The name Wetmore dates back to Frederick and Emila Wetmore, landowners here in the late 1800s. Several owners have succeeded them, the most recent private landowner being a nationally recognized breeder of Morgan and thoroughbred horses. Some of this land was acquired by Metro Parks, Serving Summit County, then in 1984 the National Park Service purchased the remainder of the farms. The current Wetmore trails follow old logging roads and horse paths used by previous owners.

The Riding Run and Perkins Trails travel through wooded hills above the Furnace Run valley. Most of the land was acquired by Metro Parks, Serving Summit County, in the 1970s. The trails make use of some former roads and drives as well as paths used in the past for horseback riding. Both trails cross federal land as well, and the Perkins Trail briefly enters a corner of Hale Farm & Village property.

Much of the routing and clearing of the bridle trails was accomplished by volunteers from the Cuyahoga Valley Trail Riders, the Medina County chapter of the Ohio Horseman's Council (OHC), in cooperation with the National Park Service. The horsemen have a camping area on Akron Peninsula Road that they use on trail work weekends. Riders also gather at Howe Meadow in CVNP for competitive trail rides. Cuyahoga Valley Trail Riders continue to help maintain the bridle trails in partnership with Cuyahoga Valley Trails Council volunteers and the National Park Service trail crew.

In 2003, heavy rains and floods damaged much of the horse trail system in CVNP and the trails were closed soon after. Now some sections of these trails have been redesigned and rerouted, and are once again open for riding. One trail is still under study and may be closed altogether and therefore is not included in this book.

Wetmore Trailhead

Wetmore Trail

Situated entirely between Wetmore and Quick Roads, the Wetmore Trail's four miles go through most of the area drained by Dickerson Run. Ironically, the trail name, which comes from an earlier landowner in the area, also aptly describes the trail's condition: the bottom lands here can be very muddy, especially in the spring! However, besides the wetness, you'll find clear-running creeks, deep woods, wildflowers, and acres of solitude. The Wetmore Trailhead has ample parking, restrooms, and picnic tables.

Directions: From I-77 exit at Wheatley Road. Take Wheatley east to Riverview Road. Turn right on Riverview Road one quarter mile, then left on Bolanz Road across the Cuyahoga River. Turn left (north) on Akron Peninsula Road; go about two and a quarter miles, then turn right on Wetmore Road. The trailhead is about half a mile up the road.

From SR 8, exit at SR 303 and go west into Peninsula. Turn left (south) on Akron Peninsula Road to Wetmore Road. Turn left on Wetmore Road to the trailhead.

Trail Description: The Wetmore Trail starts at the trailhead bulletin board at the east end of the Wetmore Trailhead parking lot. From the bulletin board, follow the trail down along the fenced pastures and into a mixed woods of aspens, red maples, and sycamores. In about a quarter mile you will come to the sign indicating the start of the Wetmore Trail loop—take the circular trail in either direction at this point. Our description will follow the trail to the right (counterclockwise).

Here in the lowlands the trail crosses bridges over tributaries of Dickerson Run and passes fields that were formerly pastures. It can be very muddy in this section. Follow the fence line until you reach the intersection with the Dickerson Run Trail. Here the Wetmore Trail turns uphill, away from the creek, and enters a forested area. At the top of this ridge you find fairly level ground for about one mile. Even this high ground can be quite muddy where it is not well drained. Dickerson Run valley is off to your right but well out of sight.

Along this high ground, you come to the intersection with the Dickerson Run Trail coming in on your right. The Tabletop Trail used to go to the left just after this intersection, but it was damaged by floods and will likely not be reopened. Continue on the Wetmore Trail in a generally south-to-southeast direction. About halfway around the four-mile loop, you enter an area of planted trees—mostly white and red pines and spruces—then pass over a bridge spanning a tributary, and follow along a large meadow, now swinging north towards Quick Road. Go past a tiny pond which is slowly filling in.

Leaving the meadow and high ground, descend into the bottom lands and cross a bridge. Come out of the creek valley on an uphill stretch of trail, then parallel Quick Road. You are now heading northwest. Grasses, field wildflowers, and young tulip trees favor these sunnier, open sections of the trail.

After paralleling Quick Road for about half a mile, the trail turns left to drop down to the bottom lands. Follow this down and across a branch of Dickerson Run. Cross a second time, then leave the valley, winding up a relatively steep climb. Large old oak trees dominate the ridge here, and if the branches are bare you can glimpse the meandering course of the stream below.

Soon you reach a switchback down into the stream valley. In this lowland, the Valley Trail intersects, going west, then north, towards Akron Peninsula Road. Cross Dickerson Run and bear to the right, past a grove of Ohio buckeye trees. This Ohio state tree can be recognized by its five leaflets forming a single leaf. In early spring, the buckeye's large buds swell and open to reveal inner green and rose-colored scales. The five-part leaflet emerges fanlike, followed by pale yellow-green flower clusters, some of the first tree flowers to appear in spring. Hummingbirds feed on the flower nectar. Even more familiar to Ohioans, however, is the tree's fruit—a thick, prickly, round capsule which breaks open to release the shiny, brown nut resembling a "buck's eye."

Follow the trail on a short climb out of the bottom land and into an old pasture. You might see deer here—watch for the white flag of their tail as they signal alarm. At the signpost, you have completed the four-mile loop; turn right to climb back up to the parking lot.

Dickerson Run Trail

The Dickerson Run Trail, in the Wetmore Bridle Trail system, is only one mile long, but you must take the Wetmore Trail to reach it, so the overall length is at least two and a half miles. The trail follows Dickerson Run; half of the distance is in the creek valley, the other half on the ridge above the stream.

Directions: From I-77 exit at Wheatley Road. Take Wheatley east to Riverview Road. Turn right on Riverview Road one quarter mile, then left on Bolanz Road across the Cuyahoga River. Turn left (north) on Akron Peninsula Road; go about two and a quarter miles, then turn right on Wetmore Road. The trailhead is about half a mile up the road.

From SR 8, exit at SR 303 and go west into Peninsula. Turn left (south) on Akron Peninsula Road to Wetmore Road. Turn left on Wetmore Road to the trailhead.

Trail Description: To reach the Dickerson Run Trail, start from the Wetmore Trailhead bulletin board. Follow the trail down to where the Wetmore Trail splits to the right and left (less than a quarter mile). Turn to the right and go about another quarter mile to the intersection of the Dickerson Run and Wetmore Trails.

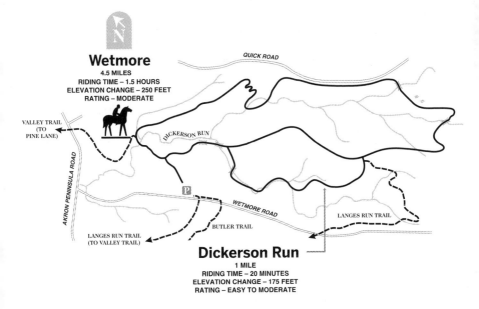

Turn to the right to begin the Dickerson Run Trail. For the first half mile or so, the trail stays in the stream lowlands and can be quite muddy. There are rewards, however. Many wildflowers thrive in these wet places, and you can also find several different fern species, including the delicate black-stemmed maidenhair fern.

About halfway on the Dickerson Run Trail you begin the climb out of the creek valley and onto the ridge. In fall and winter there are some nice views off to the right. The Langes Run Trail comes in from the right near the intersection with the Wetmore Trail. Climb some more to reach the Wetmore Trail. At this point you have several options for returning to the trailhead. Turning to the left on the Wetmore Trail is the shortest way back. Longer trips can be made taking the Wetmore Trail in the other direction or the Langes Run Trail to the southwest.

Best Hikes for . . .
Wintertime

- Buckeye Trail—Egbert Rd. to Alexander Rd. (p. 53)
- Buckeye Trail—Alexander Road to Frazee House (p. 53)
- Buckeye Trail—Red Lock (Jaite) to Boston (p. 66)
- Hemlock Loop Trail, Brecksville Reservation (p. 124)
- Deer Lick Cave Trail, Brecksville Reservation (p. 120)
- Brandywine Gorge Trail, Jaite/Boston Area (p. 145)
- Ledges Trail, The Ledges (p. 169)
- Tree Farm Trail, Oak Hill Area (p. 197)

Langes Run Trail

The Langes Run Trail in the Wetmore Bridle Trail system includes a bit of everything: high meadows, ponds, stream bottom lands, and steep, wooded slopes. To make a loop trip, combine this trail with the Dickerson Run and Wetmore Trails (six to nine miles long, depending on your chosen route).

Directions: From I-77 exit at Wheatley Road. Take Wheatley east to Riverview Road. Turn right on Riverview Road a quarter mile, then left on Bolanz Road across the Cuyahoga River. Turn left (north) on Akron Peninsula Road. Go about two and a quarter miles, then turn right on Wetmore Road. The trailhead is about half a mile up the road.

From SR 8, exit at SR 303 and go west into Peninsula. Turn left (south) on Akron Peninsula Road to Wetmore Road. Turn left on Wetmore Road to the trailhead.

Trail Description: To begin the Langes Run Trail, leave the Wetmore Trailhead parking area and cross Wetmore Road. A sign indicates the start of the trail, on an old farm lane. Follow the mowed path around the edge of the pasture. From this 870-foot elevation there are good views of the valley to the west. Nestled in the fields are two farm ponds. The fields themselves are full of sun-loving plants.

At the far end of the meadow, the trail begins to descend into the woods. At the bottom of the slope follow an old fence line bordering a field. Akron Peninsula Road can be seen beyond the field. Half a mile farther along, and while still down in the lowlands, you come to the intersection with the Butler Trail. Continuing on the Langes Run Trail, cross Langes Run then switchback up a hill to an oak-hickory forest.

The trail stays in the woods until coming to a utility right-of-way clearing. Turn left into the right-of-way, then in a short distance, turn right, back into the woods. Next, the trail goes through two old fields. Aspens are pioneer species here, helping revert the meadows to forest. Still on the ridge, you come into a dense woods of maples, ashes, aspens, tulip trees, and sassafras.

The trail swings north now and descends once again to cross Langes Run. The trail leaves the creek valley by way of an old road and comes out to Wetmore Road. Cross Wetmore Road and continue on the Langes Run

Trail as it parallels the road through a field and into some pines, then back into the field. The trail borders the edge of a ravine, then comes out close to the road to get around the head of the ravine, and comes out onto a private driveway. Turn left and follow the driveway for a short distance, then head left again into the woods. After the woods you go into a large meadow, then descend to a stream. Make a right turn to make the final climb out of this valley and reach the end of the Langes Run Trail where it meets the Dickerson Run Trail, just before Dickerson Run intersects with the Wetmore Trail.

To return to the parking lot by the most direct route, follow the Dickerson Run Trail to the left or go on to the Wetmore Trail and turn left.

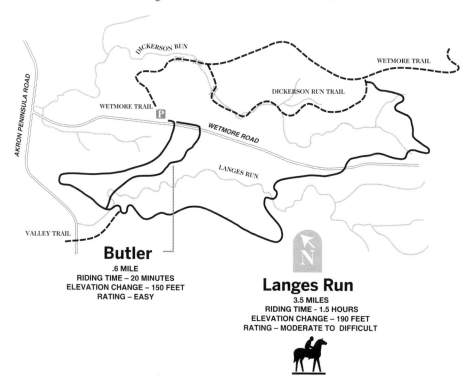

Butler
.6 MILE
RIDING TIME – 20 MINUTES
ELEVATION CHANGE – 150 FEET
RATING – EASY

Langes Run
3.5 MILES
RIDING TIME - 1.5 HOURS
ELEVATION CHANGE – 190 FEET
RATING – MODERATE TO DIFFICULT

Butler Trail

The Butler Trail, part of the Wetmore Bridle Trail system, connects the Wetmore Trailhead to the Langes Run Trail, partially using an old brick road. Reach the trail from the Wetmore Trailhead.

Directions: From I-77 exit at Wheatley Road. Take Wheatley east to Riverview Road. Turn right on Riverview Road a quarter mile, then left on Bolanz Road across the Cuyahoga River. Turn left (north) on Akron Peninsula Road; go about two and a quarter miles, then turn right on Wetmore Road. The trailhead is about half a mile up the road.

From SR 8, exit at SR 303 and go west into Peninsula. Turn left (south) on Akron Peninsula Road to Wetmore Road. Turn left on Wetmore Road to the trailhead.

Trail Description: From the Wetmore Trailhead, turn left on Wetmore Road and go along the road for about one-sixth mile. Turn right onto an old brick road that used to connect Wetmore Road to Akron Peninsula Road. Follow the road downhill into the bottom lands of Langes Run. For about half its length, the Butler Trail follows the meanders of Langes Run through a wet bottom land habitat of cottonwood and sycamore trees. Coltsfoot, an early spring wildflower, is abundant in this area.

The Butler Trail crosses Langes Run and intersects with the Langes Run Trail near Robinson Field, OHC's camp area.

Return on the same trail, or follow the Langes Run Trail in either direction. The Valley Trail also intersects here: it goes south and west to the Everett Covered Bridge and access to the Riding Run and Perkins Trails.

Enjoying Wetmore Trail

Riding Run Trail

The Riding Run Trail starts at the Everett Covered Bridge, follows Everett Road, then forms a loop trail in the forested area between Everett and Wheatley Roads. The trail has several steep climbs and about two miles of wide, graveled path. In the spring, daffodils brighten the secluded meadows and you are very likely to see deer bounding ahead on the trail.

To reach the Riding Run Trail, begin at the Everett Covered Bridge, on Everett Road, half a mile west of Riverview Road. The combination of the covered bridge, the cultivated fields, winding roads, and historic Hale Farm & Village nearby, creates an atmosphere that takes you back in time a century or more.

For longer trail rides, you can begin at the Langes Run Trail in the Wetmore Bridle Trail system, and use the Valley Trail to reach Riding Run (a round-trip length of ten miles).

Directions: From I-77, exit at Wheatley Road. Take Wheatley east about two and a half miles. Just after a very tight turn, turn right into the Everett Covered Bridge Trailhead.

Trail Description: Cross the covered bridge and go straight, following the trail as it goes alongside Everett Road and Furnace Run. Make a right turn at the Everett Road/Wheatley Road connector, using the stone equestrian trail alongside the road. The trail bears right, towards Furnace Run, winding its way through a grove of white pines. The trail then takes a left turn to cross the connector road and climbs a small slope. Here the loop trail begins. Our description follows the trail in a counterclockwise direction.

To begin the loop, bear to the right and climb a short distance. The trail emerges onto a wide, graveled roadbed, formerly Meirs Road. This section of township road was abandoned in the 1950s, and the western end was officially abandoned in 1994. Follow this road uphill for three-quarters of a mile, passing a pine woods along the way. The reward upon reaching the top of the ridge is a secluded meadow filled with wildflowers and apple trees. Look closely for the remains of a chimney and other signs of the barn and two houses that once stood here.

The trail turns towards the south and continues on the old roadbed for another mile. This nearly level stretch of trail provides great vantage points for seeing down into the steeply cut Riding Run valley. Everett Road is visible as you reach the trail sign marking the halfway point. A clearing near here with domestic plants marks another house site. The trail turns now and parallels Everett Road.

About a half mile farther along, a connector trail to the right crosses Everett Road and links the Riding Run loop to the Perkins loop on the south side of the road. Past the intersection, Riding Run continues straight ahead through a wooded area. Two bridges take you across streams before climbing back up to the top of the ridge, where the scent of pine sweetens the air. From this high spot you can glimpse the Cuyahoga River to the east.

Leaving the ridge, the trail descends a steep switchback and crosses a small stream before reconnecting to the start of the loop. Turning right, you soon reach Everett Road and can retrace your route to the Everett Covered Bridge.

Perkins Trail

The Perkins Trail is shaped like a narrow balloon at the end of a long string. It begins at the Everett Covered Bridge; about a mile from the start a connector trail links the Perkins Trail to the Riding Run Trail, across Everett Road. The steep hills and narrow paths of the Perkins Trail contribute to its "difficult" rating. Much of the trail also tends to be muddy. Nonetheless, it is worth the effort, as the trail takes you into some of the valley's more remote and quiet forests and stream ravines, areas beautifully typical of this northeast Ohio landscape.

This trail was named after Simon Perkins, the founder of Akron. Perkins was a friend of Canal Commissioner Alfred E. Kelley who convinced Perkins to donate land around and in Akron for canal development. This move resulted in the present route of the canal and assured the prosperous future of Akron. County maps for 1856 show that Simon Perkins owned land here as well, south of Everett Road.

To reach the Perkins Trail, park at the Everett Covered Bridge Trailhead on Everett Road, half a mile west of Riverview Road. For a longer ride, begin at the Langes Run Trail in the Wetmore Bridle Trail system, and use the Valley Trail to reach Riding Run (a round-trip length of ten miles).

Directions: From I-77, exit at Wheatley Road. Take Wheatley east about two and a half miles. Just after a very tight turn, turn right into the Everett Covered Bridge Trailhead.

Trail Description: Cross the covered bridge and continue straight ahead alongside Everett Road for a hundred feet or so. This is a scenic rural road with little traffic. (Hale Farm & Village is located about a mile to the south on Oak Hill Road, but be cautious if you decide to explore in that direction. The road is narrow, hilly, and winding.) At the trail sign, turn left and cross Everett Road.

A severe storm in the summer of 1996 damaged many of the trees in this area. In a short distance the trail passes through an opening and heads towards the wooded hillside. The climb up the hillside begins with switchbacks up the steepest section, then becomes more gradual. The entire ascent to the ridge top is about one mile. Mature beeches and oaks border the trail; near the top you go into an old clearing that is now filling with hawthorns and other pioneer trees.

The trail picks up an old lane, and soon reaches the intersection where the loop part of the trail begins. Go straight to follow the trail clockwise. The

Everett Covered Bridge

trail swings to the south and follows a pretty beech ridge. Large shagbark hickories and oaks also surround the trail here in this high, open woods. The trail leaves the woods and comes into a clearing above Hale Farm & Village. For a short distance you are on Hale Farm property. An oil well is here in the center of a grassy meadow. On a clear day you can see across the Cuyahoga River valley to Cuyahoga Falls and beyond.

Go past the oil well, following a buried cable right-of-way, and watch for where the trail makes a sharp turn to the right. (This is the outermost point along the trail and it now turns to complete the loop.) Descend the steep trail into the creek valley, cross the creek, and begin a more moderate climb partway up the opposite hillside, then follow the trail down again to parallel the creek, a tributary flowing to Furnace Run. Watch for where the trail crosses back across the main creek the last time. The trail used to continue north along the stream but has been rerouted here to pull it away from the stream and create a riparian buffer along the water. The trail now climbs diagonally away from the stream and reaches a three-way intersection. The trail to the north goes to Everett Road, crosses the road, and connects to the Riding Run Trail. To finish the Perkins Trail loop, turn right (east) at this three-way intersection and go uphill another 300 feet.

At the top of this climb, the trail continues on level ground a short distance until it reconnects to the point where the loop trail began. Turn to the left and retrace the beginning of your ride to return to the Everett Covered Bridge, a downhill trip of about one mile.

Valley Trail—Everett Covered Bridge to Wetmore Trailhead

The Valley Trail is a long, linear trail connecting the bridle trail system in the south part of CVNP with the bridle trails in Brecksville and Bedford Reservations in the north end of CVNP. The sections of trail from Peninsula to Brecksville Reservation were the last to be built, and are the newest trails in the CVNP system. With the addition of this fourteen-and-a-half-mile-long trail, equestrians visiting CVNP have unlimited opportunities for trail rides. Additionally, the bridle trails in CVNP reach some of the most remote and beautiful parts of the Cuyahoga Valley.

This section of the Valley Trail connects the Riding Run and Perkins Trails on the west side of the valley to the Wetmore Bridle Trail system on the east side of the Cuyahoga River valley. The Valley Trail goes along the Cuyahoga River, skirting a number of sweet corn fields. The trail is basically flat, with a quarter mile of road riding and one railroad crossing, until it climbs to the Wetmore Trailhead.

There is horse trailer parking at both the Everett Covered Bridge Trailhead and the Wetmore Trailhead. Both trailheads have small picnic areas and restrooms.

Directions: From I-77, exit at Wheatley Road. Take Wheatley east about two and a half miles. Just after a very tight turn, turn right into the Everett Covered Bridge Trailhead.

Trail Description: Begin the Valley Trail at the Everett Covered Bridge Trailhead. This is also the starting point for the Riding Run and Perkins Trails, reached by crossing the covered bridge. The Everett Covered Bridge has achieved almost legendary status in local Cuyahoga Valley lore. One night in the winter of 1877, John Gilson, a local citizen, and his wife were swept into the icy waters of Furnace Run while attempting to ford the stream on their way home. Mrs. Gilson survived, but Mr. Gilson lost his life in the rapidly flowing stream. In his memory the local residents pressed to have the Everett Covered Bridge erected to provide a safe crossing. The bridge served travelers for nearly a century and became a local attraction. It later suffered a series of hard times, sustaining damage from a truck over its weight limit, and finally, being swept away in a flood. Today's Everett Covered Bridge is a reconstruction of the bridge that was first built in the 1800s. The National Park Service built this bridge in 1986, using new timbers, but in a design true to the original construction.

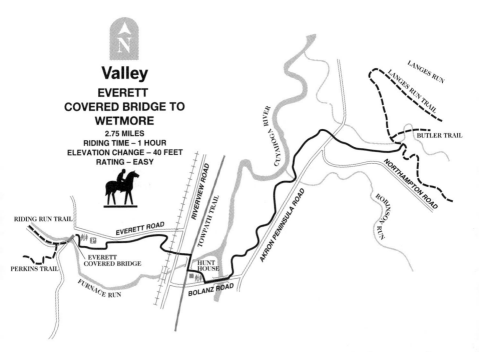

Next to the Everett Covered Bridge Trailhead is the Seiberling Wayside, an area honoring John F. Seiberling and other founders of Cuyahoga Valley National Park. The wayside exhibits are in a small outdoor room created by sandstone walls, sandstone seating areas, and plantings. The covered bridge was one of Congressman Seiberling's favorite places.

The Valley Trail leaves the trailhead and parallels Everett Road between the road and the cultivated fields. It passes near an interesting historic spot. Near the intersection of Riverview Road and Everett Road and west of the railroad tracks, was a tree nursery operated during the Great Depression. Metro Parks, Serving Summit County, owns this land where a Civilian Conservation Corps crew grew trees in the late 1930s to be planted throughout the metropolitan parks. One of the primary reasons that early parks in Ohio were established was to counteract the negative results of deforestation. Here in Everett, three and a half million seedlings helped reforest the valley. Many of the pines you find in the Virginia Kendall unit today came from this tree nursery.

The trail goes south along the old tree nursery, and just before reaching Riverview Road the trail crosses the Valley Railway (used by the Cuyahoga Valley Scenic Railroad for excursion trips) on a crossing designed especially for horses. Cross Riverview Road and go fifty feet, coming out of the woods at the Ohio & Erie Canal Towpath Trail and the bridge over Furnace Run.

Turn right and cross Furnace Run. The Valley Trail immediately leaves the Towpath Trail and drops down a small slope to go behind the Hunt House (open seasonally). A hitching rail for the horses allows you to take some time to explore the visitor center, fill up on water, or stop at Szalay's Farm for sweet corn, fresh fruit, or a cool drink.

The crossroads hamlet of Everett, which included Hunt and Szalay Farms, residences, and various small enterprises, is now recognized as the Everett Historic District. The National Park Service has restored the houses and commercial buildings, which now house park offices, the park library, partnering non-profits, and interns who teach at the Cuyahoga Valley Environmental Education Center.

The Valley Trail comes out to Bolanz Road just east of Hunt House. Follow Bolanz Road for a quarter mile, using the road bridge to cross the Cuyahoga River. At the farm field (private property), turn left and follow the trail through the field to the tree line. Here the trail turns right, then left (north), crossing through the tree line to reach another field. For a short piece the trail parallels Akron Peninsula Road, then winds away from the road to pass behind the historic Point Farm. This farm is part of CVNP's Countryside Initiative Program, managed by the non-profit Cuyahoga Valley Countryside Conservancy. The farm is owned by the National Park Service and leased to a private farmer to help preserve the rural landscape and agricultural function of the Cuyahoga Valley.

Past the Point Farm, the Valley Trail goes around another farm field, then turns east again alongside Robinson Run. It crosses the stream very near Akron Peninsula Road. It swings back towards the river again, then north, before again turning towards Akron Peninsula Road. Just before the road it joins a farm lane and then crosses Akron Peninsula Road.

On the east side of Akron Peninsula Road you reach Robinson Field, a camp area used by the Ohio Horseman's Council on trail work weekends. Here you will find hitching lines along the open fields. Follow the trail signs through the Robinson Field area to Langes Run. The Valley Trail crosses the stream, and just after crossing you reach the intersection with the Butler Trail and join the Langes Run Trail.

From here to the Wetmore Trailhead, the Valley Trail follows the Langes Run Trail, first staying fairly level, then climbing from the valley to the hill top. The trail comes out of the forest, along some fields, and through a thorny tree tunnel. From this high ground you can get some good views, both back to the valley and off across the fields. Summer wildflowers are plentiful in these sunny fields. At the end of the fields the trail reaches Wetmore Road and the Wetmore Trailhead.

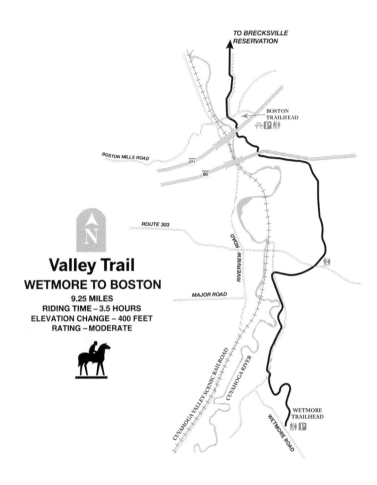

Valley Trail—Wetmore Trailhead to Boston Trailhead

This section of the Valley Trail connects the Wetmore Trailhead and the Wetmore system of bridle trails to the Boston Trailhead via the beautiful Boston Run valley. The trail crosses both federal property and property owned by Metro Parks, Serving Summit County. It is described here from south to north.

Directions: From I-77 exit at Wheatley Road. Take Wheatley east to Riverview Road. Turn right on Riverview Road a quarter mile, then left on Bolanz Road across the Cuyahoga River. Turn left (north) on Akron Peninsula Road. Go about two and a quarter miles, then turn right on Wetmore Road. The trailhead is about half a mile up the road.

From SR 8, exit at SR 303 and go west into Peninsula. Turn left (south) on Akron Peninsula Road to Wetmore Road. Turn left on Wetmore Road to the trailhead.

Trail Description: Begin this section of the Valley Trail at the Wetmore Trailhead on Wetmore Road, half a mile east of Akron Peninsula Road. From the trail kiosk, take the horse trail north, along the pasture, and then down into the Dickerson Run valley. You reach a trail sign that marks the start of the Wetmore Trail loop. Turn left onto Wetmore Trail and follow it through the floodplain of Dickerson Run, then across the stream. Here where two branches of Dickerson Run meet, the Valley Trail and Wetmore Trail part company.

Take the Valley Trail to the left. It climbs twenty to thirty feet above the creek valley, then cuts back to the west to follow Dickerson Run for a ways. A woods borders the stream here, with an open field to the right of the trail. Metro Parks, Serving Summit County, is managing this field as a bird habitat, so you might see bluebirds or other field birds. In late summertime, this field turns gold from all the goldenrod flowers. You are also likely to stir up the many grasshoppers living among the grasses and shrubs.

The Valley Trail comes out to Akron Peninsula Road, then crosses the road and continues on the west side of the road, between the road and the river, for another two and a half miles. For a ways the trail either runs beneath or crosses a major power line right-of-way. To stay on the trail watch carefully for trail signs in these areas. Deer—and occasionally, wild turkeys—can be seen feeding in these open areas. As the trail comes closer to the river, the land to the left of the trail slopes steeply down into the floodplain and some beaver-created wetlands.

At Salt Run, the trail drops steeply and crosses the stream on a bridge. The trail continues north, through fields and woods, and at one point you can see an old oxbow of the Cuyahoga River below and to the left. Farther along, the river's course comes very close to the trail, as the river takes its widely meandering route downstream.

The Valley Trail crosses Haskell Run on a bridge, then climbs up alongside the Par 3 course of Brandywine Golf Course. At the end of the road guardrail, near the cabin club house for the Par 3 course, the Valley Trail turns east and crosses Akron Peninsula Road. It goes uphill alongside the road, through a thorn apple grove, then joins a gravel road leading up to a communications tower.

Turn right (east and uphill) and follow the gravel road uphill. Near the summit, the communications tower road turns right. Stay straight ahead to stay on the Valley Trail. There are some nice views back down into the hilly and wooded back nine of the golf course. The trail swings a bit to the right and is raised and filled in this area to reduce the muddiness. The trail goes through some pines, then winds out to SR 303 and crosses this major two-lane road. Across a shrubby area full of autumn olive trees, the trail reaches and crosses Pine Lane. A hitching post here allows you to stop for a break. The Pine Lane Trailhead serves the Buckeye Trail as well. There are restrooms just a few yards away.

From the Pine Lane Trailhead, the Valley Trail continues north. This next section is an exceptionally beautiful part of the trail. It begins in a hemlock grove, paralleling the Buckeye Trail, then descends through a mixed hardwood forest with large, mature oaks, hickories, American beeches, maples, and scattered dogwoods. In springtime the slopes running towards Boston Run are covered with wildflowers—violets, trilliums, Mayapples, many other species of flowers, and numerous ferns.

At the bottom of the slope, the trail crosses Boston Run on a bridge, then climbs partway out of the valley and turns west on a more gradual uphill grade. Climbing more steeply towards the top, the trail comes out to Akron Peninsula Road (closed to vehicular traffic between here and Peninsula). Some daffodils brighten the spring woods here, having escaped from someone's garden.

The Valley Trail crosses to the north side of the road (the Buckeye Trail also crosses the road, a few yards west of here), and takes a straight route north, following an old single-lane road. Here a younger forest is growing up from old fields, and you can still find some raspberry bushes and plenty of wild roses. This lane ends (and once again the Valley Trail is very close to the Buckeye Trail) and the bridle trail continues north into a planted pine forest. The BT runs parallel here, also in the pines. To the west of both is the borrow pit for the Ohio Turnpike (I-80), an interesting spot botanically because several less common plants grow there, including fringed gentian.

Nearing Boston Mills Road, the Valley Trail and the Buckeye Trail cross over each other, the Buckeye Trail heading out to Boston Mills Road, and the Valley Trail turning west towards the open borrow pit. The trail dips down to the south side of I-80 and begins the least scenic part of the route. For the next half mile, the trail leads alongside the highway, at first separated only by a fence, then dropping below and away from the highway on a maintenance road. Here you can get some very good views of the river valley. The Towpath Trail can be seen below and away to the south, winding around the Stumpy Basin wetland. Beyond it, the Cuyahoga River makes a wide, sweeping bend.

The Valley Trail passes through an opening in a fence and turns right. It now goes under the twin bridges of I-80, through some fields, then on a gravel lane towards Boston. The Buckeye Trail comes out of the woods from the right and joins the gravel lane. Just before reaching Boston, the Valley Trail joins the Towpath Trail and goes under the I-271 bridges. The Towpath Trail turns off to the left to go to the Boston Store Visitor Center. The Valley Trail goes straight to the Boston Trailhead, located east of the Boston Store. There are hitching posts here at the parking lot. The Boston Store Visitor Center and restrooms are just across the canal, west of this parking lot.

Valley Trail—Boston Trailhead to Brecksville Reservation Stables

From the Boston Trailhead to Brecksville Reservation, the Valley Trail travels through many different habitats, from old farm fields, past active farms, through floodplain forest, to steep slopes and ravines. In some places it is quite remote and rugged. It is the bridle trail equivalent of the Buckeye Trail, and in one place crosses and parallels the Buckeye Trail. It is described here from south to north.

Directions: I-77 to Exit 145, Brecksville Road. North a quarter mile to Boston Mills Road. East on Boston Mills Road, jogging left and right to go over I-80, about three miles to Riverview Road. Cross Riverview Road and the Cuyahoga River. Pass the Boston Store and Towpath Trail. Turn right into the Boston Trailhead. From the east side of the park, take I-271 to SR 8. South on SR 8 three and a half miles to Boston Mills Road. West on Boston Mills Road three and a quarter miles to the trailhead.

Trail Description: Begin at the Boston Trailhead, just east of the Boston Store Visitor Center. The Valley Trail going north crosses Boston Mills Road at the corner of Stanford Road and goes along the edge of the woods, between the canal basin and Stanford Road. In this section along Stanford Road, there are a lot of Ohio buckeye trees, most evident in the spring when they are in full flower. For a few hundred yards the trail follows the edge of Stanford Road, then crosses Stanford Road, climbs partway up a hillside, parallels the road, and in six-tenths of a mile reaches a connector hiking trail that goes from the Stanford House to the Towpath Trail. The bridle trail follows Stanford Road until the road takes a sharp turn to the right.

The Valley Trail leaves Stanford Road and goes onto an old single-lane road. It goes uphill into a forested area, then winds its way back off the slope and into the floodplain of the Cuyahoga River, passing through an old orchard and wet meadows before nearing the Ohio & Erie Canal Towpath Trail. Turn right—paralleling the Towpath Trail—then cross the Towpath Trail and follow the old Jaite Mill road past the site of the historic paper mill. Continue north on the road, parallel to the Towpath Trail, to Highland Road.

At Highland Road, turn left (west) and follow the road shoulder across the Cuyahoga River bridge. Near the Cuyahoga County boundary sign, turn right (north) to leave the road and continue north.

The next half mile of trail winds through the floodplain forest alongside the west bank of the Cuyahoga River. This area often floods, so you might find piles of debris where floods washed logs up into the woods. The trail crosses a side stream on a bridge and continues in the low woods. The Cuyahoga Valley Scenic Railroad tracks are to the west, and beyond is a beaver-created wetland. The trail swings west to cross the railroad tracks north of the wetland, then turns northwest, generally paralleling Riverview Road. The trail crosses a bridge near the road, then begins a climb from a 650-foot elevation to about an 820-foot elevation. The trail comes into the open, passes behind a barn, and continues along the edge of a steep slope, with views down into the wooded ravine. On the left, you will pass a stand of bamboo, very rare here and probably planted by a former landowner.

The Valley Trail now nears a farm that is part of CNVP's Countryside Initiative, managed in cooperation with the Cuyahoga Valley Countryside Conservancy. Follow the trail around this farm and west towards Riverview Road. The Valley Trail crosses Riverview Road alongside the farm and immediately enters a forest, dropping below the level of the road and again heading northwest. It can be difficult to follow the trail here—in some places you will find a white horseshoe symbol painted on the trees. The trail follows a creek valley, staying away from the creek to provide a riparian buffer zone. In the words of one of the trail volunteers, this part of the trail is "wet-muggy-buggy."

The Valley Trail crosses the creek then reaches the Buckeye Trail. Turn left and head onto the Buckeye Trail for a few yards, then watch for where they part. The Buckeye Trail will stay in the low lands for a little while, and the Valley Trail soon begins a long, sometimes slippery, climb. At the top of this climb, the Valley Trail comes out of the woods onto an abandoned section of Parkview Drive. Bear left and follow this asphalt road about half a mile. Watch for where the Valley Trail leaves the road to the right. You will now see brown trail signs used by Brecksville Reservation. The Valley Trail goes through a pine woods, crosses Meadows Drive, and continues on. Near the stables, the Valley Trail meets up with the bridle trail system of Brecksville Reservation. A stone-paved bridle trail circles the stables. Follow this path to reach the parking lot.

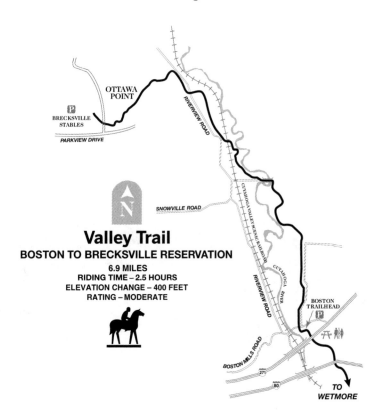

Valley Trail

BOSTON TO BRECKSVILLE RESERVATION

6.9 MILES
RIDING TIME – 2.5 HOURS
ELEVATION CHANGE – 400 FEET
RATING – MODERATE

O'Neil Woods Metro Park

O'Neil Woods is one of those places in the Cuyahoga Valley that has an interesting human history as well as an equally interesting and still-unfolding natural history. We are indebted to the staff of Metro Parks, Serving Summit County, for their research into the land use history of O'Neil Woods. According to their research, William O'Neil, the founder of General Tire and Rubber Company, and his wife Grace, bought two farms in Bath Township in 1936. These would become their weekend retreat and a place to practice gentleman-farming. One property was the Carver farmstead on Martin Road, and the second was a farmstead on Bath Road, where they would live while at the farm. The O'Neils' primary residence was a Tudor mansion in west Akron (now the O'Neil House Bed and Breakfast). At their farm, the O'Neils raised thoroughbred horses and cattle. One barn, across from where the house once stood, still stands on Bath Road and continues to be used by Metro Parks, Serving Summit County.

In 1937, William O'Neil granted permission to the General Tire Boy Scout troop to construct a camp on the farm, known as Camp Waupaca. It was a small camp, and was used until after World War II. Some older park visitors still remember seeing remains of the cabins alongside the Deer Run Trail. William O'Neil died in 1960, and in 1969 the O'Neil family leased the family farm to the metropolitan park district for park purposes. In 1972 they donated the land outright. These few hundred acres are ecologically diverse and include mature woods, a portion of Yellow Creek, an alder swamp, and fields managed for Eastern bluebirds and American woodcocks. Today thousands of visitors enjoy this park for its natural beauty, quiet remoteness, and challenging hiking.

A picnic grove is located near the remains of the Carver farm barn. Part of a foundation and an animal trough are still there, though overgrown. Picnic tables, grills, and restrooms are all near the parking lot. The Buckeye Trail (a 1,400-mile long trail) also goes through O'Neil Woods Metro Park. A 2007 master plan update for this park has proposed adding a shorter, easier trail and a deck overlook.

Deer Run Trail

The Deer Run Trail is located in O'Neil Woods, a unit of Metro Parks, Serving Summit County. The trail follows high ridges, drops down to Yellow Creek, then climbs back up a steep hillside to finish a 1.8-mile loop. Though the trail is relatively short, the climbs provide a good workout. Areas of mature upland oak forest, a scenic overlook of the Yellow Creek valley, streamside sycamores and willows, fields of goldenrods, and an alder swamp are all found along this trail. The diversity of habitat here makes the trail a favorite for birders.

Directions: From I-77, exit at Ghent Road. Turn north on Ghent Road to Yellow Creek Road (about half a mile) and turn right. Take Yellow Creek Road to Revere Road. Left on Revere Road a quarter mile to Bath Road. Right on Bath Road a quarter mile to Shade Road. Left on Shade Road one-eighth of a mile to Martin Road. Right on Martin Road to the park entrance on the right.

Trail Description: Begin the Deer Run Trail at the eastern edge of the parking area to hike the loop in a clockwise direction. Note the sandstone retaining wall alongside the parking lot. According to park history, these stones were salvaged from the demolition of the Summit County Jail in 1965, and were originally quarried at Deep Lock Quarry, now also a metro park.

The trail is marked with signposts bearing a deer print symbol. As you begin the trail, you pass through old fields that are managed for bluebird-nesting habitat. These fields are also a favored habitat for woodcocks, or "timberdoodles," which perform their mating rituals here in early spring. The woodcock is an unusual looking bird, with a disproportionately long bill for its small head. Woodcocks are secretive and rarely seen, except in early spring when the males perform an elaborate display, including a spiraling flight and rapid descent, all to attract females.

Just a short ways from the start of the trail, you reach an intersection with the Buckeye Trail. This statewide trail does not always take the shortest route, but instead chooses the more scenic or interesting route. In this part of the Cuyahoga Valley, it follows part of the Deer Run Trail through O'Neil Woods Metro Park, and then departs here to go north towards Brecksville Reservation. There the 1,400-plus-mile trail splits at a three-way junction. (See Buckeye Trail, page 51.)

Entering an oak woods, you will find a bench strategically placed at the

Deer Run
1.8 MILES
HIKING TIME – 1 HOUR
ELEVATION CHANGE – 200 FEET
RATING – MODERATE

trail summit and an overlook view of the valley down below. As you descend the many steps along the ridge, you can get some nice views off to the southeast. More steps and switchbacks take you to the valley below, a total descent of 180 feet. Large sugar maples mark the site where the O'Neils' old farmhouse once stood.

Cross Bath Road and follow the trail towards Yellow Creek, a major tributary which enters the Cuyahoga River about one mile farther downstream. Here large sycamores, willows, cottonwoods, and black walnuts line the path along the stream. You can also find several varieties of ferns, many wildflowers, plus three kinds of vines—rope-like bittersweet, greenbrier, with its prickly stems, and virgin's bower, which is a wild clematis. Small bridges take the trail across side drainages. Flooding in 2003 changed the course of Yellow Creek here and forced a rerouting of the trail. Since then, Metro Parks, Serving Summit County, has completed restoration work on the creek, using bioengineering techniques. Bioengineering uses native plants combined with built structures, such as log cribs, to repair unstable bank areas. By using an understanding of the mechanics and biology of streams, these methods help reestablish native plant communities that are

Deer Run Trail

capable of self-repair in changing conditions. This has greatly improved the water quality and habitat of the creek for various aquatic creatures.

Leaving Yellow Creek, the Deer Run Trail passes through another blue-bird field and along an alder swamp, one of few in Summit County. Alders are shrubs or small trees that like moist conditions. You can identify them by their fruits, formed in catkins, clusters of tiny flowers that resemble caterpillars. They appear in early spring before the leaves. When mature, the female catkins turn woody and look like little pinecones. Alongside the trail, opposite the alders, is a mossy slope covered with an interesting plant called rattlesnake weed. It has purple-veined leaves that closely hug the moss. The leaves remain even when the flower has gone by.

The trail crosses a creek on a bridge, then again crosses Bath Road and begins the climb back to the picnic area. You will climb about 150 feet in a third of a mile, edging a narrow ravine cut by the side creek. This gets your heart pumping! A bench along the way provides a place to rest and enjoy the view. The cabins of Camp Waupaca were located near here, perched on the edge of the ravine. This must have seemed like a great wilderness to the Boy Scouts who visited here in the 1930s and '40s.

The trail emerges from the woods at the top of this great climb, and you find yourself in the picnic area near where you began.

Yellow Creek

Hampton Hills Metro Park

Hampton Hills Metro Park is within the boundaries of Cuyahoga Valley National Park and is owned and managed by Metro Parks, Serving Summit County. The rugged topography from the floor of the Cuyahoga Valley to the eastern ridge makes the hiking here moderate to difficult. The trails reach back from the river's floodplain into these hills sculpted by water and erosion. You can even see the ongoing sculpting—in one place, raw soil is exposed where a high bank has dropped away, and in other places the ever-changing streams have carved into the land to either side.

The 278 acres of Hampton Hills were acquired in two main parcels. In 1964, the City of Akron leased 116 acres of wooded ravines along Akron Peninsula Road to the park district in exchange for land at Goodyear Heights Metropolitan Park, where the city wished to erect a water tower. In 1967, Rhea H. and E. Reginald Adam donated to the park district 162 acres of adjacent farm land. The farm area is known as Top O' the World—for good reason, as you will see when you visit it. There are two trails in Hampton Hills: the Adam Run Trail and the Spring Hollow Trail. The Spring Hollow Trail came first; the longer Adam Run Trail was built in 1979 by the Youth Conservation Corps, a program operated through the Ohio Department of Natural Resources. Both trails leave from the parking lot on Akron Peninsula Road.

Hampton Hills Metro Park is located east of Akron Peninsula Road, between Steels Corners Road and Bath Road. At present, there are three ways to enter this park: from Akron Peninsula Road, from Steels Corners Road, and from Bath Road. A master plan calls for removal of the entrance off Akron Peninsula Road and improvements to the other entrances. Plans also call for adding a trail that would connect to the popular Ohio & Erie Canal Towpath Trail.

A picnic area (with grills but no water) and restrooms are located near the start of the trails. A soccer field off Steels Corners Road can be reserved.

Adam Run Trail

The Adam Run and Spring Hollow Trails in Hampton Hills Metro Park start out together. The Adam Run Trail, marked by a stream symbol on sign posts along the way, follows Adam Run upstream, climbs steeply to the east rim of the Cuyahoga River valley, and descends back again to the valley floor.

Directions: From SR 8, exit at Steels Corners Road. Go west on Steels Corners Road five miles to Akron Peninsula Road. South (left) on Akron Peninsula Road a quarter mile to the entrance on the left.

From I-77, exit at Ghent Road. Go north half a mile to Yellow Creek Road. Take Yellow Creek Road to Bath Road and continue straight on Bath to Riverview Road. Cross Riverview Road to Akron Peninsula Road. Left on Akron Peninsula Road a quarter mile to the park entrance on the right.

Trail Description: From the trail kiosk, follow the path to the start of the trails. Bear to the left to begin. When you start these two trails, you are following the old East River Road which was relocated and renamed Akron Peninsula Road in the late 1920s. The path is wide and straight, and ahead you can see a plain, iron-railed bridge that was part of East River Road. The stone and concrete abutments are visible from the trail as you follow the path to the right, paralleling the stream. Other remnants of East River Road can be found up and down the valley between Bath Road and Peninsula.

During the first half mile or so, the trail follows Adam Run upstream. It used to cross the creek eight times, but flooding in 2003 washed out the bridges and led to a rerouting of the trail. The trail now crosses the creek twice. Spring wildflowers are abundant in the creek valley, as well as an unusual-looking plant with hollow, evergreen, grooved stems. This is scouring rush, or horsetail, in the genus of plants called *Equisetum*. Equisetums are in a category of plants that thrived and dominated plant life 180 to 500 million years ago. Only this genus survives today. The common name for this plant comes from the fact that the stems, containing silica, have been used for scouring and polishing. The rushes are often found along stream borders where their underground horizontal branching system can help anchor the soil along the banks.

After this first half mile, the two trails split. Bear left to stay on the Adam Run Trail, which follows the main course of the stream. Continue to climb the ravine; as it steepens, a set of 100 steps built into the steep hillside makes your climb a little easier. A Civilian Conservation Corps-style bench at the top is a good place to enjoy the views into the ravines full of black walnuts, elms, and sycamores. As you continue, the trail climbs at a gentler grade before passing through a white pine plantation planted by Girl Scouts in 1968, shortly after this area became a park.

After the pines, you come out into the open and crisscross fields and old fence rows. These fields and fence rows create an edge effect which is favored by birds and other wildlife. In the fall, goldenrods gild the fields with their arching, yellow-gold flower branches. By now you have climbed near the top of the east ridge of the valley and can begin to enjoy the views to the west. The Adam Run Trail reaches the east boundary of the metro park and swings back to the southwest. This is approximately the halfway point. This part of the route goes through what used to be the farm fields for the Adams' farm. A side trail from the Top O' the World area intersects with the Adam Run Trail near where the farm house used to be. There is still the farm pond, an old orchard, and fields which now feed a variety of wild, rather than domesticated, animals. Some of the fields in this high expanse are lined with shrubs, and the whole area is alive with birds and butterflies in summer months. Walking these fields can be both exhilarating and pleasantly relaxing, having made the great climb and now seeing wide expanses of sky and wildflowers.

After leaving the Top O' the World area, follow the trail through a young woods and across three bridges. Right after the third bridge, the Adam Run Trail rejoins the Spring Hollow Trail. Bear left and parallel Bath Road. Some evergreens outline the road and mark where an old lane crosses the trail. Soon the trail starts to drop off the hill and you begin to get views of the valley to the west. A long set of steps and a handrail make the descent a little easier. The trail rolls along for a while longer, then descends again on more steps near where the trail turns back to the north. You end this hike along a section of trail that again follows the old East River Road alignment, leading back to the parking lot.

Spring Hollow Trail

The Spring Hollow Trail in Hampton Hills Metro Park starts out along with the Adam Run Trail, both following the route of the former East River Road. This road was relocated and is now Akron Peninsula Road. Trail signs with an oak leaf symbol mark the Spring Hollow Trail. It makes a shorter loop than the much longer Adam Run Trail, going just partway up Adam Run, but still includes a strenuous climb up a side creek.

Directions: From SR 8, exit at Steels Corners Road. Go west on Steels Corners Road five miles to Akron Peninsula Road. South (left) on Akron Peninsula Road one-quarter mile to the entrance on the left.

From I-77, exit at Ghent Road. Go north half a mile to Yellow Creek Road. Take Yellow Creek Road to Bath Road and continue straight on Bath to Riverview Road. Cross Riverview Road to Akron Peninsula Road. Left on Akron Peninsula Road a quarter mile to the park entrance on the right.

Trail Description: From the trail kiosk, bear left (north) to begin the trail in a clockwise direction. Soon the trail bears to the right (just before a historic East River Road bridge) and winds its way up the Adam Run valley, crossing the creek twice. In just over a half mile, the two trails split at a trail sign and bench. Bear right for Spring Hollow Trail, following a side creek.

You now head up a deep, picturesque ravine. There are many fallen trees along the steep banks, with several moss-covered trunks straddling the narrow stream bed. As the hollow narrows even more, boardwalks and log bridges makes the going easier over the stream-soaked base of the ravine. Side hollows such as this one give you an idea of how intricately and tightly sculpted are the hills of the Cuyahoga Valley. There are ninety-three steps to climb here, with seventy-six in the last, steepest section. A bench at the top provides a welcome resting place.

At the top of the hill, rejoin the Adam Run Trail which enters from the left. The two trails, now joined, proceed through a young woods and across an old lane. Soon you begin the descent back down into the valley; two long sets of steps make the going a little easier. You can find plenty of large oaks up on the drier upland sections of this trail, and walnuts, slippery elms, maples, and sycamores on the slopes and wetter lowlands. In places, wild grape vines have created openings in the forest canopy where you might find birds feasting on the grapes.

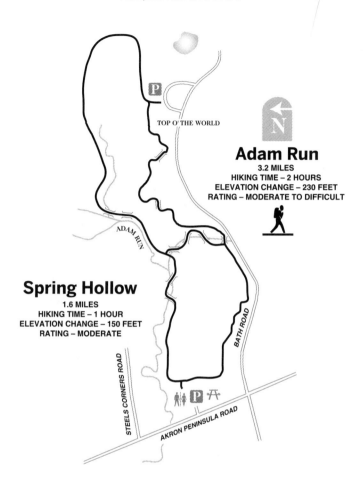

Adam Run
3.2 MILES
HIKING TIME – 2 HOURS
ELEVATION CHANGE – 230 FEET
RATING – MODERATE TO DIFFICULT

Spring Hollow
1.6 MILES
HIKING TIME – 1 HOUR
ELEVATION CHANGE – 150 FEET
RATING – MODERATE

TOP O' THE WORLD

ADAM RUN

BATH ROAD

STEELS CORNERS ROAD

AKRON PENINSULA ROAD

Near the intersection of Bath Road and Akron Peninsula Road, the trail swings to the north and again follows the old East River Road alignment. Between this old road and the newer Akron Peninsula Road are low wet areas that fill with spring peepers and other frogs in March and April. The tiny peepers pierce the spring air with their high-pitched, incessant chirps and trills. On the old road bed, soon you reach the parking lot where you began.

Appendix

General Information

For more information on park areas and facilities referred to in this guide, write or call:

Cuyahoga Valley National Park
Superintendent
15610 Vaughn Road
Brecksville, OH 44141
216-524-1497
800-445-9667
www.nps.gov/cuva
For information on the National Park System, visit www.nps.gov.

Cleveland Metroparks
4101 Fulton Parkway
Cleveland, OH 44144
216-635-3200
www.clemetparks.com

Metro Parks, Serving Summit County
975 Treaty Line Road
Akron, OH 44313-5837
330-867-5511
www.summitmetroparks.org

Visitor Centers/Nature Centers

NATIONAL PARK SERVICE:

Canal Exploration Center
216-524-1497
800-445-9667

Boston Store Visitor Center
1548 Boston Mills Road
Boston Township, OH 44264
330-657-2752

Peninsula Depot
1630 Mill Street
Peninsula, OH 44264
330-657-2039

Hunt House
2054 Bolanz Road
Peninsula, OH 44264
216-524-1497
800-445-9667
330-657-2309

Frazee House
7733 Canal Road
Valley View, OH 44125
216-524-1642
800-445-9667

CLEVELAND METROPARKS:

Brecksville Nature Center
Chippewa Creek Drive
Brecksville, OH 44141
440-526-1012

METRO PARKS, SERVING SUMMIT COUNTY

F.A. Seiberling Nature Realm
1828 Smith Road
Akron, OH 44313
330-865-8065

Reservable Picnic Shelters

A fee is charged for use of these areas, including use of a covered picnic shelter or enclosed pavilion with meeting space. Each reservable shelter is surrounded by a large outdoor play area and access to hiking trails. All have cooking grills and restrooms.

Cuyahoga Valley National Park
(216-524-1497 or 800-445-9667)
Ledges Shelter
Octagon Shelter

Cleveland Metroparks
(216-635-3200)
Brecksville Reservation:
Ottawa Point
Bedford Reservation:
Lost Meadows

Metro Parks, Serving Summit County
(330-867-5511)
Furnace Run:
Brushwood Pavilion

Organizations

Cuyahoga Valley Trails Council is an all-volunteer non-profit group dedicated to building and maintaining trails in the Cuyahoga Valley. The group conducts monthly trail work sessions throughout Cuyahoga Valley National Park.
Cuyahoga Valley Trails Council
1403 West Hines Hill Road
Peninsula, OH 44264
www.cvtrailscouncil.org

Buckeye Trail Association, Inc., which maintains the Buckeye Trail, is an all-volunteer non-profit group organized and operated exclusively to construct, maintain, and encourage use of the Buckeye Trail. For membership information and guides to the Buckeye Trail in other parts of Ohio, write or visit:
Buckeye Trail Association, Inc.
P.O. Box 254
Worthington, OH, 43085
www.buckeyetrail.org

Cuyahoga Valley National Park Association (CVNPA) is a non-profit organization created to assist the National Park Service in preserving Cuyahoga Valley National Park by fostering community awareness, support, and enjoyment of the park. CVNPA provides educational programs, raises funds, assists the park in various program areas, and encourages volunteerism.
Cuyahoga Valley National Park Association
1403 West Hines Hill Road
Peninsula, OH 44264
330-657-2909
www.cvnpa.org

Cuyahoga Valley Environmental Education Center, operated by the Cuyahoga Valley National Park Association and the National Park Service, is a residential learning center specializing in environmental education for grades 4 through 8. It also has special weekend and summer programs for adults and families.
Cuyahoga Valley Environmental Education Center
3675 Oak Hill Road
Peninsula, OH 44264
330-657-2796 or 800-642-3297

Ohio & Erie Canalway Association is working to develop the Ohio & Erie National Heritage Canalway from Cleveland to New Philadelphia.
Ohio & Erie Canalway Association
P.O. Box 609420
Cleveland, OH 44109
216-520-1825
www.ohioanderiecanalway.com

Hiking/Trail Riding and Orienteering Clubs

Cleveland Hiking Club
P.O. Box 347097
Cleveland, OH 44134-7097
www.clevelandhikingclub.com

Akron Metroparks Hiking Club
www.papays.com/amphc/

Cuyahoga Valley Trail Riders
Medina County Chapter, Ohio Horseman's Council
P.O. Box 247
Richfield, OH 44286
www.medinacountyohc.com

North Eastern Ohio Orienteering Club
P.O. Box 5703
Cleveland, OH 44101-0703
866-812-8316
www.neooc.com

Overnight Lodging

The Inn at Brandywine Falls
George and Katie Hoy, Innkeepers
8230 Brandywine Road
Sagamore Hills, OH 44067
330-467-1812 or 888-306-3381
www.innatbrandywinefalls.com
Call for reservations.

Other Attractions

Cuyahoga Valley Scenic Railroad
P.O. Box 158
Peninsula, OH 44264-0158
800-468-4070
www.cvsr.com

Hale Farm & Village
2686 Oak Hill Road
Bath, OH 44210-0296
330-666-3711
800-589-9703

Boston Mills/Brandywine Ski Resorts
P.O. Box 175
Peninsula, OH 44264
800-875-4241
www.bmbw.com

The Conrad Botzum Farmstead
3486 Riverview Road
Akron, OH 44313
Mailing address and Contact:
George and Maureen Winkelmann
996 Endicott Drive
Akron, OH 44313
330-867-6681
www.botzum.org

Outfitters:

Appalachian Outfitters
(hiking, backpacking, canoeing, kayaking, climbing)
60 Kendall Park Road
Peninsula, OH 44264
330-655-5444
www.appalachianoutfitters.com

Century Cycles
(bike sales and rentals)
1621 Main Street
Peninsula, OH 44264
330-657-2209
800-201-7433
www.centurycycles.com

Buckeye Sports Center
(cross country ski rentals)
4610 State Road
Peninsula, OH 44264
330-929-3366
www.buckeyesportscenter.com

The Trails

Trail	Hike	Ski	Bike	Horse	Length	Elevation	Difficulty
Adam Run	🚶				3.20	230	• • •
All Purpose Trail-Bedford	🚶		🚲		5.25	120	• •
All Purpose Trail-Brecksville	🚶		🚲		4.50	410	• •
Bike & Hike	🚶		🚲		10.50	min	•
Blue Hen Falls	🚶				0.50	80	•
Boston Run	🚶	🎿			3.10	80	• •
Brandywine Gorge	🚶				1.50	160	• •
Bridal Veil Falls	🚶				0.25	30	•
Bridle Trail-Bedford				🐎	14.10	270	• • •
Bridle Trail-Brecksville				🐎	9.00	260	• • •
Bridle Trail-Pinery Narrows				🐎	3.00	8	•
Buckeye Trail							
Egbert to Alexander	🚶				6.10	90	• • •
Alexander to Frazee	🚶				1.50	200	• •
Frazee to Station Rd.	🚶				2.50	8	•
Station Rd. to Jaite	🚶				7.00	200	• • • •
Jaite to Boston	🚶				5.60	250	• • • •
Boston to Pine Lane	🚶				4.00	240	• •
Pine Lane to Hunt House	🚶				4.10	150	•
Hunt House to Botzum	🚶				4.00	160	• •
Butler				🐎	0.60	150	•
Chippewa Creek	🚶				1.50	50	•
Cross Country	🚶	🎿			2.50	160	• •
Deer Lick Cave	🚶				4.00	205	• • •
Deer Run	🚶				1.80	200	• •
Dickerson Run				🐎	1.00	175	•
Egbert Loop	🚶				1.10	min	•
Forest Point	🚶				0.50	min	•
H.S. Wagner Daffodil	🚶	🎿			0.60	min	•
Hale Farm	🚶		🚲		1.00	120	•
Haskell Run	🚶				0.50	70	•
Hemlock Loop—Bedford	🚶	🎿			0.80	min	•

Trail	Hike	Ski	Bike	Horse	Length	Elevation	Difficulty
Hemlock Loop—Brecksville	🚶				2.50	220	• •
Lake	🚶				1.00	min	•
Langes Run				🐎	3.50	190	• • •
Ledges	🚶				2.20	105	• •
Oak Hill	🚶	🎿			1.50	50	•
Ohio & Erie Canal Towpath							
Lock 39 to Frazee	🚶	🎿	🚲		3.75	20	•
Frazee to Station Rd.	🚶	🎿	🚲		2.50	8	•
Station Rd. to Red Lock	🚶	🎿	🚲		2.50	20	•
Red Lock to Boston Store	🚶	🎿	🚲		1.75	15	•
Boston Store to Lock 29	🚶	🎿	🚲		2.50	30	•
Lock 29 to Hunt House	🚶	🎿	🚲		3.00	25	•
Hunt House to Ira	🚶	🎿	🚲		1.75	6	•
Ira to Botzum	🚶	🎿	🚲		1.75	25	•
Old Carriage	🚶	🎿			3.25	180	• • •
Old Mill	🚶				1.00	min	•
Perkins				🐎	2.75	260	• • • • •
Pine Grove	🚶				1.80	100	• •
Plateau	🚶	🎿			4.80	200	• • •
Praire	🚶				0.50	20	•
Quarry	🚶				1.20	120	•
Riding Run				🐎	4.00	260	• • •
Rock Creek	🚶	🎿			1.20	min	•
Sagamore Creek	🚶				3.60	200	• •
Salamander Loop	🚶				1.50	100	•
Salt Run	🚶				3.25	160	• • •
Spring Hollow	🚶				1.60	150	• •
Stanford	🚶				1.50	190	• •
Tree Farm	🚶	🎿			2.75	80	•
Valley: Everett to Wetmore				🐎	2.75	40	•
Valley: Wetmore to Boston				🐎	9.25	400	• •
Valley: Boston to Brecksville				🐎	6.90	400	• •
Viaduct Park	🚶				0.40	80	•
Wetmore				🐎	4.50	250	• •
Wildflower Loop	🚶				0.75	50	•

Photo Credits

Page xiv, Jim Goulthrop; p. 3, Rob Bobel; p. 5, National Park Service; p. 8, D.J. Reiser; p. 16, National Park Service; p. 22, D.J. Reiser; p. 26, Jackie Teeple; p. 27, Rob Bobel; p. 30, Rob Bobel; p. 33, D.J. Reiser; p. 36, D.J. Reiser; p. 40, Rob Bobel; p. 44, D.J. Reiser; p. 46, Patty Stafford; p. 48, Rob Bobel; p. 50, National Park Service; p. 54, D.J. Reiser; p. 56, Robin Dubin; p. 63, Rob Bobel; p. 64, Ken Colwell; p. 69, Bob Lucas; p. 72, D.J. Reiser; p. 74, D.J. Reiser; p. 81, Kris Hartley; p. 82, National Park Service; p. 89, D.J. Reiser; p. 90, National Park Service; p. 96, D.J. Reiser; p. 97, Bob Lucas; p. 98, Rob Bobel; p. 102, Rob Bobel; p. 110, D.J. Reiser; p. 112, Cleveland Metroparks; p. 114, Rob Bobel; p. 116, Rob Bobel; p. 122, D.J. Reiser; p. 127, Rob Bobel; p. 133, Joe Williams; p. 134, National Park Service; p. 139, Peg Bobel; p. 146, Walt Kauppila; p. 148, Ken Colwell; p. 150, National Park Service; p. 152, Rob Bobel; p. 154, Bob Lucas; p. 156, D.J. Reiser; p. 158, National Park Service; p. 160, Rob Bobel; p. 164, Rob Bobel; p. 166, National Park Service; p. 167, Rob Bobel; p. 168, Rob Muller; p. 169, John Spitzer; p. 175, Bob Lucas; p. 176, National Park Service; p. 181, Rob Bobel; p. 186, Rob Bobel; p. 187, Bob Lucas; p. 188, National Park Service; p. 190, Rob Bobel; p. 192, Rob Bobel; p. 193, Rob Bobel; p. 194, National Park Service; p. 198, Rob Bobel; p. 202, Frank Smrdel; p. 204, Rob Bobel; p. 206, National Park Service; p. 208, Rob Bobel; p. 215, Denise Setteur-Spurio; p. 219, Denise Setteur-Spurio; p. 230, Metro Parks, Serving Summit County; p. 234, Peg Bobel; p. 235, Rob Bobel

Acknowledgments

The Cuyahoga Valley Trails Council's motto could well be, "Many hands make light work," and that is true for this trail guide as well. From the start, this book has been a group effort. The first edition, published independently by the council in 1991, was researched and compiled by the "Big Guide" committee and many volunteers. Each volunteer brought to the project his or her unique talent and personal familiarity with the trails of the Cuyahoga Valley. There is no way that all these talents could be found in one person alone. Their unabashed love of the valley and never-failing humor imbued the project with a joy and spirit that kept us persevering through all the deadlines and details.

That first edition, completed only a decade and a half ago, was compiled when many of us were acquiring our first desktop computers. The maps were carefully, and by today's standards, tediously hand-drawn. For the second edition of the book, CVTC contracted with Jef Sturm Graphic Design to improve and computerize the maps and completely redesign the book. Those first two editions of the trail guide provided income for the CVTC, making it possible for the volunteers to purchase tools, conduct training sessions, and contribute materials to trail projects. For more than a decade and a half, volunteers managed all the distribution and sales of the book.

In 2006, the CVTC trustees decided to approach Gray & Company with a request to publish the third edition, and Gray & Company accepted. We were delighted with this news, and equally delighted to be asked by CVTC to once again work on updating this guide. It has been our great pleasure to work with David Gray and Rob Lucas at Gray & Company on this new edition. Their creative ideas and enthusiasm for the guide have made this edition the best ever.

We thank our good friends in the Cuyahoga Valley Trails Council for their dedication to this book project and for their thousands of hours of volunteer labor spent building, maintaining, and improving the trails we all enjoy. We wish to especially acknowledge and thank our good friends Dave Daams, president, and Mike Wendelken, trustee, for encouraging and guiding the updating of this book. In addition, we appreciate the volunteers who walked the trails, reviewed text and maps, and gave helpful advice: Dave Burgan, Bill O'Brien, Penny and Mark Bruce, and Troy Russell. We are grateful to Jim Sprague, former CVTC trustee and Buckeye Trail Association trustee emeritus, for writing the Buckeye Trail introduction and for answering our many Buckeye Trail questions. This third edition is illustrated by all-new photographs donated by many wonderful volunteers, whose work we appreciate whether or not we were able to use their photographs.

Much of the work completed by the original "Big Guide committee" and later CVTC volunteers forms the underpinnings of this third edition. Therefore we'd like to again thank some of those who made those earlier editions possible: Jay Abercrombie, Carl Bochmann, Dave and Cindy Burgan, Tom Fritsch, Dave Gates, Jan Geho, Glen Jenkins and the late Tom Jenkins, Kim Norley, Karen Parsons, Kathleen Pettingill, Carolyn Sullivan, Jerry Welch, Jack Wenrick, and Gene Wimmer.

For all editions, we are grateful for the review and information provided by the staffs of Cuyahoga Valley National Park, Cleveland Metroparks, and Metro Parks, Serving Summit County. Special thanks go to Patty Stevens and Jim Kastelic from Cleveland Metroparks, Dave Whited from Metro Parks, Serving Summit County, and Kim Norley from Cuyahoga Valley National Park.

We are grateful to all these friends and associates for sharing with us their knowledge and appreciation of the trails in our great national park.

—Rob and Peg Bobel

About the Editors

Rob Bobel is a civil engineer in the Resource Management division of Cuyahoga Valley National Park and serves on the board of the Ohio & Erie Canalway Coalition and on the Towpath Trail Partnership Committee. He was a founding trustee and charter trail boss for the Cuyahoga Valley Trails Council and currently advises on publications projects.

Peg Bobel is a freelance writer and editor, often combining her interests in nature and local history. For thirteen years she was the executive director of the Cuyahoga Valley Association and was a founding trustee of the Cuyahoga Valley Trails Council. She currently serves on a chapter board of the Western Reserve Land Conservancy.

Index

Cuyahoga Valley National Park

Map courtesy of National Park Service

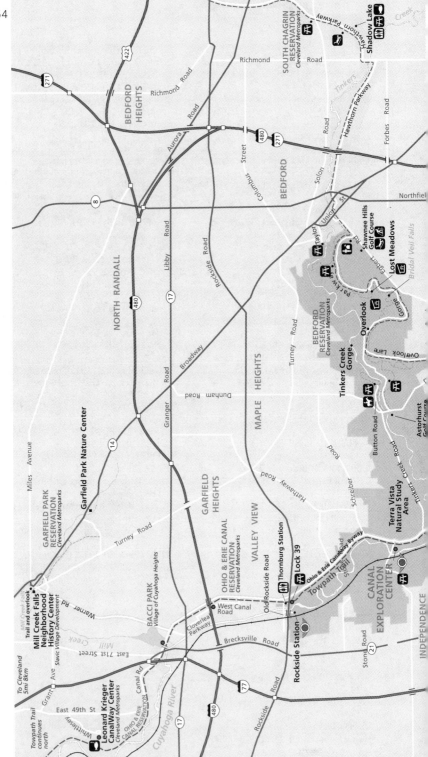

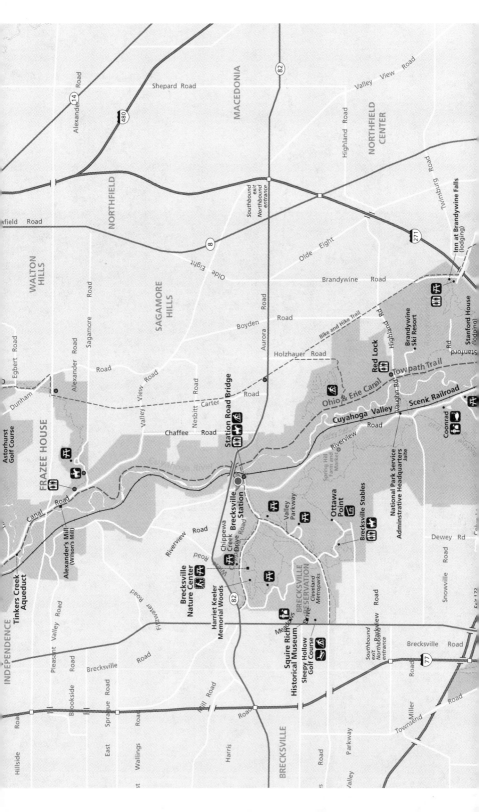

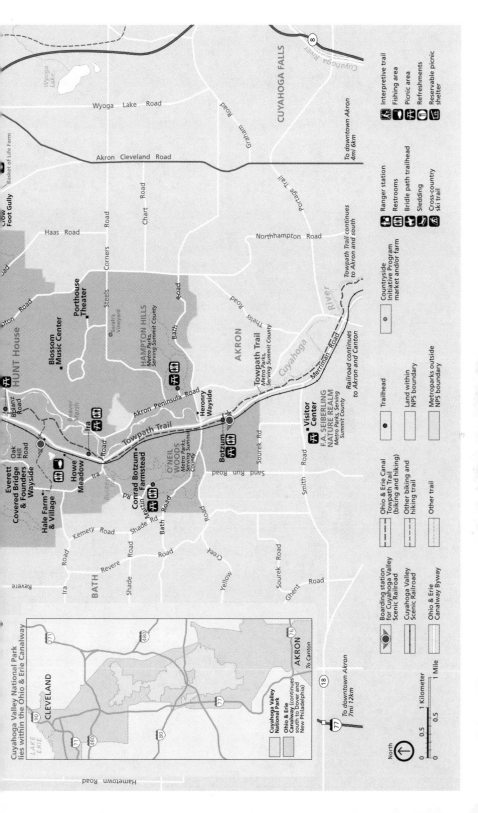